If You Want To Be A SUCCESS, Learn From 100+ People Who Already Are!

Fireflies For The Heart Series
Volume 1

Ginny Dye
Sandi Valentine
Suess Karlsson

Together We Can Change The World Publishing
Bellingham, WA

Fireflies For The Heart

All over the world fireflies are known as magical little creatures.

We love to watch them on warm summer evenings as they flit through trees with their glowing beauty.

Kids love to catch them, hold them in their hands to delight over their flashing body, and then either release them into the wild or capture them in a glass jar to be mesmerized for hours.

What is it about fireflies that attract all of us?

Beyond their magical beauty fireflies have a great lesson for us.

90% of the energy a firefly uses to create light is actually converted into visible light.

In contrast, a light bulb only emits light equal to 20% of the energy used!

Hmmm... obviously technology has a long way to go before it can catch up with the magic surrounding us in nature. It also can't teach us the same lessons...

Think about the Firefly...

How effective is the energy you use in your life?

Does the energy you expend radiate through the world, lighting the way to
all you want in life, or does it fizzle out before it creates
the results you long for?

Too many of us are in the fizzle category.

Fireflies for the Heart
was created to teach you how to glow like the
Firefly.

How to create the most effect from your life – just like
the Firefly.

And how to create a life of radiance that attracts
everyone
and everything you dream of.

Learn how:

To create the success you dream of...
overcome any obstacles and challenges...
live a life of grace and love.

Learn how to make a difference with your life.

Learn how to become the best you possible.

Visit our website at:

www.FirefliesForTheHeart.com

Dear Friend,

In our many years of working with people we have watched as person after person falters when they reach the "Real World." You start out with such great dreams. You are full of energy and hope - determined to make your mark on the world. Then you face the reality of unkind people; cruel words; failed attempts; unforeseen obstacles; and a myriad of other "Real Life" situations. Your dreams crumble before the onslaught. It doesn't have to be that way! If you are prepared; equipped; and strengthened by the SECRETS OF SUCCESS learned by people who have come before, you can conquer everything that comes your way - making your dreams come true!

We have learned that a ***single moment of Epiphany will not create lasting change.*** It is repeated impacts of stories, ideas & thoughts that change patterns and habits in order to achieve your goal.

Knowing that, we began to collect stories of successful people. We read about their lives. We learned the true definition of success. We studied how they achieved success. We saw their struggles and fears. We saw how they overcame them to accomplish great things. Meeting these people began to create change in our own lives as we applied what we learned.

The change wasn't always easy but it was so worth the journey.

In 2004, we created Someone Believes In You (www.SomeoneBelievesInYou.com), an online service that gives the Gift of Confidence to people by sending a very special certificate in the mail, and then sharing DAILY stories via email. As the number of stories continued to grow, we knew we needed to compile them into books. If You Want To Be A SUCCESS, Learn From 100+ People That Already Are! is the result.

You'll get to know:

A 19 year old girl who moved beyond self-doubt and abuse to found the largest cookie company in the world!

A 42 year old man who barely survived as a child, yet grew up to become the owner of one of the largest hotel chains in the world!

A young girl who had her arm bitten off by a shark, yet came back to become a national surfing champion!

A penniless Russian immigrant who founded a multi-million dollar brassiere company!

A single mother of 7 who discovered the way to make a difference in millions of lives!

You'll meet people who:

* *Have overcome debilitating fears.*
* *Come back from devastating physical challenges.*
* *Started their journey to success with NOTHING.*
* *Have discovered their real purpose for living.*
* *Came back from despair to find great JOY.*
* *Made the choice to overcome huge obstacles*

Within the life lessons of ordinary people who have lived extraordinary lives you'll learn to:

* *Overcome whatever obstacles are before you!*
* *Harness the power of persistence!*
* *Master the secrets of how to gain great wealth!*
* *Make a difference with your life!*
* *Master how to attain the goals you have for your life!*
* *Build deep, meaningful relationships!*
* *Live a life of incredible joy!*

And so much more....

You may feel you are all alone in your quest for
Success and Joyful Living. You're NOT!

Millions have gone before you. There are so many who discovered what they were looking for. People who have succeeded are not stingy with their secrets. They are eager to share them with others who are looking for their own success. And, we are eager to share them with you!

This Journal/Book will give you an opportunity to journal your dreams and feelings, chronicle your achievements and challenges, and ask you some tough questions that will help you move forward. We want this book to become a valued treasure and portion of your life!

We hope you enjoy reading this book as much as we enjoyed creating it for you!

Joyfully,

Ginny Dye
Sandi Valentine
Suess Karlsson

Table of Contents

8

9

Here's the first thing you need to know as you strive toward accomplishing your goals and dreams.

There are NO SECRETS TO SUCCESS!

Webster's Dictionary defines a <u>secret</u> as something kept from public knowledge; something mysterious that is beyond general knowledge or understanding.

If that were true then it would mean success is only possible for those few who have access to the great mysterious secrets of success. Nonsense! People *believe* there are hidden secrets that will propel them to success. *There are no secrets.* There are truths, lessons, insights and actions you can take to get you where you want to be. They're not hidden, but neither are they dancing in front of you as you walk through life. You have to WANT to know them. You have to LOOK for them. You have to DO something with them once you know them.

Do you ever wonder what your life is going to be like in 1 year; 5 years; 10 years; 20 years; longer…? Of course you do. Everyone does. As we begin this journey together there is a very basic truth you need to hear, and hopefully accept.

Your life will be whatever you decide to make it. You've got a choice to make. Today. And every other day of your life. Let me clue you into another secret of life. *Where you are in your life today is a direct consequence of every decision you have ever made.*

Ouch. I know. It was pretty tough on me when I had to face this truth. I didn't like some of what I saw – other things I felt pretty good about. I figure we might as well get this out of the way right at the beginning. I have discovered it is best to face the reality of where you are starting from before you begin a journey. It's the only way you can know how far you have to go – or how far you have come.

So go ahead… take a few minutes (or longer) to think about these two secrets. You may discover the same kind of freedom I did. While it was tough to accept I am ultimately responsible for whatever the condition of my life is right now – there is also incredible freedom in knowing I have the power to make it anything I want it to be. Wow!

I get so tired of people complaining about their lives. Complaining they can't do certain things because they're just not smart enough. Complaining they will never excel in anything because they just don't have the talent others do. Complaining they will never make much money because no one else they know does. It goes on and on…

I hear it all the time. People selling themselves short because they simply don't believe life will be exciting for them – they don't believe their dreams will ever come true. As long as they believe that – it will be true for them.

Okay… did you hear that? This is another so-called secret of life. *If they believe it, it will be true for them.* I didn't say it was true. I simply said it was true for them because they have decided to believe it. That MAKES it true for them. Too bad!

Especially because the opposite is equally true. If you choose to believe in your ability to excel; to succeed; to make your dreams come true – then you will. *Your decision to believe it makes it TRUE FOR YOU!*

Today is a day you can use to change your life. Change the way you think about things.

Decide to believe your entire life is going to be an exciting adventure. *Decide* to believe you will be a success. *Decide* to believe today is going to be better than yesterday.

<u>*Decide*</u> *and it will be TRUE FOR YOU!*

As we travel the adventure of SUCCESS together, we'll be asking you many questions for you to consider. Let's start with the most important one, however. None of the other questions matter until you lay the foundation. Before you answer, let me tell you the best way to get all you can from our adventure together. *Be brutally honest. Dig deep into your feelings and thoughts.* You're not taking a test someone is going to grade. No one will ever read this unless you want them to. This is for YOU.

We call the questions POWER BOOSTERS because we know the power they have to change your life if you're brave enough to truly answer them.

<u>POWER BOOSTERS</u>

WHY are you reading this book? What do you hope to gain from it?

_____

_____

_____

_____

_____

_____

_____

_____

How do you define success? (Think about more than money...)

_____

_____

_____

_____

_____

_____

_____

_____

_____

_____

_____

★ _She's On Her Way_ ★

Eilleen was born in the tiny town of Timmons, Ontario in Canada. She grew up used to bitter cold and a gnawing stomach. There were days on end when bread and milk was the entire diet for her and her 3 younger siblings. She learned to hide her poverty and hunger from friends at school but it didn't ease the suffering.

About the only thing that could do that was her music. When life was more than she could handle, she would retreat to her bedroom with her guitar, singing and writing until her fingers ached. The music fed her soul even while her stomach was growling.

Her talent was recognized early and this little tomboy was shuttled all over to perform in clubs, bars, and anywhere else they could get her booked to make some extra money. Yet Eilleen never really thought music was her future.

When she could no longer stand the poverty she managed to convince her mother to leave their father and head for Toronto. The shelter they stayed in for a long time provided the first regular meals she had ever experienced.

Eilleen got her first job when she was 14, working at a McDonalds. Later, she spent summers working as the foreman of a dozen-man reforestation crew in the Canadian bush, where she learned to wield an axe and handle a chain saw as well as any man. She was tough because she had to be tough.

Then things got tougher. Both parents were killed in an auto wreck and suddenly she was the parent to her siblings. She managed to survive by getting a job singing at a local resort. The experience was invaluable – giving her exposure to every aspect of theatrical performance. It prepared her for what was to come.

In 1990, her siblings were grown and 23 year old Eillen was on her own. The first thing she did was change her first name to an Ojibway Indian name meaning **_"I'm on my way."_**

Shania Twain was indeed on her way. She has turned the world of Country/Pop music upside down, winning many awards along the way. Unless you live on another planet, you have probably heard of her!

One of her songs really sums it up. She has this to say about the irresistible _I'm Gonna Getcha Good!_ "There is a typical Shania attitude in the lyric, a definite female confidence. It's all about a girl who knows what she wants, she not only knows how to get it, but she's going to get it good."

All of us make a choice everyday how we are going to live our lives. No one would have been surprised if little Eilleen had simply become another person sunk in poverty – trapped by the reality of a hard life.

Shania Twain, however, saw her future differently. She was not content to stay where she was – determined to pay whatever price necessary to achieve her dreams. Each hard thing did nothing but strengthen her resolve and determination, teaching her how to press through to success!

She learned to do the hard things. She learned how to spot opportunity in every situation. She learned how to ask for what she wanted – and just keep asking until she got where she wanted to be. She learned how to fail, then pick herself back up and do it again.

> _"Develop an attitude of gratitude and give thanks for everything that happens to you, knowing that every step forward is a step toward achieving something bigger and better than your current situation."_
> ~_Brian Tracy_

★ *He Started What?!* ★

Can a kid from a broken family change the world?

Pierre was born in Paris, France and attended a bilingual school so he was able to speak English when his family moved to the United States when he was six. Pierre's family lived in the Washington, D.C. area for most of his schooling. Although his parents were separated when he was about 2 years old they stayed in close contact and Pierre felt loved and valued. Even though living with his mother, he spent many weekends with his father who was a surgeon. Pierre enjoyed tagging along on his father's rounds, *"We would spend maybe 45 minutes in the car going from one hospital to the next and we'd have some great conversations. That's one of my fond childhood memories."* Pierre was raised with the belief he could do anything he wanted to do, and this gave him confidence in himself from an early age.

Pierre's love affair with computers started in the third grade. He would cut gym class in order to play on the school's computer, which the teacher hid in a closet between classes. Unafraid to try new things, Pierre was soon writing computer programs. The first program he designed was for printing out cards for the high school library's card catalog (he charged $6 an hour). In 10th or 11th grade (he isn't sure which); he wrote software that helped schedule classes. *"I resisted the temptation to put in some code in there to make sure I never had classes on Friday, because I wouldn't have been able to get away with it, but I thought about it."*

Not surprisingly, Pierre majored in computer science in college. One of the classes designed to weed out students was a C programming class called "Data Structures." Pierre excelled in the class and went on to teach himself how to program the Macintosh (Apple) computer. The summer before graduating from college, Pierre took a summer job in California working at a software company for the Apple Company.

"I was just pursuing what I enjoyed doing. I mean, I was pursuing my passion. . . the ability to create software that could have a benefit or an impact on people that was what was driving me. . . And so, like people have said, it is not really work, you know, if you are having fun, it's not work so that was the case with me."

In 1995, Pierre's fiancée (who had a master's degree in molecular biology and was working as a management consultant) was having trouble finding other collectors of Pez candy dispensers – her favorite hobby. The web was still in its infancy (having been created in 1993) but Pierre was intrigued with the idea of using it as a way to help Pamela. He created a page on his personal website as a way to help the collectors connect with each another. After a short period of time, visitors started posting offers and requests for other items. *"It was just an idea I had, and I started it as an experiment, as a side hobby basically, while I had my day job. And it just kind of grew."* He named the site Auction Web. In 1997, he incorporated the enterprise and named it eBay.

Pierre based the entire enterprise of eBay on members treating one another with honesty and courtesy and offering them a Forum with which to communicate and rate each other. *"It's all about treating one another the way you want to be treated yourself so you can do business with one another."*

Pierre's main belief is that a person must pursue his or her passion. *"If you're passionate about something and you work hard, then I think you'll be successful."* He believes that all entrepreneurs should be about making the world a better place, *"I want people to be entrepreneurs, but I want them to do it for the right reasons, because they think they can change the world, because they think they have got something of value to give to the world. Not because they think they can make a lot of money. That is the wrong way to do anything."*

Pierre and Pamela Omidyar are now in the process of giving away all but 1% of their income. Their goal is to help people get involved with their communities and change the world by doing so.

Passion – integrity – respect – optimism – generosity – these are virtues that made Pierre Omidyar successful. Add to those, belief in yourself and not being afraid to try something new, and you've got the formula to not only help yourself, but help others as you achieve success!

Merri pulled the covers over her head hoping that if she wasn't seen perhaps her adopted stepmother would ignore her. She could hear birds chirping outside the window. . . if Merri had only been a bird, she could have flown away from the torment a long time ago.

This small soul began life as a loved little girl. However, the deaths of both her parents over a period of a few years resulted in her being adopted by her stepmom. Not only adopted, but also terribly abused. Fearing the night and fearing the day, Merri could only dream of a safe, free, loving existence. Eventually her stepmother put her in an orphanage, changed her name so no one in her family could find her, and refused to pay for her education after she turned fourteen.

As a young girl, she endured much and vowed that when she was older she would do something to help other adopted children live in safety. And once grown, Merri did just that and more. After 30 years in *broadcasting*, Merri Dee served as Director of Community Relations at WGN-TV in Chicago, Illinois, USA. This enabled her to supervise the programs that reach over 55 million homes. She also works as a manager of the TV channel's Children's Charities where over 25 million dollars have been raised. The monies raised have been given solely to children's organizations. As of this writing, she retired at 71 to join the Leadership Council of AARP Illinois.

Because of Merri's efforts in raising awareness about the needs of orphans, the adoption rate in Illinois increased over 50 percent. The credit is given to her and WGN-TV.

As the host of the United Negro College Fund's annual "Evening of Stars," Merri has helped raise over 30 million dollars for educational scholarships.

These 3 accomplishments are only a small representation of what she has accomplished. Her life is characterized by giving, giving and giving some more.

These feats take on even greater awe when you learn that Merri was kidnapped one night, very early in her career, after taping a TV show. Her kidnappers shot her in the head and left her for dead in rural Illinois. She was abandoned, cold and bloody with two bullet holes in her head.

Miraculously, Merri's lifelong will and fight to survive came to her rescue once again and she crawled for help. Finding a nearby highway, she managed to flag down a passing car and received the needed medical care that would save her life. It was a long road back but she was determined to accomplish all she had dreamed of. Nothing would stop her.

Blinding headaches from the bullet shrapnel still left in her head gives her daily pain. But after more than a year of recovery, Merri returned to the journalistic life she loved for 30+ more years!

She also decided to bring good from her experience. Her near-death experience fueled a new passion - victim's rights. Merri was instrumental in getting the first Victims Bill of Rights legislation passed in Illinois. That bill has since become the example for the rest of the USA's victim's legislation.

Merri lived a lonely and sad life as a child. Neglected and beaten, she knew no love. Then she suffered an almost-fatal attack that would have made most people give up. She could be bitter and angry – the choice too many people make. Instead, she has taken her desperate past and made her present world better – changing the lives of thousands of other children and victims along the way.

Today Merri lives a rich fulfilling life. A survivor's life. Her life has left scars on her body and her soul, but she chooses each day to live a Victor's Life!

★ *You're Not Going to Believe This* ★

How many times have you been discouraged because someone else didn't see the brilliance of what you created, thought of, or wanted to do? How many times have you walked away from something because you decided it wasn't a good idea, too?

Consider these…

+ The movie Star Wars was rejected by every movie studio in Hollywood before 20th Century Fox finally produced it. It went on to be one of the largest-grossing movies in film history.

+ As a child, Sylvester Stallone was frequently beaten by his father and told he had no brains. He grew up an unhappy loner. He floated in and out of schools. An advisor at Drexel University told him that based on his aptitude tests he should pursue a career as an elevator repair person. It's not a bad profession but it's certainly not where "Rocky" ended up!

+ Einstein was criticized for not wearing socks or cutting his hair. He didn't speak until he was four, and didn't read until he was seven. One observer noted, *"He could be mentally retarded."*

+ An expert said of Vince Lombardi: *"He possesses minimal football knowledge. Lacks motivation."*

+ Beethoven handled the violin awkwardly and preferred playing his own compositions instead of improving his technique. His teacher proclaimed him hopeless as a composer.

+ Walt Disney was fired from his job as a newspaper editor for lack of ideas. He also went bankrupt several times before he created Disneyland.

+ Henry Ford failed and went broke 5 times before he finally succeeded.

+ Louisa May Alcott, the author of Little Women, was encouraged to find work as a servant or seamstress. She would certainly never be a writer.

+ In 1944, the director of the Blue Book Modeling Agency, told modeling hopeful Norma Jean Baker (Marilyn Monroe), *"You'd better learn secretarial work, or else get married."*

So… *what are your ideas? Your thoughts? Your dreams?* Who cares if anyone supports what you want to do?

The important thing is for YOU to believe. For **you** to ignore the people who say you can't do it – and *do it anyway*! It takes courage. It takes persistence. It takes believing in the "voice inside" when no one else does.

Ideas, dreams, and visions are planted within you because you have the ability to make them happen. You'll learn, grow, scramble, fail, and get back up again. The important thing is to simply never give up. The people I told you about never did – and they made great things happen!

★ *How She Got Her Crown* ★

It's so easy to look at really successful people and think they just woke up one day that way. Nothing could be further from the truth. Every successful person I know had their share of failures and hardships. The "Queen of Television" was no different...

Born to teenage, unwed parents, Oprah had a lot of things going against her. She was poor, black, a female, and born to parents out of wedlock. Her early years with her grandparents were wonderful, but from age six to thirteen her life was full of abuse and trouble-making. Her mother's failed attempt to put her in a detention center landed her with her father. He helped her turn her life around and she went on to college and then moved into journalism.

Oprah was fired as a TV reporter because she broke the "cardinal rule" of journalism -- remain objective. Oprah started crying while interviewing a woman who had lost seven children in a fire. That show of sympathy cost Oprah her job.

At age 22 and a new anchorperson, she was sitting around a table with men in suits when they suggested she change her name to Suzie. They counseled that it was a "friendlier" and more easily remembered name than Oprah. Oprah rejected their suggestion and decided to stay true to herself.

She knew she was different and liked it that way. So she worked hard to launch her own media career by creating a talk show with heart and a helping hand to people in need. The Oprah Winfrey Show was born. Today Oprah is a one-woman media empire worth billions of dollars. More importantly, to her, she has the ability to influence millions every single day – and she does! She has used her success to change millions of people's lives.

If Oprah had listened to the "professionals" and followed their advice, I wonder if we'd even know who she is today. But because she rejected the "tested formula" of journalism and built upon her uniqueness, millions of people around the world have been touched and helped because of her.

Each of us is unique, with special gifts and talents. If others recommend you make changes, honestly consider if such changes would diminish who you really are. Some changes might be for the good -- others might cause you to compromise your uniqueness. And your uniqueness might just be what the world is waiting for!

Be willing to evaluate yourself honestly. Be willing to be true to who you are. You have the choice to be brave enough to embrace what makes you unique and different. It's easy to be like everyone else. True courage comes from choosing to be true to yourself. Will you join Oprah in making that choice? You may not be the next Queen of Television but you'll be on the path to your OWN success!

> *Do the one thing you cannot do. Fail at it. Try again. Do better the second time. The only people who never tumble are those who never mount the high wire. This is your moment. Own it.*
>
> *~ Oprah Winfrey*

POWER BOOSTERS

What hard things have kept you from success?

_____

_____

_____

_____

_____

_____

_____

_____

_____

_____

How do you define success? (Think about more than money...)

_____

_____

_____

_____

_____

_____

_____

_____

_____

_____

★ _She Was The First!_ ★

The sun rose and Wilma awoke. Pulling herself together she faced the glowing sunrise. Breathing in the fresh morning air she thought to herself. . . _"No more days watching the old way of life die. No more days feeling the pointed barb of despair."_

Wilma was alive in a time when the Native American culture was at a low point. Want to guess when that was? No, not in the 1700's or even the 1800's but in the 1980's! Less than forty years ago!

For the Cherokee, teamwork and working together, both men and woman for the common good of the whole tribe was a traditional and an honored way of life. However, deep discouragement, broken promises and a completely male dominated culture had replaced their historical ways. Now the women were cast aside and forgotten. They lived hopeless and powerless. And the whole culture fought alcoholism and unemployment.

The year was 1987... Wilma dressed as the morning sun warmed the air. Preparing for her first official day as the elected Chief of the Nation, all of her life's work, hopes and beliefs lay around her mind. Her anticipation of a brighter future began to bubble up.

This day brought the end of much prejudice and ridicule, hardship and skepticism. She dressed and remembered. Wilma knew the sweetness of life could be short.

She remembered the car accident that killed her best friend and nearly killed her. She carries the scars of 17 surgeries. Each scar reminded her as she dressed, that life can only give back to you what you put into it.

She remembered the death threats she received as her popularity with her people grew and the tension grew with her enemies. She remembered buying new tires for her vehicle when its tires were slashed in protest.

She remembered 1985, when she first "inherited" the position as chief of the Cherokee nation. Inherited it because her boss left the position and she was the next in command.

However, this year, 1987, she was freely elected... the very first female ever to hold that position. She knew her people had high expectations for her. She had high expectations herself... for all of them.

As she left for her office, her head held high with pride and hope, she offered silent thoughts of respect for the people who had gone before, and deep gratefulness and sincere appreciation for the opportunities ahead of her. _She knew her day had finally come._ She knew her Nation's day had come as well.

Her high expectations, hard work and deep commitment paid off as she was elected twice more as the Nation's chief.

This remarkable woman passed away in 2010 but her influence is still felt within the Nation. The Cherokee Nation is a vast organization, with over 140,000 in population, an annual budget of more than $75 million, and more than 1,200 employees spread over 7,000 square miles!!

Wilma's election and her tackling of their problems did much to restore and revive the Cherokee economy, education and equality. She restored faith to a desperate people.

She didn't take the easy way or the quick way. She took the way that was necessary and needed.

So many times we look for the quick way. Wilma is a wonderful reminder that often times it takes a willingness to work within the existing structure. It takes patience to wait for the opportunity that we desire to present itself. But by doing those two things, Wilma created an environment where now, present day young Cherokee girls dream of becoming chief. Before her election, those girls would never have believed that possible.

Success is not always fast and easy. It can take patience and perseverance. It can take great courage. We encourage you to dream like Wilma did of the changes coming. You have the power to create your own bright future!

★ _Do You Believe In Miracles?_ ★

I'd like to introduce you to the miracle of Chinese Bamboo...

It all begins with a seed - and with the vision of someone willing to wait... A Chinese farmer, usually struggling to survive and provide for his family, plants the seed and sets his hope and vision on all it will provide when it towers 90 feet above his head. With a heart toward the future, he digs hole after hole, plants the seeds, then begins their care. Day after day he carries water to the spots he has marked. And because it's human nature to want to see results he carefully inspects "the spots" every day.

Nothing.

Knowing he has to feed his family he plants other crops, carefully sewn around "the spots" that contain the real hope for his future. He continues to water them every day, feeding them carefully, and watching...

Nothing.

The other crops sprout within weeks, providing nourishment for his family within months, but provide nothing for the future. These crops will not make his dreams come true - they will simply provide for the present. The Chinese Bamboo seeds contain all his hopes, his dreams... A whole year goes by...

Nothing.

He continues to haul water. He stares endlessly at "the spots" but sees nothing but barren ground. His hopes, his dreams, seem so very far away. There is no evidence of life. Has the seed rotted? Has it died before it ever had a chance to grow? Another year goes by...

Nothing.

His neighbors - those who don't know and believe in the miracle of the Chinese Bamboo - laugh at him. They mock his vision for the future. They look on with scorn as he hauls buckets of water to "the spots". He begins to question himself. Will it ever grow? Is he pouring water, and his life's energy, into something that will reap no reward for him?

Another year goes by...

Nothing.

3 years of pouring water, energy and hope into the Chinese Bamboo. Nothing to show for it. Yet he's heard of the miracle of the Chinese Bamboo. He's heard of the huge rewards that come to those who believe. One day he stands over "the spots" and he cries his frustration and fears. "The spots" reveal nothing, the barren ground seeming to mock him, yet the wind whispers hope to him. He sighs and hauls yet more buckets of water.

Another year goes by...

Nothing.

4 years.... 4 years of hoping, wishing, and diligently tending his dream. Surely the miracle will happen now. His neighbors have quit laughing. They no longer even care - yet they talk quietly among themselves of the farmer who "isn't quite right." At this point the farmer isn't even sure... Yet he's fallen into a habit so he continues to water "the spots." He continues to feed them. It's simply what he does now, with no knowledge of reward - just the simple, now unspoken hope that life resides beneath the spots he so carefully tends. Another year passes...

Nothing.

5 years... The farmer is tired. Tired of hauling buckets. Tired of growing and tending so many other crops to feed his struggling family. Tired of trying to keep his dream alive. Tired of seeing no results day after day. He stares hopelessly at "the spots." There can not possibly be life after so many years. He must have watered them wrong. He must not have fed them correctly.

If only he had done things differently, there would be growth. Despair rocks his soul. 5 years he has poured into his dream - into his hope for a better future. His dream mocks him. The vision of a better life for his family melts away under harsh reality. Tears fill his eyes as he grabs for the last hope residing in his soul and slowly lifts the bucket to pour water on to his dream.

After 5 years he realizes it would be folly to give up now...

Then comes the morning when the whole village is jolted awake by the cries of joy from the farmer. They watch startled from their windows as he runs down the dusty road calling for his family to come see. As his family races back up the road after him, the rest of the village pours from their houses to see what has the crazy farmer so excited. They find the family clustered around "the spots", talking excitedly. From the edge of the road they can see green sprouts thrusting out from the barren ground. They seem to be growing before their very eyes! The farmer is dancing.

"The miracle has happened!" he cries.

"The miracle has come!"

"The spots" become the place for everyone in the village to come - watching in amazement as the bamboo grows, and grows, and grows. *5 feet. 10 feet. 20. 30. 40. 50. 60. 70. 80. 90...* In just 6 weeks the bamboo has grown 90 feet tall! 5 years of nothing and now this... 90 feet in 6 weeks! It is truly a miracle!

The farmer stands to the side. He is aware all his dreams have come true. The harvest of the bamboo will provide all he dreamed of for his family. He also realizes the lessons he has learned are far more valuable.

He learned to plant a dream.

He learned to do the daily things that would make it a reality.

He learned to ignore those who said it couldn't happen.

He learned to push past his own fear and doubt and keep taking action.

He learned to have faith when there was no reason to have faith.

Now he smiles every time he walks through the village.

Everyone is hauling buckets of water to their own "spots." Gazing over at his towering 90 feet tall bamboo, they know what can happen.

Because of him.

Because of his willingness to blaze the trail and make his dream come true.

What about you? What are you willing to do to make your dreams come true? How long are you willing to work? How long are you willing to go to school? How much faith and belief are you willing to have? How long are you willing to persevere?

We hope your answer is one that will help you achieve all you dream of in life!

★ A Radical Idea ★

Muhammad walked slowly down the muddy road in Bangladesh, his heart breaking as starved faces gazed at him pitifully, their blank eyes begging for help. Children who should be playing in the streets lay helplessly, their life ebbing away because of starvation. He knew most of them would die. His heart was ripped by the looks of desperation on the faces of parents who knew their children were dying but could do nothing to help them.

Bangladesh, caught in the grip of yet another natural disaster these parents could do nothing to stop, was losing more than a million people who were dying horrible deaths.

Muhammad's eyes filled with tears as he remembered his own beginning...

By all accounts, Muhammad had every reason to make excuses for his lack of opportunity. Born the third of nine children in 1940 in a small village in Bangladesh (then known as British India), Muhammad was four when his family moved to the city of Chittagong – escaping a famine that claimed millions of people. When he was nine, his mother was afflicted with a mental illness. But even with the resulting family difficulties, little Muhammad excelled at school – he had an insatiable thirst for knowledge. By the age of 21, he had received his Master's Degree in Economics.

Over the next few years Muhammad continued his schooling and held government and teaching positions in both Bangladesh and the United States. Little did he know that his love of learning, his understanding of economics and his years of living in the U.S. would change the lives of millions of people.

And now here he was... once again Bangladesh was in the grip of a horrific famine that was claiming innocent lives.

An idea started to take root in his consciousness and soon his vision became very clear. Ask him what that vision is and he'll tell you it's the total eradication of poverty from the world. A huge vision, right? Yet it was a natural progression for Muhammad -- his years of study and research in economics, coupled with his deep understanding of both Eastern and Western culture, gave birth to his solution.

What is the one thing the poorest of the poor cannot get? Credit -- loans. Muhammad had the crazy idea of opening a bank that gave credit to those who could **never** receive it. It would be a bank that would empower the **very** poorest people by helping them become entrepreneurs.

And so, in 1976, Muhammad created the Grameen Bank which gives microcredit (small loans) to the poorest of the poor so they can launch businesses and lift their families out of poverty. Is it working? Oh, yes – it is – in a BIG way!! The World Bank recently acknowledged Muhammad's radical idea: *"This business approach to the alleviation of poverty has allowed millions of individuals to work their way out of poverty with dignity."*

Muhammad says, *"Grameen is a message of hope, a program for putting homelessness and destitution in a museum so that one day our children will visit it and ask how we could have allowed such a terrible thing to go on for so long."*

This amazing man has won many, many awards around the world because of his far-reaching, sustainable ideas. In 2006, he was awarded the Nobel Peace Prize and was named by Business Week as one of "The Greatest Entrepreneurs of All Time."

But Muhammad's sharp mind and huge heart have not stopped with the creation of the Grameen Bank and microcredit. He has recently published a book entitled *Creating a World Without Poverty* in which he challenges and empowers businesses to make a difference in the world.

What would have happened if Muhammad had spent his time thinking about what he couldn't do instead of imagining and acting upon what he could do? Just think of the millions of lives around the world that his simple but profound and revolutionary ideas have changed!

Have you ever caught yourself limiting yourself by thinking, "I can't do that" or "I'm only one person" or "If I only had more money, a different upbringing, lived in a different neighborhood. . . I could do this or accomplish that"?

Your potential – like Muhammad Yunus' – is unlimited. It doesn't matter where you were born or who your parents are. It doesn't matter what your past was like or where you find yourself today. Take the word "can't" out of your vocabulary and replace it with the word "can." Exchange the word "problem" with the word "opportunity" and watch your world change!

You hold the power to change the world in your hands!

Frustrated, Scott stops. He puts down the ink and reaches for the computer mouse. Turning on some music, he sighs. With a little patience, he knows he can make his deadline. But still, drawing and writing when your hands don't want to cooperate is hard.

Scott Adams needs his hands every day to produce his livelihood and yet he never knows when they will fail. Without notice, they can suddenly twist and move on their own because he has a disorder called focal dystonia.

Maybe you've read DILBERT, the cartoon about a micromanaged U.S. business office with an engineer named Dilbert as the main character. DILBERT appears in 2000 newspapers worldwide in over 60 countries and multiple languages. However, few people realize how difficult it is for Scott Adams to continue to create.

A typical day might mean having to endure uncomfortable convulsions and spasm-like tremors. Scott has learned to "trick" his brain into working with his hands instead of against them. His body may betray him, but he knows that in order to continue his life's dream, he must be determined to never quit.

So, he and thousands like him, take injections or medications. But most importantly, Scott uses his mind. His most powerful tool in overcoming his physical limits is his thoughts.

Your most valuable tool in overcoming your obstacles is also your thoughts.

You have to decide that for today you are going to do whatever it takes to reach your goals. Today you will make the telephone call or write that letter. Just for today, you can see yourself living the life you want to have. I know it can be difficult at first, but be like Scott – don't quit! Keep up the hard work. As you do, you'll find it easier to keep going.

Scott had to decide that his art and drawing are worth the persistence it takes to produce it. Because he chooses to fight through his physical challenge, we know and love his goofy business comic strip with its quirky characters and humorous one-liners.

Living with obstacles is not easy. Persevering is a choice.

Choose this day to live determined to overcome your obstacle and one day you will find it easier and easier to make that choice.

Some people know really early what their destiny is, and they begin to prepare for it. Ichiro Suzuki is one of those people. In August of 2004 he broke an 84 year old record for most hits in a season. He was only 20 years old when he won his first batting title.

What has made Ichiro great? Knowing what he wanted, and knowing what it would take to get there.

Ichiro picked up his first ball and bat when he was 3 years old. When he was eight, he insisted he wanted to play baseball and joined a baseball club. His Dad supported him by becoming the manager. It wasn't good enough for Ichiro because the team only played and practiced on Sundays. He wanted to play every day.

Every day of the week you would find Ichiro and his father outside – playing baseball. They practiced together every single day for 4 years, until Ichiro was old enough to join a team that would give him daily playing time. By the time he was in high school he participated twice in "Koshien" - the National High School Baseball Tournament in Japan.

He went professional as soon as he graduated from High School – racking up honor after honor in his homeland of Japan. He continued to practice just as hard, determined to be the best by doing his best – every day. The Japanese fans responded by making him an idol.

Then a new opportunity presented itself. The Seattle Mariners wanted him. His determination to be the best paid off when the Mariners paid $13 Million dollars to bring him to the United States. Not knowing English, he followed his dream, ignored his fears and came to the United States.

In his first year he was named "Rookie of the Year" and "Most Valuable Player of the Year" for the League. He became an instant sensation.

All the while he kept working hard, focused on being the best he could be, taking nothing for granted. He was where he was because he worked hard. He would continue to work hard.

In 2004 it all came together under the bright lights of the Seattle Mariners home field when he broke the record George Sisler had held on to for 84 years. He made 262 hits in just one season. Amazing! The fans went wild – both here and in Japan. Fireworks exploded. His teammates mobbed him on the field.

262 hits in one season.

It all began when he was just a little boy, determined to be the best by doing his best. Every one of us has that choice to make. You might not have the ability or the desire to be a baseball player, but you have a dream. You have something you want to do with your life.

You get to choose. Choose to be the best by doing your best.

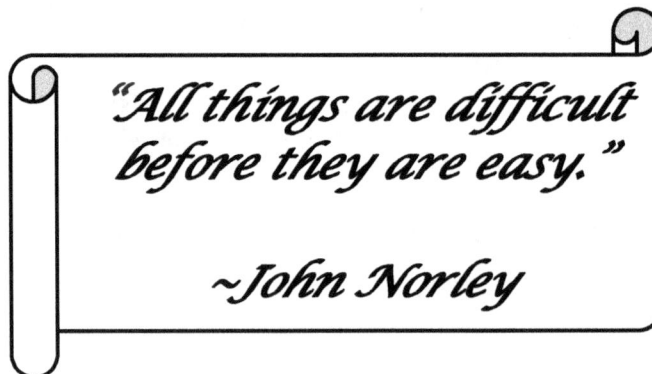

"All things are difficult before they are easy."

~John Norley

POWER BOOSTERS

What are you passionate about?

_____

_____

_____

_____

_____

_____

_____

_____

_____

How can you use your past to create an exciting future?

_____

_____

_____

_____

_____

_____

_____

_____

_____

_____

★ _He Chose Life_ ★

Lying on the bed, Buckminster Fuller looked at the ceiling. Roaches and filth surrounded him.

His purpose for living was gone. His passion for discovery - also gone. Ending his life seemed the only answer.

The year? 1927. Alcohol was the easiest drug to abuse. And he did. At age 32 he should have had much going for him.

He had attended Harvard University just a few years earlier. Twice. Most folks never go to Harvard once in their life but he attended twice AND he got kicked out…twice. He was a self-proclaimed non- conformist. The fraternity misfit. Harvard did not tolerate his actions, even if he was brilliant. He lost his spot there the first time because of throwing a wild, inappropriate party. The 2nd time, he got kicked out for lack of interest.

And now, here he was - bankrupt. Even though he was a machinist by trade, and had served in the United States Navy, he had no money.

Despondent over those facts and over the recent death of his 4-year-old daughter, Fuller dropped out of life.

Lying there deciding how to end his life, he stumbled upon a challenge. A challenge to himself that would ultimately lead him back to living, creating, designing and researching.

The challenge? Fairly simple, but life changing. Suicide wasn't the answer to his depression.

The solution was _"to find what a single individual can contribute to changing the world and benefiting all humanity."_

The challenge to himself got him up and out of bed. Having been a regular at a bistro in Greenwich Village New York, he _bartered_ for his meals in exchange for redecorating the restaurant. By talking to people and risking trying again, he slowly began his journey back.

Buckminster Fuller went from bankrupt and suicidal to author, designer, futurist, inventor, and even served as the second president of Mensa (an exclusive society for certifiable geniuses). Before his life ended in 1983 at the ripe old age of 87, this "guru of design" invented the geodesic dome, traveled the world, wrote over 25 books, lectured in some of the most renowned halls around the world, and named a family of complex Carbon structures "Buckminsterfullerene" or Bucky Balls.

All this, and more, happened because he chose to believe that life is worth living. Not because he had all the answers at once – he certainly didn't. Nor was putting his life back together an overnight process. Buckminster had a complex mind filled with questions that he chose to use to change his world. He wrote in a journal about his life every 15 minutes from 1915 to 1983. . . possibly the most documented human life in history. Buckminster took seriously the challenge of life over death and went on to fulfill his life's interests.

To try and fail is no disgrace.

We want to encourage you today if you are discouraged or depressed. There is hope. We know it is hard sometimes to choose. You are not alone. Like Buckminster, you may have to reinvent your life. But it is worth it. The world needs what you have to offer.

> _"Follow your own vision, despite what others think you are supposed to do. Don't try to be like someone else, because you'll only be second best. Honor your authenticity. Stand tall in who you were meant to be." ~Cynthia Kersey_

★ _It Was In His Blood_ ★

Carlos closed his eyes and could see them as if he were sitting in their kitchens. He watched with anticipation as they patted the tortillas between their experienced hands. He could already smell and taste those wonderful corn patties as they cooked on the outdoor clay oven. As they cooked, their voices blended together in his memory as he heard lively tales of Mexico and family heroes.

He didn't know which was better – eating his grandmothers' spicy, flavorful meals and their handmade tortillas, or listening to their colorful stories. Both fed, nurtured and satisfied him.

Carlos was born in 1928 to a Mexican diplomat and grew up straddling multiple cultures. His pre-teen years were basically spent in Washington, D.C. where his father served as legal counsel to the Mexican embassy. During the summers while his U.S. friends were on vacation, Carlos was sent back to Mexico to live with his grandparents and attend school there.

From his grandmothers, Carlos learned Mexican history and folklore. He says, _"They were the storehouse of these great tales of migrants, revolution, highway robberies, bandits, love affairs, ways of dressing, eating – they had the whole storehouse of the past in their heads and their hearts."_

From his elementary schooling in the U.S. he learned North American culture. From the dinner table he was introduced to and followed international politics.

Since members of the diplomatic corps are moved frequently, Carlos also lived in and adapted to life in Chile, Argentina and other South American countries. He learned many cultures and became acutely aware of the shared cultures of the Latin countries. _"Being the son of a diplomat, you are constantly forced as a child to change schools, language, friends, ambience. So I had to go from Spanish to English to Portuguese, back to Spanish, back to English, make new friends – but it was challenging."_

Carlos became an avid reader and decided at an early age that he wanted to be a writer. At the age of 7 he was writing his own magazine and distributing it throughout the 7 stories of the apartment building in which they lived. Writing was in his blood. _"I had published my first stories in Chile when I was 11 years old, and went on from there and won contests in high school."_

But his parents insisted he needed a career besides writing and wanted him to pursue a law degree. _"... the pressure in Mexico at the time was if you are a writer, you will die of hunger, so you must have a professional title."_ To appease his parents, Carlos attended the National University of Mexico, received his law degree in Switzerland and followed his father's footsteps into diplomatic service.

But Carlos never lost his love of writing, nor his desire to fulfill his dream of becoming a writer. Long days became much longer as he continued to write while fulfilling his government duties. His first novel, _Where the Air is Clear,_ allowed him to leave the Foreign Service and write full time.

Carlos Fuentes became more and more famous as both a writer and political commentator in South America and Spain. Then his novel, _The Old Gringo_, became a best-seller (and a movie) in the United States. He was the first Mexican author to achieve this honor and distinction. Carlos is a prolific writer and popular speaker. He's even taught at Cambridge, Harvard and Brown Universities.

When asked what he felt is the most important thing in life, Carlos replied _"Life and love. The quality of love around me. Yes. And the quality of your life."_

When it comes right down to it, who we are and how we live and love is the most important thing. If we treat others the way we want to be treated; if we respect others and the planet on which we live; if we embrace our differences and choose to live in peace and harmony with one another, then we can't help but become successful!

If you are not living your dream right now because of other responsibilities, do whatever it takes to move that dream forward. Even fifteen minutes a day, carved out of other pressures, can make your dream come true. The important thing is to never give up – just like Carlos never gave up his dream!

★ *Destined To Be A Failure* ★

Sandi Watkins was doomed to be a failure.

At least that's what people believed. That's what they said. By the time Sandi got to high school she had the reputation as the biggest trouble-maker in town. She had a long arrest record, mostly for petty crimes, but everyone knew she was on the fast-track to prison.

Teachers cringed when they say her name on their class list. Sandi was sullen; sat slumped in her seat, and ignored everything going on around her. She had flunked every class in high school but she kept moving up because not one teacher in her school wanted to have her back again. Sandi was moving on - but she was most certainly not moving up.

No one tried to get to know her. Teachers, and most kids, were afraid of her. No one knew when she would erupt with anger, and fights were common. By her senior year, everyone was simply counting the days until Sandi was gone.

Then Sandi did a strange thing. She signed up for a leadership conference designed to get students involved in their communities. It was only because she wanted to get out of class, but something happened that first day...

At first she merely stood against the wall and watched with disdain. She would join the discussion groups but only mumbled a few words when it was her turn to speak. But slowly the interactive games drew her in. She really began to open up when her group was asked to make a list of positive and negative things that had happened at school that year. She certainly had some things to add about that.

You could see the surprise on her face when the other kids in the group actually listened to her. She kept talking. Her group told Sandi her ideas made a lot of sense. They began to treat her like a leader. Suddenly everyone realized Sandi was really smart and had some great ideas.

The next day Sandi continued to share her ideas, signing up to be part of the Homeless Project Team. It was clear she knew something about poverty, hunger and hopelessness. No one was more surprised than Sandi when they elected her to be co-chair of the team.

Okay, maybe the teachers were more surprised - *appalled* actually. They insisted Sandi couldn't do it, that it was ridiculous to put something so important into Sandi Watkins' hands. The principal held firm, however - telling them they might be surprised. I'm sure he was hoping he was right.

Sandi and her team put together a Homeless Scavenger Hunt. They went to the Homeless Shelters to find out what they needed most. Then they made a list of things they planned to collect, assigning the most points to those items the shelters needed most. She found out the homeless rarely get dessert, so she gave high points to cookies, brownie & cake mixes, etc. High scores also went for blankets and coats.

Two weeks later, 100 kids hit the streets of their town, followed by support vans to carry their haul. 4 hours later they met back at the school to load everything into a school bus and take it to the shelter.

There was a slight problem, however. By the time the school bus was loaded, there was room for only one person - the driver. Every seat, every square inch of floor, all the way to the ceiling, was packed with what they had collected. Coats, blankets, clothing, food, a lot of desserts - it was the most the Shelter had ever received.

The shelter residents had huge smiles on their faces as they filed out to help unload the bus. They cheered Sandi and her team. The paper was there to take pictures and tell stories. Sandi was a hero. A leader.

She was definitely a changed person. The rest of her senior year she actually talked in class. She made good grades. She put together 2 more projects for the Homeless Shelter, each time bringing them what they needed most. There were no more arrests.

Sandi graduated in the spring and went on to college - with glowing recommendations from many teachers at her school. Every year she leads 4 projects for the Homeless Shelters in the town where she goes to school.

Here is what Sandi has to say, *"I was on the fast-track to nowhere. I was the only one who could change where my life was going. It was scary but I knew what would happen if I didn't change was worse. I learned I really could make a difference. It changed my whole life. And I learned that other people could believe in me if I only gave them a chance."*

Sandi asked us to share her story to let you know you can be whatever you want to be. It's always your choice. She also wanted us to tell you that a little belief goes a long way. ☺

ഇ‍ാരു

Listen very carefully
To the cry rising from the earth,
Does anyone really love me
Do I really have any worth?
Does anyone know who I really
am?
Does anyone really care?
Is there anyone I can lean on?
Is there anyone with whom to
share?
Is there anyone who will see my
faults
Look beyond my mistakes –
what I try to begin,
See what's beyond the surface
things
And see what's deep within?
Please!
If there's anyone who really
cares,
If there's anyone with whom I
can share,
If of my hurt and pain you are
aware,
Won't you please let me know
you are there?

ഇ‍ാരു

31

★ _Infectious!_ ★

The spicy meat of the hot dog causes her to roll her eyes and scrunch her face. _"This is soooooo good!"_ she manages to squeak out between bites. Her eyes twinkle and her contagious smile is absolutely irresistible. Watching her eat that hotdog makes you drool as she opens wide…and bites.

Rachael loves food, people, and life, itself. Her enthusiasm for what she does is as infectious as her wholesome smile. And she's always on the move… It's fun just watching her; she's so down-to-earth, warm, curious and willing to try most anything. She makes the simplest food irresistible.

Rachael Ray's family owned several restaurants on Cape Cod, Massachusetts. She grew up surrounded by food and cooks. Her mother's side of the family came from Sicily and cooked Italian dishes and her father's side of the family was from Louisiana and he cooked Cajun-style.

"Everyone on both sides of my family cooks," she says.

The allure of New York City called to Rachael and success followed. She soon managed a gourmet food market.

Her love of food, fun and family were displayed in everything she touched…her warmth and openness oozed out of her market displays and food creations. But while successful and happy, Rachel wasn't content.

As glamorous and exciting as New York City was, Rachael knew she didn't want to spend the rest of her life there, so she moved back home to Lake George, New York. Soon after the move, Rachael became the chef of an upscale gourmet market. Wanting to increase the sales at both the market and the market's in-store restaurant, she used her personal pizzazz and created what we now know as _"30 Minute Meals with Rachel Ray."_

It was so popular that the local CBS station signed her to do a weekly cooking show. _"I did 30 Minute Meals for five years on local television, and I earned nothing the first two years. Then I earned $50 a segment. I spent more than that on gas and groceries, but I really enjoyed making the show and I loved going to a viewer's house each week. I knew I enjoyed it, so I stuck with it even though it cost me."_

And the rest is history…

This young woman never attended a culinary training institute, didn't train under a famous chef, nor did she ever work in a five-star restaurant. In fact, she never took a single cooking class. And she is criticized because of it. Her critics don't think she should be teaching cooking because of her lack of professional credentials and her too-bubbly personality. But Rachael doesn't let it get to her. She says, _"It's all true and I can't do much about it at this point."_

I think that's the key to Rachael's wild success. She doesn't try to be someone she isn't. She's just fun-loving Rachael. And you feel like she's letting you in on some great secrets as she shares with you what she knows and what she's discovered. She includes you in the fun – and that's why people keep coming back to watch her shows. Rachael keeps everything simple, real and up-beat. But her success was not easy -- she wasn't an "overnight success." She worked hard, stayed open to opportunities and change, walked through doors that opened for her, and stayed true to herself and her values.

Whether she's doing a cooking show, compiling another cookbook, producing her magazine, appearing on her talk show or running her non-profit organization for kids, Rachael keeps it simple, easy and enjoyable.

I hope you'll consider Rachael's "secrets to success" while you work toward your own success. Be real. Be yourself. Keep life simple. Give to others. And have fun!

"If you have courage to begin, you have the courage to succeed."
~David Viscott

★ *He Did the Impossible* ★

Everyone knew it couldn't be done.

Roger Bannister had no real motivation to prove them wrong. The young Englishman loved to run, but from the time he was a child he also had a passion to be a doctor. This was the passion that drove him. His parents were unable to afford a University education so it was up to him to make it happen.

He knew early on that to achieve his dream of being a doctor he would have to be exceptional – so he set about being exceptional. His studies were paramount, but that didn't mean he couldn't improve his track skills by running to and from school. While he was on his way to earning a scholarship from Oxford University, he was also gaining a name for himself as a runner.

"It is physically impossible for a human being to run a mile in under 4 minutes." This statement was the accepted wisdom of the time during the late 1940's and early 1950's. Runners tried, but failed, proving the words of athletes and doctors – cementing a belief in runners' minds that it couldn't be done.

Roger didn't set out to prove them wrong. He simply loved to run and he was fast. He was also learning a lot about the human body in his studies at Oxford. The day arrived when he was firmly convinced it WAS possible for a human being to run the mile in under 4 minutes.

His decision to be that person was formed by a humiliating defeat in the 1952 Olympics. In order to redeem himself he decided to break the world's record for the mile. No one believed he could do it.

Adding to his challenge was the fact he was now a full-time medical student and he could devote only 45 minutes a day to training. People scoffed at the idea he could accomplish such a wild goal, but Roger believed slow and steady training would allow him to break the record. He painstakingly researched mechanical aspects of running, and developed scientific training methods to help him achieve his goal.

His opportunity came 2 years later – on a blustery day with 25 MPH gusts of wind to hamper his efforts. It didn't look promising. So what? He had trained. He was ready. He *believed* it could be done.

So he simply went out and did it. Roger ran the race of his life, breaking the tape and collapsing as the announcer delivered his time to a wildly cheering crowd:

3:59.4

Within two months his record had been broken by John Landy – proving the 4 minute mile was as much a psychological barrier as it was a physical barrier. As the years have passed the mile has been run in shorter and shorter times, but it was Roger Bannister who proved it was possible.

When he was asked to explain that first four-minute mile – and the art of record breaking – his answer was simple: "It's the ability to take more out of yourself than you've got."

Did you get that?

"It's the ability to take more out of yourself than you've got."

How did Roger do it? First, he BELIEVED he could do it. He understood the size of his success would be determined by the size of his belief.

Here is where we're going to depart from some more common thoughts that are spread around a lot today. While belief is critically important – in fact, he couldn't have accomplished what he did without it - belief alone is not enough. It is not enough to repeat affirmations over and over to yourself, even though they are important.

At some point you have to do the *work*. Roger Bannister ran day after day. He researched the human body. He created scientific methods to enable him to stretch his limits. He did what it would take to fulfill his dream.

What are your goals? What is it you dream of accomplishing? ***BELIEVE it can be done. Then do the work. Apply yourself to success. Apply yourself to excellence. Figure out what it is going to take and then go DO IT!***

You may have no interest in breaking a world record, but we know you have an interest in being the best you that you can be – or you wouldn't be reading this book! ☺

POWER BOOSTERS

Have you walked away from what you thought was a great idea because someone didn't believe in you? What was it?

_____

_____

_____

_____

_____

_____

_____

_____

_____

What is unique about you?

_____

_____

_____

_____

_____

_____

_____

_____

_____

★ *With Only One Hand* ★

Jim struggled. *"Put on the glove. Catch the ball. Take off the glove. Throw the ball. . . . "*
Jim's family struggled silently from the sidelines as well.
Jim kept on. *"Put on the glove. Catch the ball. Take off the glove. Throw the ball."*

As little Jim grew up his desire was to play sports. His parents and family watched in agony as his determination grew with each mistake made. The sun and sweat of the playing fields didn't make learning or watching any easier. In team sports, each player is essential. Each position sets up the next player for success or failure. One dropped ball can mean failure for the entire team. Each player needs to be able to fully play his position and help take care of the next player. Jim knew he had to figure out a way to be a true team player.

Jim kept trying. *"Put on the glove. Catch the ball. Take off the glove. Throw the ball. Put on the glove. Catch the ball. Take off the glove. Throw the ball."*

Finally he found a system that worked… You see, Jim was born with only one hand. He also loved sports - especially football and baseball. He simply wanted to play. He didn't know why he couldn't. He could throw and catch. He just had to do it differently than two-handed kids. I guess no one thought to tell him you can't play these sports very long with only one hand.

Finally, Jim mastered that *"Put on the glove. Catch the ball. Take off the glove. Throw the ball"* technique.

Jim started figuring out how to do what he wanted… when he was only 4 years old! Because he wanted to play -- pure and simple. To Jim, only having one hand meant nothing more than doing things differently from everyone else.

Looking over Jim Abbott's many sports accomplishments and *professional* sports awards (including being the pitcher on the U.S. OLYMPIC baseball team) you will read:
. . . *"Starting* quarterback on his high school football team which went to the *finals* of the Michigan state championship…went to the University of Michigan on a baseball scholarship…led the U of M Wolverines to *2* Big Ten titles…won the prestigious Golden Spikes Award, the U.S. Baseball Federation's Golden Spikes awards, awarded (twice) Michigan's Most Valuable Pitcher…won gold medal in the 1988 Olympics…*and the list goes on and on.*

Yet when you listen to Jim speak, it is to hear a thankful man with a big heart who loves to share the lessons he has learned from his life experiences. He gives back to kids and to life every time he sees the opportunity.

Retired from professional sports now, Jim's reputation as a public speaker is one of respect and courage.

Do you know what he says about who is responsible for whatever good he has done? It's always the people in his life who BELIEVED he could…his parents, family and friends. He speaks often of that simple truth, *"they believed in me… so I believed in me."*

No one ever told him he couldn't and he just never realized that he shouldn't be able to do the stuff he did. How about you? Can you justify NOT doing what you love? It is not about what life gives you that makes a difference, it is what you DO with what life gives you that makes a difference.

Don't quit just because you feel like a one-handed ball player. Keep figuring out how to do it differently because you will succeed if you don't stop!!

> **"The will to win, the desire to succeed,
> the urge to reach your full potential…
> these are the keys that will unlock the
> door to personal excellence."
> ~Eddie Robinson**

Nothing Could Stop Her ★

★

How much courage does it take to follow your passion? *Ask Bethany Hamilton...*

Bethany, who lives in Hawaii, was in grade school when she started her quest to become a professional surfboarder. Surfing is her passion. She spent every available minute in the water; even homeschooling so she had more time to pursue her goal. At 8 years old she entered her first major competition and eventually took the division championships that year. She obviously had what it took.

It was almost all taken away from her on Halloween morning, 2003. Bethany was 13 years old. She was surfing with her best friend, Alana, and Alana's brother and father. The waters were calm, not good for surfing, so Bethany was just lying on her board, her left arm dangling in the cool water.

She remembers a flash of gray, a lot of pressure, and a couple fast tugs. She also remembers watching the jaws of a 15-foot tiger shark cover the top of her board and her left arm. She watched in shock as the water around her turned bright red.

The shark was gone as fast as it appeared. So was her arm – bitten off almost to the armpit.

Bethany was horrified but not in pain at that point. She yelled to her friends and their father, Holt. *"I just got attacked by a shark!"*

It was a combination of miracles that saved Bethany at that point. High tide allowed them to make it over the reef without going around. Holt knew enough to wrap his shirt around the wound to act as a tourniquet while they paddled the quarter-mile to shore. While Bethany drifted in and out of consciousness; a nearby vacationer who was a paramedic, rushed to help her.

Surgery saved her life but her arm was gone for good; and everyone, Bethany included, thought her surfing days were over. Balance is everything when surfing. How could she balance with only one arm?

Within a week, spurred by her passion for surfing, Bethany was thinking something different. *I can do it. I know I can do it!* She wasn't ready to give up what she loved so much, but it would take time for her body to heal.

There was a huge outpouring of love and support from Hawaiians and people all over the world. Love, food, flowers, cards, money... Bethany gathered hope and courage from the waves of love aimed toward her.

It was only a few weeks later – the morning before Thanksgiving when Bethany headed back for the water. Her love of surfing wouldn't let her wait any longer. Her family and friends were there to cheer her on when she stepped into the warm water for the first time since the attack. It was like coming home.

Bethany smiled and waved, then jumped on her board to paddle out – pushing down the fear of what might be waiting under the water. She knew too well...

She failed at her first attempts to ride the board, struggling to push herself up with one arm and keep her balance. Tears rolled down her face, and the crowds cheered when she caught her first wave and rode it in. *Bethany was back!*

Really back. Only months after her vicious incident, Bethany amazed thousands by achieving the unimaginable, including taking 5th at the 2004 National Scholastic Surfing Association Nationals Championships. That September she struck again, winning the Open Women's Division of the NSSA's Hawaiian conference season opener. After placing in the finals of the National Surfing Championships, Bethany secured a spot on USA's National Surfing Team.

Ask Bethany if she is afraid of sharks and she'll say yes. Her heart pounds when she sees a shadow in the water. She has nightmares. But she also has a dream, and moving beyond her fears is the only way to accomplish her dreams – the only way to fulfill the passion she has for surfing.

Is there a fear keeping you from following your passion? I would encourage you to do what Bethany has done. Stare it in the face, acknowledge you are afraid, then go out and do it anyway!!

★ _Evita_ ★

Eva delighted in the love and cheers of the crowd. She couldn't believe it was all for her. "I've come such a long way," she thought to herself. As she smiled and waved to the sea of faces in the courtyard below, she let her mind float back over time. . .

Eva Ibarguren Duarte was born in 1919 as the fifth child to an unwed mother. It wasn't unusual for wealthy men to have several families in rural areas of Argentina at that time. When Eva was one year old, her father returned to his legal family, leaving her mother impoverished. All Juan Duarte left to his "illegitimate" family was a document declaring the five children were his so they could bear his last name. Doña Juana was reduced to living in the poorest part of town. She supported her children by sewing clothing for neighbors. Eventually Eva's older brother moved the struggling family into a larger house which they turned into a boarding house and restaurant. It was during this time that Eva became enthralled with acting and participated in all of her school's plays and concerts.

She still shudders at the memory of her mother's plans for marrying her off to one of the boarders in their house. Eva begged and cajoled her mother to allow her to go to the big city of Buenos Aires. _"Mama, please – there is no future for me here,"_ she pleaded. Eva's mother finally gave in and accompanied her daughter to the big city where Eva was hired as an actress at a radio station.

Changing her name to Evita, she spent the next 9 years working in radio productions, as well as the theater, doing some modeling, and making movies. But radio (there was no TV in Argentina yet) was where she thrived, and she became one of the highest paid radio actresses in Argentina.

Evita was suddenly pulled from her reverie. The crowd was chanting her name. She lifted both hands to her mouth and y threw kisses to the adoring throng. Their roar dimmed as she remembered the first time she saw her husband – the man whose side she'd never left for the past 7 years.

A devastating earthquake had mobilized Colonel Juan Perón, Secretary of Labor, to establish a fund for the victims. He organized an "artistic festival" and invited performers to participate. It was during these festivities that he met and fell in love with Evita. They became inseparable.

Eva and Juan were married in December 1945, the year the Labor Party chose Perón as their candidate for President. For the very first time in Argentina's history, a candidate's wife campaigned and traveled with him. At each stop along the campaign trail, Eva handed out buttons and personally greeted the people. She even represented him when he was too ill to speak.

When Perón assumed the Presidency, unlike other first ladies, Evita chose to take an active political role. She immersed herself in serving her country, devoting her tireless energy to the disadvantaged, the working class, the elderly, children, and women (she was instrumental in getting them the vote in 1951).

In 1950, Evita was diagnosed with cancer, but she refused to slow down. She created medical clinics for the workers, and distributed subsidies to the poor, as well as clothing, food and household goods. She created entire neighborhoods of affordable housing, school food programs, jobs for the unemployed, equipment for hospitals, water and sanitary facilities for low income neighborhoods, and pensions for people over 60. (This is just a tiny, tiny list of her vast accomplishments.) _Evita became a legend in her own time._

At age 33, Evita died of cancer. While there is a great deal of legend, myth and misinformation circulating about this driven woman, no one can deny the passion she had for her country and the incredible work she did on its behalf.

Evita never forgot what it felt like to be poor or have to work hard. She understood how it felt to be discarded, criticized and degraded. What she accomplished in seven short years was remarkable.

You are not expected to do what you cannot do – you are only responsible for doing what you can. When you find yourself in the position of being able to stand up and make a difference, be like Eva Perón and do everything you can to make it happen. Like a song says, _"It's not who you knew, it's not what you did, it's how you lived."_ By living with passion and purpose you can't help but be successful!

★ *Belief!* ★

"Watch out! Help!" Surprised and scared, Stephen shouted as he fell down the stairs of his lofty Cambridge University hall.

His head bloody, his pride shattered, this 21-year-old rowing captain had suddenly lost control of his body. Fearing damage to his brain from the resulting head injury, he took a Mensa (a high IQ society) test to make sure his mental abilities were okay.

Stephen found his mind was okay, but his body was not. Weakness in his arms and legs remained.

"What do I do now? How can I live?" Steve agonized as the doctors gave him only 2-3 years to live.

The diagnosis was technically Amyotrophic Lateral Sclerosis. This condition is called also Maladie de Charcot, or Lou Gehrig's Disease. It starts out causing physical weakness and rapid loss of use of the body, paralysis, and then death. Basically, the neurons in the body stop sending messages to muscles. Unable to function, the muscles weaken and waste away. The patient often loses the ability to control all voluntary movement except for the eyes.

What would you do if you were so young and heard those words? Would you give up? Would you finish your studies? Get married? Would you continue to have your sense of humor? How about pursuing your dreams?

Well, let me tell you about one young man who did not give up, has realized his dream, and has lived over 40 years LONGER than expected!!!

Stephen Hawkins is a multi-faceted man. He is a best-selling author, a husband, father, renowned British physicist, and a Cambridge University professor of mathematics. He has appeared on several TV shows, been referenced in rock songs, and received more than 10 distinguished awards for his scientific studies, theories and research in cosmology and quantum gravity.

Wow! Sounds like a busy guy!

But you have to realize, all of these accomplishments occurred *after* his diagnosis. During the time where his body was failing him, he kept on going. He had to study, research, write, love, travel, act, and live even while his body betrayed him. Through the years he went from an able bodied young man, to a total quadriplegic… unable to move anything more than his check muscle!

At one point, early on in the disease, he admits to becoming depressed and very discouraged. His outlook was dismal. But the turning point in his struggle was his then fiancée's belief in Stephen. Jane believed in him! Even with 2-3 years left to live, she married him anyway. Jane's belief was strong!

Can you catch the spirit of Stephen's life? You read his very long list of accomplishments and while you are very impressed, you may know you couldn't compete with him. Scientific knowledge of that complexity and theories about black holes are not things most people understand easily.

But believing in someone -- that life-changing, life-giving gift of belief! *That* I hope you understand!

I want you to see Stephen as a man, a brilliant scientist, a mathematician, and yes, even a quadriplegic. *He is a man at the top of his field because someone believed in him.*

You may or may not be able to discuss theories of quantum gravity, but you can believe in someone!

First, though, you need to believe in *yourself!* Stephen had to trust Jane's belief. He had to believe *he* was worth the effort it took to learn how to live without use of his hands, his feet, his mouth, and even his vocal chords. He had to believe that what he had to communicate was important – even when answering just one question took him over 6 minutes to type the answer.

Stephen had to believe in order to achieve. That's a common denominator in all successful people: they believe in their ability; they believe in their dream; they believe in their possibility.

Is *not* believing in yourself holding you back from success? Then today's the day to reverse the process! Do whatever is needed to begin your walk of confidence and achievement – it's up to you!

She picks up the small stone and admires the bright colors. *"How much do you think we should ask for this one?"* she asks her friend. They bicker for a while, and then come to an agreement just in time.

"Hurry! Look! Here comes someone!"

9 ½ year old Janine and a friend were selling their artwork (painted rocks) at a roadside stand to raise spending money. But something happened when the money started coming in – the two girls decided to put their money where it mattered, saving the rainforest around their town.

When Janine Licare was 4 years old her family moved to Manuel Antonio, Costa Rica, a beautiful area of rainforest and wildlife. *"Ever since we were little, we acknowledged the fact that it is home to many kinds of animals as well as other living organisms such as trees, plants and insects. The rainforest is an amazing place and we vow to do anything and everything we can to save it. . . If it disappears, then so does our planet."*

The girls created a non-profit organization and opened a store, *Kids Saving the Rainforest* (KSTR), in a corner of a local hotel restaurant. Nine years later, that little corner shop turned into a successful store selling donated artwork and merchandise to raise funds for KSTR's numerous projects. The store also distributes information about their organization, and important environmental issues affecting their area. 100% of the profits go directly to KSTR and Janine's ongoing quest for saving their local rainforest.

One of the first projects *Kids Saving the Rainforest* tackled involved the native, and endangered Titi (squirrel) monkeys, which were dying at an alarming rate. With some investigation, the girls discovered two problems. One problem was that the monkeys were being hit by cars as they tried to cross the roads. The other, was the monkeys were being electrocuted trying to cross over the roads on power lines.

To address the problems, KSTR instituted monkey bridges which are ropes stretched high above the roads so the animals could safely cross. Over 120 such monkey bridges have been installed with the help of the local hydroelectric company, and local experts. The bridges are maintained by *Kids Saving The Rainforest* (KSTR).

Janine is also busy helping plant indigenous trees around the town in which the monkeys and other wildlife feed and live. So far they have planted over 5,000 trees which were also in danger of extinction.

Janine had yet another idea. Why not sponsor a kids' camp every Saturday where she and others teach children about the rainforest, its destruction, and how to help save it? *"Kids are the future. We are the generation that will have to make a difference. Everything depends on us,"* says Janine. Some of the artwork created by the children attending these camps is sold in the KSTR store.

Janine has been instrumental in other projects as well:
- creating a website
- raising money for and purchasing property for an animal rehabilitation center

- a gift shop that sells artwork created by kids and local people
- a program within the community teaching about why NOT to feed the monkeys
- a public library (the first in the area) with over 2000 books people can borrow.
- publishing 3 children's books
- developing sister schools in Denmark, Pakistan, England, Viet Nam, France, Canada, India, the U.S.A. and Costa Rica.

Janine says, *"With the help of volunteers, friends, classmates and the community, we've gone a long way. I believe kids can make a real difference."*

Although Janine was only 9 ½ years old when she and a friend got the idea of selling painted rocks to help save the rainforest, she didn't consider age a factor against them. They started asking for help until they found it!

Janine has remained a major force behind all KSTR's projects. With the assistance of her board of directors, and generous volunteers, Janine is truly making a difference in her world. (You can visit her website at: www.KidsSavingTheRainforest.org.)

What does it take to make a big difference? It means taking one step at a time. Janine didn't start out with a successful organization; she started out selling painted rocks at a roadside stand. Each question she asked and each request for help was a single step along her pathway to success.

Don't think you have to start out big – as the saying goes, *"the trip of a thousand miles begins with the first step."* Be like Janine and get started on your trip to success today!

KIDS SAVING THE RAINFOREST PLEDGE!
We believe that the rainforest is a storehouse of treasures.
We vow to do everything we can to save it.
With the vanishing rainforest goes the future of our planet.
We have to be the generation that makes a difference!

POWER BOOSTERS

What do you need to do to make your dreams come true?

_____

_____

_____

_____

_____

_____

_____

_____

How long are you willing to work for your success?

_____

_____

_____

_____

_____

_____

_____

_____

★ _Imagine Life without These_ ★

Imagine a world with no ATM Machines; no passbook savings; no car or home-improvement loans; or no installment-plan credit. Hard to do, isn't it? Well, you owe a huge thanks to one man who refused to be told it couldn't be done.

Most people want to know how to create success in their life. Regardless of who you are, I know you're thinking about what you are going to create with your life. I'm here to tell you that if you have a strong vision, and a will to overcome whatever obstacles get in your way, you can accomplish anything. Just ask Amadeo Peter Giannini (A.P.).

A.P. certainly had his share of obstacles. When he was only 7, his father died in a fight over one dollar. Things were hard for him and his mother. She remarried a man who went into the produce business. A.P., at age 14, quit school to work with him. By 19 he was a partner in the thriving enterprise, built largely on his reputation for integrity and honesty. At 31 years of age he had all the money he needed or wanted, and announced his retirement. _**One year later his real career began…**_

At 32, A.P. was asked to join the board of the Columbus Savings & Loan society, a modest bank in the Italian section of town. It wasn't long before A.P found himself at odds with the other directors. A.P. wanted the bank to loan money to hard-working immigrants, but at that time banks were in business only for business men and the wealthy. His ideas of loaning money to the working class were scoffed at.

No problem. A.P. had a vision and he was determined to make it reality. He raised $150,000 (a massive amount of money then) from family and friends, bought a converted saloon right across the street from the Columbus S&L; kept the bartender on as an assistant teller; and opened the Bank of Italy.

In those days it wasn't considered proper to solicit banking business. He ignored the "proper way" and began ringing doorbells and talking to everyone he could about what a bank did. He advertised. He kept the bank open longer hours, and on weekends, to fit into working people's schedules. Business boomed.

A.P. believed in making other people's dreams come true. He helped the California Wine Industry get started. He bankrolled Hollywood when they were trying to make movies popular. When Walt Disney ran $2 million dollars over budget on Snow White, he stepped in with a loan.

A.P. believed integrity and "giving back" were the formulas for success. What began in 1904 as the Bank of Italy transformed into the Bank of America – now the world's largest bank.

What about A.P.? Did he die a billionaire? When he passed away at age 79, his estate was worth less than $500,000. _It was purely by choice._ He disdained great wealth, believing it would make him lose touch with the people he wanted to serve. He worked for no pay for years. A surprise $1.5 million bonus one year was promptly given to the University of California. It was far more important for him to give and make a difference.

All of us have that ability and opportunity. As you strive for success, remember you can use it to make a difference in the world. A.P. strove to make a difference every day of his life. Follow your own formula for success, and then look for ways to give back to the world that has given you so much.

There are always ways. They are out there waiting for you to find them!

> _"The real act of discovery
> is not finding new lands,
> but in
> seeing with new eyes."_
> ~Marcel Proust

Columbian Rap Singer

Even though life may throw you curves and move you in directions you didn't plan or anticipate, that doesn't mean you have to become a victim. Choose to overcome those challenges and take control of your life, like young Andrés has!

Ricardo Andrés Tabares grew up on a farm in the countryside near Bogotá, Colombia before rebels forced his family to leave. First the rebels demanded food, then the family's livestock. When Andrés was 13 years old, the rebel leader demanded his father give up their 3-year-old daughter. At that point, Andrés' father refused to comply with their demands. When the rebel leader became angry and threatened the family, the Tabares family grabbed what they could carry and left everything else behind.

The family hitchhiked into Bogota and found themselves living a subsistence existence in the city's slum. Andrés' father thought his family in Bogotá would take them in, but that wasn't the case. Eventually Andrés' father was able to find work and saved enough money to purchase a small 20 x 20 foot piece of land in the barrio called Cazuca.

Andrés says *"Things are better now and we have what is most important – a floor and a roof to live under."*

"Coming from the countryside has been hard. We were used to the river and raising our animals. But here in the city it is very different because you can't even keep a small chicken... there's no place to keep it or money to feed it." Andrés continued, *"Here, everything comes in a bag... water in a bag, milk in bag. On the farm we ate what we grew. Here, everything costs money. If you have money, you buy stuff. If you don't, you can't."*

Others in the barrio have escaped the violence of rebels just like Andrés' family. Unfortunately, they left rebels in the countryside only to inherit "social cleansing" groups within the barrios. These groups take the law into their own hands by trying to silence people and keep them under their control. Andrés says: *". . . there's a war to win, and we'll win it: for all those doing something positive for our community, and above all, for our families."*

Because of the threats to him, Andrés practices capoeira, a Brazilian martial art. But even though he fears these cleansing groups, he expresses what's on his mind through his guitar music and his rap. He takes on the problems of his neighborhood through his music and speaks out about what's happening in his barrio.

Andrés says, *"My dream is to be a great rap artist, but that is just a part of my dreams. The other part is to help my people in Cazuca, the people of my neighborhood by singing and rapping the truth."*

As a 13-year-old, Andrés created a video entitled *Rapping At Fear* for a project entitled Beyond Borders: Personal Stories from a Small Planet. Eleven short films were chosen. The films were produced by teenagers who are overcoming huge obstacles that have defined their lives. The teens shot, edited, and wove their documentaries with animation and archival footage to tell their personal stories on fear and insecurity.

After filming *Rapping at Fear*, Andrés joined *City TV Bogota* as a children's TV host where he worked for about a year. He continues to perform rap in Cazuca and belongs to a theater group in Taller de Vida.

http://www.youtube.com/watch?v=jfxHFuOt5pU

Andrés could view himself as a victim and succumb to the violence and destructive lifestyle around him. But he has chosen to rise above what is wrong and work at making it right. It isn't easy, but he has the passion and the belief to help make it happen.

Life isn't easy. And it isn't fair. But it is your life, and you can choose to live it victoriously. Let Andrés' story inspire you to take the steps you need to take in order to move forward with intention and determination.

At first glance, the pizza looks and tastes like most home delivery pizza. Hot, cheesy, and wafting of oregano and parmesan, Dominos Pizza has kept many a college student going. We've probably all eaten our fair share of the stuff! But did you know founder Tom Managhan has donated hundreds of MILLIONS of dollars? HUNDREDS of millions! He also made some big mistakes in his life... but he didn't quit!

"But Mom, I want to come home. I don't want to be here at the children's home."

"But Mom, I'm sorry. I was just having fun at seminary. I didn't know the nuns would kick me out for that!"

"But Mom, I'm sorry! I thought I was joining the Army. Yes, I know how tough the Marines really are!"

"But Mom, James <u>wanted</u> to trade the store for the VW!"

These conversations could have taken place in Tom's life. His mother loved him, but because she could not care for him, she took him to a Catholic children's home. He did get expelled from seminary; did accidently join the wrong branch of the U.S. military; and did trade his brother a VW Beetle for his brother's half of a little known pizza restaurant.

However, what I learned after taking a second glance at Tom Managhan's life was the millions of dollars he has invested, donated, and given away... despite his mistakes. He took each large mistake he made and tried again.

That is the key to success you know -- trying and trying again!

While still in college, he and his brother James bought a little pizzeria in Michigan. Tom worked and worked and worked that little business until it was the Domino's pizza empire! Then he was able to buy and sell land, furniture and even entire professional baseball teams with MILLION dollar price tags.

But even with his affluence, Tom wasn't very happy deep inside. He knew he was missing something, so he took a break - a 2 year hiatus from work. He reexamined his purpose, his passions, and his beliefs.

He wound up a different man. His "reawakening" brought him peace. Purpose. Meaning. He discovered that *he had more by giving to others.* So he channeled his business savvy and talent into more philanthropic endeavors.

He sold his pizza business and now spends his life creating, funding, building, supporting, and sustaining businesses, colleges, investments and communities that he feels best represent his personal beliefs.

Tom didn't allow being given up as a child, his mistakes or his disillusionment with life to stop him from living. He took the punches, the failings and kept on going. Not everyone in this world agrees with his new directions. They question his religious zeal. The business world wonders at his new enthusiasm. But Tom knows he has to do what gives him the most inner peace.

I wonder; do you know that you too need peace? You don't have to have millions of dollars to give away to find it. All you have to do is to ask yourself, *"Is what I am doing bringing me peace?"* Your honest answer will reveal much. I sincerely hope if you don't have that calming power of peace in your life that you do whatever it takes to get it. I know it is not easy, nor does it happen overnight. But one small step today will bring you a little closer to it tomorrow.

Next time you take a bite out of a Dominos pizza, remember the man who didn't do it all correctly, but kept on trying until he made it right!

> *We are what we repeatedly do. Excellence then, is not an act, but a habit."*
> *~Aristotle*

★ *Meet A Tiny Dynamo* ★

Mary Lou Retton has a list of accomplishments that is impressive no matter who you are. She is the…

- 1st and only American ever (including today) to win the Olympic All Around Title
- 1st American woman to win gold in gymnastics in the Olympics
- 1st female to appear on a Wheaties® cereal box as well as the first female spokesperson for Wheaties® plus scores of other achievements.
-

As extraordinary as all that is, it is encouraging to note that Mary Lou is not perfect. Her gymnastics scores were often times a "perfect 10." As a teen, this petite powerhouse awed the multitudes in each of these sporting events: Uneven Bars, Vault, Team and Floor Exercise. Yet as a baby she was born with a hip condition called hip dysplasia that required a hip replacement. Not only that, but she has suffered with both an overactive bladder and arthritis. As part of her public persona as a sports celebrity, she admitted her problems and gave her support to the medications that combat these conditions.

Mary Lou battled competitors on the mat and her body off the mat. A severe wrist injury and knee surgery forced her to decide whether to quit her beloved gymnastics or try to overcome the injuries. Sitting on the sidelines was not where this dynamo wanted to be. She worked hard. She exercised. She did the strength training exercises. She sweated. She cried. But she did not give up. She kept on and on until one day she was back. She could participate again in the sport she loved and that loved her back. Mary Lou went on to be inducted into both the National Italian American Sports Hall of Fame and the International Gymnastics Hall of Fame.

As an engaging public speaker Mary Lou tells audiences *"to never give up on your dreams! Work hard!"* She knows what it is to feel the applause of millions worldwide, and she knows the solitary agony of pain and rehabilitation.

I want to encourage you to think about your life story. How do you want it to read? You may not want to compete for the gold and hear the applause of millions. But even if your goal is more common than Mary Lou's - keep at it until you get it. Never give up. Refresh your determination and revise your target.

"There is no great achievement that is not the result of patient working and waiting."
~ J. G. Holland

"High achievement always takes place in the framework of high expectation."
~ Jack Kinder

★ *Thinking Big* ★

Life was different back in the 1800's. Charles Tiffany was only 15 when he completed his formal education and went to work managing a general store for his father who owned a Connecticut cotton mill. He worked long, hard hours – learning new things every day. Over the next 10 years he was given some additional education, as well as working in the office of the cotton mill, but by the time he was 25 he still had nothing to call his own – and very little money.

It was time to change his life – time to create his own success. I can imagine the conversation he had with his friend, and new partner, John Young.

"We're going to New York!"

"To do what?" John asked warily.

"We're going to open our very own stationery & notions store on Broadway!"

By now John was looking at him like he'd lost his mind..."With what money?"

"I've talked my father into loaning us $1000."

"$1000! That's all? How are we supposed to start a new business and have money to live on with just $1000?"

Charles had the perfect answer. "It's either that or be stuck here for the rest of our lives."

The two young men went to New York… It was 1837.

The first three days of business in their new store on Broadway were certainly not promising. Tiffany & Young raked in a dismal $4.38 in sales. No matter. With their sights set on success, the young men worked hard to provide products people wanted. Within two years they were selling glassware, cutlery, porcelain, clocks and jewelry.

They had also learned a tremendous amount. They knew to search for every opportunity. They knew to take advantage of ways to expand their business. They knew each year would bring new challenges and opportunities. But Charles still had no idea what they would become.

In 1841 they added a new partner because they needed someone to travel abroad to increase their purchasing power.

Six years later they recognized a growing market for quality gold jewelry and began to manufacture their own.

Just one year later, in 1847, Europe was rocked by disturbances. One of the results was diamonds declining 50% in Paris. They took advantage of the situation to purchase huge amounts – gaining huge profits back in America.

4 years later they began the manufacture of sterling silver ware.

All the while they were moving into bigger and better storefronts.

The Civil War became another opportunity for them. They supported the raging war by manufacturing swords and other articles the Union army needed.

In 1867 they moved into the famous store still on Broadway – Tiffany's.

The young man who had left Connecticut to open a stationery store became the owner of a $2 Million dollar business (the equivalent of a multi-billion dollar business now) that was acknowledged as the greatest jewelry company in North America.

There are so many "Success Secrets" to learn from Charles Tiffany. The one that stands out most to me is the knowledge that your original dream may be just a shadow of its true potential. Tiffany never dreamed of being the greatest jewelry company in North America. He simply moved toward every opportunity – keeping his mind and heart open to every possibility.

What is your dream? Follow it. Take the steps to bring it to reality. But don't let your own ability to dream limit you. Give the dream room to grow. Give it every opportunity to become more. Take advantage of your lessons learned and continue to forge ahead. You never know what it can become!

POWER BOOSTERS

What can you do to make the world a better place? What can you contribute?

_____

_____

_____

_____

_____

_____

_____

_____

_____

Do you have to overcome anything to make your dreams come true? What is it?

_____

_____

_____

_____

_____

_____

_____

_____

_____

_____

"Come on ma'am... time to move on."

Kimball peeked at the park worker through sleepy eyes. The morning songbirds serenaded her as she gathered her bags. The singer drew in a deep cleansing breath and glanced at her watch... only an hour until her shift started at Grady Memorial Hospital in Atlanta, Georgia. Kimball was a respected volunteer. She was also homeless. Her home that day was a park in downtown Atlanta.

Kimball believed there were people less fortunate than herself – and they were the patients in the hospital. Every day she gave of her time, her heart and her song to help those recuperating from surgery, accidents and disease.

An accomplished singer and orator, Kimball had not always been homeless. But sometimes life forces us down a rough and rocky road in order to get us to a beautiful place. Kimball knew the only way to get off that rocky road was to *give* herself out of that bad place.

So, Kimball William's literally sang and volunteered her way onto a smoother road. She became an advocate for the poor, abused and destitute. As she took care of so many others, local leaders noticed and took care of her. She had left the rocky pathway and found herself on the way to a more successful life again.

Kimball never forgets where she has been. She is known throughout Georgia for her outlandish but gorgeous hair bows, her generosity and her voice. She is not a part time volunteer. She does not work on others' behalf in her spare time. Now that she has a home and a career as a sought after singer and speaker, she still devotes her time to several causes and events. She has become the voice of *"'Feed The People Christmas Party,"* a Christmas party for homeless, abandoned, abused and generally underprivileged children. Kimball is also involved in a long list of fundraisers. She knows only too well that poverty, abuse and disease never rest and so neither does she.

As I read over her life, I was amazed at this beautiful woman. Sometimes you read of someone you'd like to meet and take to dinner. Kimball is one such lady. Undaunted in her life's passion and mission to serve others, she let nothing stop her. Not even being homeless. I'm sure there were times she wanted to give up and quit. But she didn't.

What about you? What are you willing to do to keep your dream alive and make it come true?

★ *What Do You Really Want To Do?* ★

Have you ever had someone comment on something you said or did and you responded with, "that's just how I am"? Perhaps it was something astute that you said, a keen observation that you made, or something you did that they thought was extraordinary, but to you it wasn't especially impressive.

Jane was born in 1934 in London, England and grew up on the southern coast of England. As long as she can remember, she'd loved animals.

When Jane was two years old, her father gave her a life-like toy chimpanzee named Jubilee. Well-meaning friends warned him that it would frighten her, but she adored the toy. (In fact, she still has it and it currently sits on a chair in her home in England.)

At age four Jane stayed on a farm and helped collect hen's eggs. When she asked the adults how the hens could lay such big eggs, no one answered to her satisfaction. So she hid in the small, stuffy hen house for four hours to find out! (If you've ever been around young children this age, you know that's pretty extraordinary. Actually, it would be amazing for any age kid, and many adults!) ☺

Unknown to Jane, the family had called the police; everyone was frantically trying to locate the missing four-year-old. Imagine her family's relief and amazement, when Jane came rushing out of the hen house in great excitement to tell them how hens lay eggs. Instead of scolding her youngster, Jane's mother sat down with her and listened intently.

Not surprisingly, Jane's favorite childhood books included *The Story of Dr. Dolittle, The Jungle Book,* and the Tarzan books. By age 10 or 11, she was dreaming of going to Africa to live with animals. But instead of discouraging her, Jane's mother said, *"Jane, if you really want something, and if you work hard, take advantage of the opportunities, and never give up, you will somehow find a way."*

Believing her mother's words, Jane did what it took to get to Africa and at age 23 finally sailed to Kenya. When there she heard of a famous paleontologist and anthropologist by the name of Dr. Louis Leakey. She got an appointment to meet him and ended up being interviewed by him about Africa and its wildlife. Dr. Leakey hired her as his assistant, and together with Mrs. Leakey, they traveled to Olduvai Gorge on a fossil-hunting expedition.

After three months at Olduvai Gorge, the group returned to Nairobi, Kenya and Jane worked at the museum there. Soon after, Jane and Dr. Leakey spoke about Jane studying a group of chimpanzees on the shores of Lake Tanganyika. *"I could have gone on at the museum. Or I could have learned a lot more about fossils and become a paleontologist. But both these careers had to do with dead animals. And I still wanted to work with living animals.*

My childhood dream was as strong as ever. Somehow I must find a way to watch free, wild animals living their own undisturbed lives. I wanted to learn things that no one else knew, uncover secrets through patient observation. I wanted to come as close to talking to animals as I could."

At first the British authorities resisted the idea of a young woman living among wild animals in Africa. But they finally agreed to Leakey's proposal when Jane's mother volunteered to accompany her for the first three months. In 1960, Jane and her mother arrived at Gombe National Park in Tanganyika (now Tanzania).

And the rest is history...

Jane Goodall's years of solitary, patient observation and research taught us that chimps hunt for meat, use tools and have unique personalities. Her few month field study turned into the longest such study of any animal species in their natural surroundings.

Jane writes: *"The most wonderful thing about fieldwork, whether with chimps, baboons or any other wildlife, is waking up and asking yourself, 'What am I going to see today?' ...It can be exhausting climbing high, far and fast. Around 3 pm you feel very weary because of spending a lot of the day on your tummy, crawling, with vines catching your hair. Living under the skies, the forest is for me a temple, a cathedral made of tree canopies and dancing light, especially when it's raining and quiet. That's heaven on earth for me. I can't imagine going through life without being tuned into the mystical side of nature. People are too busy nowadays."*

You see, Jane wasn't doing anything extraordinary on purpose – she was simply fulfilling her purpose – her childhood dream of living with and observing animals. She was living out the proclamation: that's just how I am.

Do you remember your childhood dream – what you answered when someone asked you what you wanted to do "when you grew up"? Does it still make your heart race? Can you still see yourself living it out? If your answers are "yes," you've most likely just identified your passion – your life's purpose. And it's never too late to reclaim it!

Believe Jane's mother's words: *"...if you really want something, and if you work hard, take advantage of the opportunities, and never give up, you will somehow find a way."*

Jane did – and so can you!

One of the things that may get in the way of people being lifelong learners is that they're not in touch with their passion. If you're passionate about what it is you do, then you're going to be looking for everything you can to get better at it.

~ Jack Canfield

★ *Wild Child* ★

His parents were too busy running their tavern and basically ignored their son. To cover his unhappiness, George took advantage of every opportunity to cause trouble. He stole, skipped school, chewed tobacco, and drank whiskey – all before he was 7 years old.

It was the police who finally got the parents to pay attention to their son. Their response to the problem was to place their son in a reformatory-orphanage and they rarely saw him again. George, unable to adapt to the strict regulations of St. Mary's Industrial School for boys, was quickly classified as *incorrigible.* It was probably the nicest thing they could say.

Until… one man saw promise within the boy and introduced him to the game of baseball.

Whether you're a baseball fan or not – everyone knows the name Babe Ruth. The very name draws up the image of homeruns.

When you learn more about him the name also conjures images of drinking bouts, devoured hot dogs, partying and carousing. Babe Ruth never gave up his wild ways; he simply found a way to channel some of them doing what he loved to do – play baseball.

He actually began his march to fame as a pitcher – setting many records for his prowess on the mound with the Boston Red Sox. His famed pitching, and impressive hitting, wasn't enough though… the Boston Red Sox owner, needing money to finance his dreams of Broadway, sold the Babe to the New York Yankees. It was another in a long line of rejections the Babe had experienced.

He could have let his bitterness stop his life and halt his drive to success and fame. He made a different choice. He kept playing. He kept swinging. He kept doing what he loved. He played baseball.

His ability to hit homeruns exploded. He became famous. He created homerun records that stood for decades. He smiled, laughed, lived life to the fullest – and he kept on swinging.

Here's the thing most people don't talk about. While it's true he hit more homeruns than anyone else; it's also true that he struck out more times than anyone. He only hit a homerun, on average, every 11 times at bat. He failed more times than he succeeded. Did you get that?

He failed more times than he succeeded!

Yet he went on to become an American icon; loved by millions; a household name.

Why? Because he chose to keep swinging! A strike out. A walk. A single. They were all necessary to get him to the next homerun. He kept swinging.

As I have studied the lives of successful people I have seen this truth. Most have failed more times than they have succeeded. Yet they choose to keep swinging until they finally connect with the right thing: the right business; the right relationship; the right way to do something. They learn from every failure and jump right back into the game.

Have you failed at something? More than one *something*? Great! Stay in the game. Keep swinging. You'll finally connect. You'll find that right thing; you'll meet that right person; you'll discover the right way. The only way you can fail is if you put the bat down and choose to stop swinging.

*"What you get by achieving your goals is not as important as what you **become** by achieving your goals."*
~Zig Ziglar

"I'm sorry Jim . . . It just won't work"
"Sorry guy . . . great idea . . . but not going with it."
"Sounds wonderful . . . never gonna happen, sorry."
"Jim, I wish I could help . . . but sorry, it just won't work."

Jim Stovall was used to hearing the rejections. He had been all over the TV industry looking for supporters. He knew what he had in mind would work and would revolutionize the television world for the visually impaired… if he could just make it materialize.

He had started losing his eyesight at age 7, but had pushed through his limits and become an All American athlete. At age 30 he had lost his battle – and his sight. He was tired. So tired and discouraged, he seriously considered staying in his room and never coming out. He even equipped himself with a TV, VCR, a radio and a phone . . . and originally determined to never leave.

However, at a support group for the blind and visually impaired, he was challenged to "see" beyond his limitations to what he could imagine.

Frustrated that he could only marginally enjoy his favorite classical movies, he made a life changing decision… he chose to leave his world of selfish isolation and partner with Kathy, a woman he had met at that support group who had caught Jim's vision.

Although in the beginning they had no knowledge of HOW to do what Jim envisioned, they just "knew that they knew" there was a way.

Jim's frustration with movie and TV watching was that because he was blind, he missed most of the important scenic and visual elements crucial to understanding the story. The movies simply needed more narrative to help describe what was going on so the visually impaired could "see" the images in their minds.

Using borrowed equipment and trial and error, the Narrative Television Network (NTN) was born.

"I'd like to thank the Academy for this award. I know I was told that what I 'saw' couldn't be achieved… well, I am just thankful I couldn't accept that truth and kept on trying. What did I have to lose? Nothing… and everything to gain."

This could have been Jim's acceptance speech less than one year later, when he accepted an Emmy from the National Academy of Television Arts and Sciences for "Technology that has expanded the use of Television."

Today NTN reaches over 25 million homes in the U.S. and is shown in 11 foreign countries. Numerous awards, countless articles and many, many broadcasts later, NTN is changing the lives of the 13 million blind and visually impaired people in the U.S. alone.

What exactly does NTN do? It *"adds the voice of a narrator to the existing programming sound track without any of the original audio or video."*

Jim did not stop there. He has gone on to become a highly sought after motivational speaker and award winning author. He travels the world granting interviews, making speeches, and serving as President of Narrative Television Network.

His decision to come out of his room has given millions of people new hope, new enjoyment and new life.

Thankfully, he allowed someone to partner with him and challenge him. Success isn't about accomplishing things on your own. In fact, none of us can do that! Each of us builds on what has been done before us. So don't hesitate to ask others to come alongside you in your road to success. That way you won't be lonely when you reach the top!

From Pennies to Millions ★

★

Marion Luna Brem was 30 years old when she was handed a death sentence. Marion had cancer of the breast and cervix. In the short span of eleven weeks, she had two surgeries: a mastectomy and hysterectomy. Next she suffered through the horrible effects of chemotherapy. In addition to her pain, the cancer had robbed her of her hair, her savings and her husband. He left because he couldn't deal with the pressure any more. He also left Marion with two small boys and no way to support them.

One hot morning Marion found herself on the floor of her bathroom trying not to throw up again. She was not only facing overwhelming pain and paralyzing fear; she was facing a major decision. Would she give up or would she fight back? Thoughts of her children consumed her. She needed to get a job, but she had little work experience and next to no formal education. Add to that equation the fact she was a woman - and a Latina, and the prospects looked as dismal as the bathroom floor.

Marion's best friend suggested a job in sales. At first Marion pushed the idea aside. And then she decided to act on it. She chose the male dominated car sales industry. In her healthier days she'd been a switchboard operator at a car dealership, and knew there was good money in car sales. She'd also witnessed how the salesmen talked exclusively to the men and virtually ignored the women. Her instincts told her women were a more important part of the equation than they were given credit for. Statistics now prove she was right. When couples buy a car, the woman influences the decision 80% of the time.

It wasn't an easy road. Marion was flatly refused applications (because she was a woman) in 16 car dealerships. Finally, at the 17th car dealership she told the manager what she'd observed about women car buyers. He hired her on the spot.

Her all-male colleagues welcomed the rookie. They didn't see her as competition but rather as a curiosity. It wasn't until she started outperforming them that they became cool toward her. Even so, Marion received the annual "Salesman of the Year" award -- complete with a man's Rolex watch. She accepted the recognition and enjoyed her achievement.

Marion was the top producer for the next two years. Then she approached her boss for a management position. He refused her because he didn't want to remove her from sales -- she was making too much money for the company.

Difficult as it was, Marion left the security of that position and hit the pavement again. She was finally hired as an entry-level manager at a new dealership. Two and half years later she was ready to start her own dealership.

She went to the drugstore and bought 50 school folders and created portfolios. She called them her "brag folder" and they contained her certificates, press clippings and a biography. She sent the package to 50 CPAs all over Texas. Two weeks later she received a call from one of her contacts. He became her silent partner, put up the working capital and millions in loans and Marion opened a Chrysler dealership.

In just 5 years after selling her first car, Marion Luna Brem opened "Love Chrysler" complete with a heart logo on every car. Marion's motto: *"It's not just the hearts on our cars, it's the hearts inside our people. We're spreading Love all over Texas!"*

Today Marion is cancer-free, the owner of two car dealerships, and recently celebrated the 11th anniversary of Love Chrysler. Her company is 89th on the Hispanic Business 500 with revenues of more than $45 million.

Success is a frame of mind that takes action. Believe in yourself. Keep moving forward. And remember Marion! Hopefully your journey does not begin as tragically as Marion's but use her determination and belief to keep going!

> *"Continuous effort – not strength or intelligence – is the key to unlocking our potential."* ~Liane Cardes

POWER BOOSTERS

How can you become better at what you do?

_____

_____

_____

_____

_____

_____

_____

_____

What experiences in your life have prepared you for success? (Hint: Some of the best experiences were the most painful ones.

_____

_____

_____

_____

_____

_____

_____

_____

★ _Turning Failure into Success_ ★

Jean's background certainly didn't indicate tremendous success for the future. Born in New York, she graduated from high school with a partial college scholarship, but couldn't attend because her family couldn't pay the rest. She decided to attend a business school, but had barely begun when her father died – forcing her to quit and take a fulltime job.

She moved from one low paying job to another, eventually marrying and becoming a homemaker and mother of two. She left the workplace, but devoted a lot of time to working with various organizations and charities.

And she kept gaining weight. She had been overweight as a child. She was overweight as an adult. She tried everything to conquer her problem – diets, doctors, medications. Nothing worked long-term.

She was desperate to find a way to conquer her problem so she headed for the New York Health Obesity Clinic. She was given a diet to follow but she fell right back into the cheating that always defeated her. She kept her failures to herself. The woman running the clinic had never been overweight.

"How could she understand the cheating of an overweight housewife?" Jean asked.

Desperate for someone to talk to, she invited 6 overweight friends to her house. The first meeting was so helpful they decided to meet weekly to share their successes and struggles.

The meeting kept growing as more women joined them. Soon she was organizing meetings for hundreds of women – charging just 25 cents a week to cover costs. And her weight kept coming off. When she reached her personal goal she reached out to help her family. Her husband lost 70 pounds. Her mother shed 57.

From her victory, and the victories of those she reached out to help, she began to realize this was bigger than just her original desire to lose weight.

On May 15, 1963, Weight Watchers was born.

From the living room of her small New York home, Weight Watchers grew to an international business worth millions - that helped millions. Jean Nidetch remained slim and became the spokeswoman for her exploding company, traveling all around the world – helping others change their lives the same way she did.

Her Success Secret? She found a way to solve a problem of her own, then invited other people along on the journey.

We've had people tell us, _"All the problems have been solved, and all the ideas for making money have been used."_

Hogwash! As long as there is life there will be problems. There will be ideas for success. Your job is to get out of your tiny little "box" and start thinking and dreaming of solutions.

Her other Success Secret?

She never started out to become a millionaire. She started out to solve her own problem. Then she wanted to help others. (Remember, she only charged 25 cents per meeting in the beginning.) Her great success sprang from a desire to make a difference.

Think outside the box. If you haven't experienced the success you want in life, start paying attention and see where you can make a difference. It's there. You just have to open your heart and mind to find it. The answer will probably surprise you, but that's half the fun.

> **"All endeavor calls for the ability to tramp the last mile, shape the last plan, endure the last hours toil. The fight to the finish spirit is the one...characteristic we must possess if we are to face the future as finishers."**
>
> **~Henry David Thoreau**

★ *Doing the Impossible* ★

The warm early morning California sun peeked in through the curtains, tempting George to snooze just a few more minutes.

Ring! Ring!

The alarm clock went off but George snuggled closer to Anne, his wife.

In his first year of studies for his Doctorate, George rarely was late to class. But this morning, the call of peaceful sleep overshadowed both the sun and the alarm.

Ring! Ring!

Now he had to get up and fly to his statistics class.

Quickly, he dressed and rushed to his early morning class at University of California, Berkeley.

George quietly slipped in, arriving after the lecture started. He noticed 2 new problems written on the board to be solved. Not wanting to fall behind, he jotted them down assuming they were homework.

After his day of classes, he sat down at the table and began working on those problems.

"Wow," he thought, *"these are tougher than usual. Must be a challenge of some sort."*

George worked on these problems several days. But finally after much effort, he solved them.

Relieved to have them out of the way, George put them out of his mind.

Taking his work into class, he approached his instructor. *"Professor Neymans, here's my recent homework assignment. Sorry it took so long. What do you want me to do with it?"*

"Just put it on my desk."

George was reluctant to put this work on that desk because of the clutter of papers already placed on it. But he did as he was told and left.

Again the early morning California sun peeked in through the curtains. But this time the alarm clock did not ring. Anne and George groggily heard another noise. *Bang! Bang! Bang!* There was a loud knocking on his door.

Professor Neymans excitedly rushed in; papers in hand and with great enthusiasm exclaimed something like this: *"I have the paper ready for publication. Read it so I can get it published. You don't know what you did...Those problems you solved were not homework. Not homework at all. Those problems are, well were, unsolvable. No one ever before had been able to solve them. They were examples of what could not be done. But you did it! You did it! You did what they said couldn't be done!"*

Not sure what his professor was talking about, George looked at him quizzically.

Finally, slowly, George understood what was taking place in his little California kitchen.

That day, a few weeks earlier when he overslept and arrived late to class, he missed something very important from his professors' lecture. He had arrived too late to hear that the two problems written before the class were not homework. They couldn't be solved.

Yet he had solved them both in days!! All because he never knew it couldn't be done.

Amazing, isn't it? I am not a mathematician by any means but I can understand the importance of what happened back in 1939 on that college campus. To read over George Dantzig's life, one reads of honors, awards, Pentagon jobs, professorships, publications, and degrees all involving very complicated mathematical analysis, research, and development.

Yet this story of doing what they said couldn't be done stays with me. Do you get the gem of beauty in George's life? He didn't know he was doing the impossible. He never once considered the task before him too hard . . . just a little "tougher than usual."

Think what you and I could do if we could grab hold of that concept? We would be unstoppable in whatever tasks we set out to do. Nothing would stand in our way.

I encourage you today to look at your situation as "just a bit tougher than usual." You can find a way to manage. You can find the answer to the problem. It might take a few days but I believe you'll get it right! (I think I will too!) Be like George, and work with the positive belief that every problem has a solution!

★ *A Big Dream* ★

Arnold was born on July 30, 1947 in a small second floor apartment of a large house in an isolated village in Austria. Growing up the second of two sons, his abusive father made it clear that he favored the older brother. He beat and taunted Arnold often, calling him "Cinderella." Following their father's lead, Arnold's older brother constantly picked on him.

Because of the verbal, emotional and physical abuse, young Arnold dreamed of leaving his family and becoming strong, rich and famous. His dream revolved around leaving not only his family, but his country as well. *"I love Austria and love the Austrian people, but I always knew America was the place for me. In school, when the teacher would talk about America... I would daydream about living there. I would sit... and watch for hours American movies, transfixed by my heroes like John Wayne. Everything about America seemed so big to me, so open, so possible."* His dream was beginning to take shape.

Arnold enjoyed sports but was a scrawny guy. To gain strength, he began lifting weights. *"I was always interested in proportion and perfection. When I was 15, I took off my clothes and looked in the mirror, I realized that to be perfectly proportioned, I would need 20-inch arms to match the rest of me."*

As Arnold progressed in his body building efforts, he noticed his shoulders, chest and arms were developing nicely, but his thighs and calves weren't doing as well. To motivate himself to work harder on his legs, Arnold cut his trousers off at the knees and walked around with his "chicken legs" showing. The challenge worked - comments from people passing by pushed him to keep working on building up his leg muscles. Arnold's goal was to become *"the best built man in the world."*

By the time he was 18 years old, Arnold was physically "pumped up." He easily became the 1965 Junior Mr. Europe. The legend was born... Arnold Schwarzenegger went on to claim many professional titles, including the International Power Lifting Championship, before moving to the United States. He went on to garner the Mr. Universe title as the youngest-ever winner at the age of 20. He won the title four more times. At age 23, he captured his first of seven Mr. Olympia titles.

Driven by his passion to be taken seriously and to become wealthy, Arnold obtained a correspondence degree in business and international economics from the University of Wisconsin. Along with some well-invested business money, Arnold worked his goal toward riches. He became a millionaire in business long before his success in movie making.

Arnold's big dream of becoming a movie star like his hero, John Wayne, proved more elusive. Because of his strong Austrian accent, he had difficulty landing roles. He got his first role in *Hercules Goes to New York* in 1970, but Schwarzenegger's career-launching role came with *The Terminator* in 1984. The rest is movie history.

Being truly famous was also part of his goals. After marrying the niece of former U.S. President John F. Kennedy, Maria Shriver, Arnold found himself the only Republican in a very famous and influential Democratic family! He served as Chairman of the President's Council on Sports and Fitness, and now serves as governor of California. Arnold has a great sense of humor and a huge heart for the welfare of children (he and Maria have four of their own). He has participated in the Special Olympics (started by Maria's mother) for over 25 years and supports children's programs both in and out of school.

Reflecting over the years, Arnold says, *"In the beginning I was selfish. It was all about, 'How do I build Arnold? How can I win the most Mr. Universe and Mr. Olympia contests? How can I get into the movies and get into business?' I was thinking about myself... As I've grown up, got older, maybe wiser, I think your life is judged not by how much you have taken, but by how much you give back."*

From his difficult beginnings as a beaten, abused child in a remote European village, to the fulfillment of huge dreams in his adopted country, Arnold Schwarzenegger did what it took to move beyond his circumstances. It took hard work and dogged determination. None of it came easily. And Arnold now understands that life is not about how much you get – it's about how much you give back. ***As you move forward in the pursuit of your dreams, never forget that it truly is in giving that you will receive!***

★ *Only 20 Years Old* ★

Debbi was only 19 years old when she reached a cross-road in her life. She was married to a well-known Economist and Futurist, and had quit work to play the role of a conventional wife. She hadn't expected her decision to deal such a hard blow to her self-esteem. No one seemed to think she had anything to offer – including herself.

One night, at a party, things reached a head. People were falling all over themselves to talk to her husband – they were treating her like she was an absolute zero, walking away from her in most conversations. Until the party host approached her… She *tried* to talk to him, answering his barrage of questions. She *tried* to appear sophisticated, urbane and clever – failing miserably at her attempt to be something she wasn't.

Her host finally asked, "What do you intend to *do* with your life?"

Debbi was a nervous wreck at this point. She blurted out, "Well, I'm mostly trying to get orientated."

Her host looked at her with disgust. "The word is oriented," he snapped. "There is no such word as *orientated*. Why don't you learn to use the English language?" He spat out his words and walked away.

Well, you can imagine… Debbi was crushed. She cried all the way home. But somewhere, in the middle of all the tears, she made a decision. She would never, never, NEVER let something like that happen again. She was done living in someone else's shadow. She would find something of her own.

As she pondered what she was going to do, she thought back to the old boat motor that had accumulated dust in her family's basement when she was growing up – her parents and 5 girls in a 2-bedroom, 1 bathroom home. Her father was going to buy a boat for that motor *someday*. He never did, and to Debbi that motor became a symbol of putting off dreams until it's too late to achieve them.

Debbi had watched her father die with his dreams unfulfilled. She didn't want the same thing to happen to her. She would do *something*.

But what?

The only thing Debbi was really good at was making cookies. She had been baking and experimenting with recipes since was 13. She'd add more butter; use less flour; or try different kinds of chocolate. She'd finally hit on a recipe that she believed was ideal. Her cookies were soft, buttery and crammed with chocolate chips.

She realized she had to use her gifts so. . . Debbi decided to open a cookie store. Every single person in her life told her it wouldn't work. No one believed in her.

It didn't matter. On August 18, 1977, when Debbi was 20, she opened her first store. No one came. By noon she was desperate. She stared at the empty store and decided if she was going to go out of business, she would at least do it in style.

Debbi loaded up a tray of cookies and went out in to her shopping arcade, trying to give away cookies. No one would take them. She figured she had nothing to lose at this point, so she headed out to the street. She begged, pleaded and wheedled until people finally took her samples. She smiled as their faces lit up.

She went back to the store and sold cookies to the people who had followed her wanting more. By the end of the day she had sold $50 worth. The next day she sold $75 worth.

The rest is Cookie History. . .

Debbi Fields eventually owner over 600 stores – with sales in the multi-millions. She is also the mother of 5. She did indeed find something of her own!

You will face obstacles. You will face people who don't believe in your dreams. So what? It's YOUR life. It will become what YOU decide to make it.

Debbi Fields shared this in a speech she gave: **"Whatever you do in your life, you have to be absolutely passionate about it."**

Debbi was passionate about cookies. Passionate about excellence. Passionate about living with no regrets.

Take some time to think about what you are passionate about. Make a list. It might be long. It might be short. What are you MOST passionate about? What will create the greatest joy and success in your life if you decide to do it? What will you most regret if you *don't* do it?

Right now – TODAY – you have gifts that can make a difference in how you live your life. How will you use them? What will you do? It's up to you, and I know whatever you decide, you will be successful!

Power Booster

What are you MOST passionate about? What will create the greatest joy and success in your life if you decide to do it? What will you most regret if you *don't* do it? *(Be completely honest, and this could change your life!)*

_____

_____

_____

_____

_____

_____

_____

_____

_____

_____

The Seriousness of Laughter

Norman Cousins was diagnosed with an illness and told that he had little chance of surviving it. Put in a hospital room to die, he rejected the diagnosis and took matters into his own hands. Norman started mega dosing on Vitamin C and put himself on a daily regimen of good old fashioned belly laughing. He was convinced that a positive attitude, including MUCH laughter, helped the body heal.

In his book, *Anatomy of an Illness* Cousins writes: *"I made the joyous discovery that ten minutes of genuine belly laughter had an anesthetic effect and would give me at least two hours of pain-free sleep. When the pain-killing effect of the laughter wore off, we would switch on the motion picture projector again and not infrequently, it would lead to another pain-free interval."*

Norman Cousins loved watching the Marx Brothers and his laughter could be heard up and down the hospital corridors. Occasionally other patients would complain and the nursing staff would have to ask Cousins to quiet down. Norman Cousins lived 16 years longer than his doctors predicted.

Others are learning the secrets he discovered. *Readers Digest* ran an issue dedicated to humor and laughter. They made some very important summaries:

- Laughter reduces stress, improves memory and helps keep our hearts healthy.
- Lightheartedness can lead to a more positive approach in everyday situations.
- Laughing for 10-15 minutes increases your heart rate by 10%-20%, burning an extra 10-40 calories a day, which over one year could add up to a four-pound weight loss.
- A UCLA study found that children tolerated pain better than usual when watching a funny program or video.
- Humor increases the production and effectiveness of natural killer cells that stomp out germs. These cells are elevated for at least 12 hours after just an hour of watching a funny movie or show.

As an ancient proverb says: *"A cheerful disposition is good for your health; gloom and doom leave you bone-tired."*

So take laughing seriously! It can improve your health and help you live longer and better!

You could become "successful" according the world's standards, but if your life isn't full of joy and laughter, what's the point? *Look for every reason you can find to laugh, and make a commitment to bring laughter to other's lives!*

> The human race has only one really effective weapon and that is laughter.
>
> ~Mark Twain

★ *Heading West* ★

Many years ago a movement swept through America. The call went out to all who had the courage and vision to "Head West." What a picture was drawn for them. . . *The West is where you want to be. There is land for everyone - for the taking! Beautiful. Fertile. Opportunity for everyone. Don't miss your opportunity to be one of the first to stake your claim!*

The call went out and hordes signed up to join the wagon trains pulling out of Independence, Missouri. As the pioneers bought supplies and lined up their wagons, their eyes shone with the excitement of what would be waiting at the end of the trail. I think it fair to say not one of them had a real understanding of what lay between Missouri and the far west they envisioned in their dreams.

Can't you hear the conversation. . .?

"Why, honey," one confident husband says to his rather nervous wife, *"there isn't going to be anything to this. We've got a nice, sturdy wagon. We're all together, and we have plenty of food. We're just going to roll along the trail for a while and soon we'll have everything we've dreamed of. Just think of it!"*

I don't know how long before the starry looks faded from their eyes - somewhere between broken wagon wheels and Indian attacks. Maybe it was the weevils in the flour, or the snowstorm that left them stranded in the mountains for months on end. Perhaps it was losing a child to illness because there were

not enough medical supplies, or simply the fatigue that came from fighting the dust, heat, and long days of the grueling cruelness of the trail.

Every pioneer who started down the trail, if they didn't die, had one of three things happen. Some gave up and turned back. Others decided they couldn't take any more and simply built a house where they stopped. Then there were the others... the ones who made it all the way to the West.

Yes, somewhere along the way the starry look faded from their eyes. . . *faded.* . . to be replaced by determination, broken wagon wheels, Indian attacks, weevils, snowstorms, death, fatigue, choking dust, and long days. They all became daily obstacles to be endured and overcome, but at some point each person who made it, simply decided nothing was going to stop them. They had left behind their former lives to go someplace new. ***They were going…***

So what about you? Do you have a dream? Surely you must, or you wouldn't be reading this book! ☺

Do you have something you've started, but then turned back because it seemed too hard? Or maybe you're still on the trail, wondering which obstacle will be the one to destroy what you've worked so hard for.

Maybe you're just looking at the trail, thinking, *"No way. Not me. That just looks too hard."* Yet your heart yearns to go where the trail will take you.

You have a choice to make every single day. You can stay right where you are, or you can go on an adventure to accomplish what you dream of accomplishing. Not going may seem safer, but the truth is that not going will only assure you stay right where you are in your life.

What do you want? Where do you want to go? The only way to get there is to start your journey, and then determine to not let anything stop you!

★ _Radio_ ★

"Happy Thanksgiving!" James smiled his beautiful smile at the young disheveled man.

"Want some more dressing? Here you go! Happy Thanksgiving." He eagerly serves the men at the _Haven of Rest Men's Shelter_ on this North American holiday of thanks.

The next week finds James at the _Jim Ed Rice Center_ for Senior Citizens.

"I can help you ma'm! I'll get it!" James greeted the grey headed woman while reaching out to take the bag from the elderly woman's fragile hand.

Several days later, you would find James ringing the trademark bell for the _Salvation Army,_ collecting money during the blustery Christmas season. Soon after Christmas vacation, James will return to the high school where he's volunteered for 40+ years. He helps out the teaching staff, the coaches, and the students. He will clean, straighten and organize materials as he keeps a watchful eye over the students.

The next week he travels with his long time mentor, Harold, as a keynote speaker at a regional conference. Finally, on any given night throughout the year, you will find James on the sidelines of various high school athletic events, encouraging the athletes, keeping track of sports equipment and assisting the coaches.

Who is this man?

His name is James Kennedy and his entire life has been devoted to helping others. He is passionate and devoted to all he meets. No one I have read about gets greater joy from believing in others than James. You might have heard of him - his nickname: RADIO.

Maybe you've seen his life story in the Hollywood movie, _RADIO_. He was played by actor Cuba Gooding, Jr. and his mentor Harold Jones was played by actor, Ed Harris.

You see James suffered brain damage as a young boy when he was in a car wreck. He may always be "childlike" as a man, but his work is serious. He is a highly valued volunteer with 3 organizations, an accomplished public speaker and is endeared to his entire U.S. hometown of Anderson, South Carolina.

James and Coach Jones met years ago when services for mentally challenged children were nearly non-existent. At 18 years of age, James spent all his days aimlessly wandering the streets of that sleepy country town pushing a grocery cart, mumbling to himself, and listening to a transistor radio. He was raised by a very loving single mom who had few resources for his care. In fact, there were no day programs for teens like James. He was unable to look you in the face, answer a question, or otherwise connect.

Horribly teased and rejected, and unable to defend himself, James was nobody. That is, _**until Coach Jones and the high school football staff befriended him and believed in him**_.

They believed this young man could be more. Could do more. Could have a fulfilled life.

They refused to accept the limitations of his brain damage.

Coach Jones especially believed in the quality person he saw in James. Jones believed in who James could be, and not who James had been.

The staff and the school loved him. They loved his family and slowly, ever so slowly, James "RADIO" Kennedy grew into the man I described at the beginning of this story. RADIO spends his days now volunteering and speaking and talking and loving and encouraging others . . . He has travelled all over the U.S. and gives back to everyone he meets.

You see, you never know what believing in someone will do. Coach Jones decided to get involved with James on that muggy afternoon when he first noticed the boy, mumbling and stumbling precariously down the road pushing his grocery cart. Coach Jones didn't turn away in indifference or apathy. He allowed himself to be moved with compassion and did the right thing. He believed in RADIO and now, over 40 years later, they are an inseparable team.

There are many forms of success – it looks different for different people. Don't let what someone else thinks short-circuit your achievement. You can do whatever you decide!

★ *A Huge Heart* ★

Vicki giggled while the other students in her class pressed their hands over their ears. She found it funny that almost everyone else found the squeak of the chalk on the chalkboard unpleasant. It didn't bother her in the least. In fact, Vicki looked forward to adding her own chalk squeaks to the world of school chalkboards – Vicki knew she was going to be a teacher.

Little did she know where she'd end up teaching and the thousands of lives she would change...

Raised in Ripoll, Catalonia (Spain) Vicki had a rapacious appetite for learning. She just couldn't seem to get enough. After graduating from her local university, she taught school for ten years. But then her hunger for learning kicked in again and she attended graduate classes at various universities until she ended up with a Master's Degree from Michigan State University (USA).

Have you ever had a fascination with a place you've heard about but never visited? Well, Vicki did! And her fascination became a deep longing.

There was just something about Nepal and she knew she had to get there. When she arrived in the capital city of Kathmandu in 1988, she was shocked at the poverty and terrible living conditions. After returning home, she couldn't get the images of the street children out of her mind and began thinking about what she could do for these desperate children.

A year later, still haunted by the visions of Kathmandu, Vicki moved to Nepal to learn the country's language and culture first hand. She wound up founding her first of many schools -- Dorgee School which took in 32 refugee children from Tibet. Four years later, steeped in the culture and language of Nepal, she was ready to serve the poorest of the poor – the people that really tugged on her heartstrings. Vicki started the Daleki School in Kathmandu for the most impoverished children, teaching them their culture, history and traditions.

"Teacher, Teacher... there is a girl here... She has nowhere to go." Vicki's heart grew even bigger…

A little 7-year-old girl with disabilities was abandoned in a market in Kathmandu and brought to Vicki. In response to yet another need in her adopted country, she opened the Reception Center which provides housing, education and medical attention for special needs children. The classes also prepare the children so they can attend regular schools.

*It's not hard to see why the people loved Vicki and turned to her when there was a need... Nepal had become part of Vicki even as she had become part of Nepal... but it still wasn't enough! Vicki was unstoppable...*and her huge heart moved her beyond Nepal to Pakistan and Bangladesh where she is setting up schools for the poorest of the poor.

Although Vicki Sherpa has been honored with many awards and her Daleki School is an international model school for poor and marginalized children and adults, her greatest reward is knowing she has made a difference in the lives of thousands of people. ***And the key to it all -- she did it by doing what she loves to do – teach.***

You see, the secret to success really isn't a secret at all. Harvey Mackay puts it in one simple sentence – *"Find something you love to do and you'll never have to work a day in your life."*

Life is not just about accumulating things, making money or having lots of influence. Life is about fulfilling your purpose. And your purpose is doing what you love to do in a way that helps as many other people as possible.

So don't sell yourself and others short. Take the bold step needed in order to embrace what you love to do.

Make sure that it helps others, and you will be wildly successful!

> *"Take what you have and use it and your talent will be increased."*
> ~Zig Ziglar

★ *Worth Living* ★

"No . . . no . . . help me . . . .Take me out of here . . . .Help. Mama! Daddy! Why?"

Dark and dismal... those are the only words to describe the camp. Remembering the lifeless, death-filled days of her childhood in a concentration camp, Trudi promised herself that once that hellacious period of her history came to an end, she would take care of children. Having lost her own childhood to the Nazi's, she passionately pursued giving so other children would have theirs.

Yes, life as a 6 year old during the Holocaust was tragic and horrifying. Yet Trudi defied death numerous times... once being literally snatched from the flames of the human incinerator. That unconquerable "life sprit" she possessed spilled over into her every endeavor.

As she grew up, Trudi remembered her promise and after working with immigrants and refugees, she saw her niche. Her dream: a totally free clinic in Jerusalem that would take care of the children of the poorest of the poor with the best dental care money could buy.

Not content to "put a band aid on a gaping wound," Trudi and husband, Zeev, require a time commitment from those receiving dental care – from both the children and their families. The kids and their guardians or parents agree to dental education, training and follow up care for months.

Trudi and Zeev truly desire to see their patients better themselves and to feel good about who they were created to be. In one interview she spoke of "adopting" over 50 kids and 250 families to ensure they all had an education... an education that oft times included teaching degrees as well as law, medical and dental schools.

"Ah, vacation at last!" yawned the latest visiting dentist from Norway. *"Can't wait to get started! How many do we have today?"*

"Same as yesterday... about 100!" calls out the grinning hygienist.

Today, the Trudi Birger Dental Clinic is run by the life force of the late Trudi Birger, her devoted husband, Zeev and the organization Dental Volunteers for Israel. The patients are referred through social welfare offices.

Volunteer dentists come to the Clinic from around the world with differing religious backgrounds... but with a single passion - to give! They give of their own time, talents and money to come to Israel and treat kids who can't pay them or even say "thank you" in a language the doctors understand. The clinic treats any child, all children... from Jewish to Christian to Muslim... any child in need because teeth are teeth!

I want you to understand that while this clinic has the most modern, up to date medical equipment available with some of the best trained doctors and hygienists in the world; ***in the beginning days of the clinic, she had nothing... no money, resources, no equipment, no volunteers... nothing except her devoted passion and sweet tempered will.*** It was solely Trudi's vivacious love of life, her grace and purity of heart that brought every needed resource, from professionals to equipment into reality... throughout the years!!!

Trudi loved life and passed that love along to everyone she met. It was returned to her many, many times over.

WOW! If anyone had a reason to be totally and completely against the world, it was Trudi. Losing her childhood to the horrors of the concentration camps could have tarnished her heart beyond repair. But to read her responses in an interview, is to hear of a very deep and resounding love of people, a belief that all are worthy of respect and passionate joy-filled devotion to life itself.

If that's not a recipe for success, I don't know what is!

★ *From Manya to Marie* ★

"Manya – speak in Russian, not Polish! You might be heard!"

It was hard for little Manya to remember she could speak Polish only at home – never in public. A single conversation in Polish could bring harm to herself and her family. The year was 1871. Manya was only 4 years old. Her country – Poland – had not been an independent country for almost a century. Warsaw was controlled by the Russian czar who tried to stamp out Polish nationalism by keeping the people ignorant of their language and culture. But Polish patriots (like her parents) were determined to not only retain both their culture and their language, but to ultimately regain control of their nation.

Manya's parents were both educators, but were not allowed to teach in certified schools under the repressive czarist regime. Manya was the star pupil in her class and graduated at age 15. Because women were not allowed at the University of Warsaw, Manya and one of her sisters, Bronya, attended an illegal night school dubbed the Floating University. It got its name because the location was changed frequently to help evade the watchful eyes of the authorities.

"Manya...we have to help each other...We need to go to school....You help me through school and then I will help you...we can do it if we work together... Don't you think?"

The two sisters made a pact. Manya would work to put her sister through medical school in Paris. And as soon as she could, Bronya would reciprocate.

During these years, Manya filled her hours with self-taught studies. Not sure what she was really interested in; she studied sociology, literature, physics and chemistry. She discovered that math and the physical sciences were her strength and passion. By the fall of 1891, Manya was able to leave for Paris to begin studies at the University of Paris – the famous Sorbonne.

Manya became Marie when she enrolled at the University. As lonely and difficult as her living situation was, she was able to concentrate on her studies and experienced a liberty and independence she'd never known. Because of her lack of academic preparation she was behind the other students, especially in the physical sciences which the Russians had outlawed in Polish schools. Her proficiency in technical French was also lacking, as was her mathematical background – but she loved learning – she was like a sponge. *"All that I saw and learned that was new, delighted me. It was like a new world opened to me, the world of science, which I was at last permitted to know in all liberty."*

Marie's ferocious studying paid off when she finished her master's degree in physics just 2 years later and started her second master's degree in math. But there was a problem. The math degree required lab work and there was no lab available to her at the University.

Her search for lab space resulted in an introduction to another scientist who had done pioneering research on magnetism -- Marie was introduced to Pierre Curie. This introduction would change not only their individual lives, but also the course of science.

The rest is history . . .

They were married a year later and Pierre, deeply intrigued and respectful of Marie's brilliance, helped her every way he could. (And Marie did the same for Pierre.) Their lives were fraught with deprivation and difficulties due to lack of funding and adequate lab facilities. But both understood the importance of their research and ignored their personal discomfort and pain.

Known best for her discovery of the radioactive elements of polonium and radium, Marie went on to become the first person to win two Nobel prizes. Her radium was a key to the basic change in scientific understanding of energy and matter. And her work not only influenced science, but also began an entirely new era in medical research and treatment.

As a female child growing up in an occupied country, Marie could have come up with all kinds of excuses why she couldn't finish school, go to college, or persevere in her career choice. But she didn't. Marie took the steps necessary to move from one level of life to the next. She faced each obstacle, found a solution and moved forward.

She is a marvelous example of what success looks like!

POWER BOOSTERS

Where is your life going if you don't make changes now?

_____

_____

_____

_____

_____

_____

_____

_____

Who believes in you?

_____

_____

_____

_____

_____

_____

_____

_____

_____

★ *The Human Frog* ★

"You will never walk again, Ray. I'm so sorry."

The year was 1873. The boy was just 7 years old – stricken by polio. Ray decided to prove them wrong. He couldn't imagine a life without being able to run and play through the beautiful Indiana countryside. He had no one to tell him how that might happen, since he had been orphaned at age 5, so he had to figure it out for himself. A doctor had suggested leg exercises might work, so he created a strict regimen of leg exercises.

He put his legs through "Ray's workout." Every day. Many times a day... For weeks...for months . . .

"I will walk! And not only that -- I'm gonna run again. You'll see...you'll all see," Ray answered with determination in his voice, even as tears mixed with sweat on his face.

The 1800's was not a good time (not that there is ever a *good* time) to contract polio. Most of those who survived the ravaging disease ended up crippled and stuck in wheelchairs, and/or in heavy iron leg braces. Those were the lucky ones – the unlucky ones spent the rest of their lives in an "iron lung."

Ray Ewry was among the "lucky ones." His bout with polio left him stuck in a wheelchair with heavy iron braces and the voice of his doctor resounding in his head - *"You will never walk again, Ray."*

So He pushed. He pushed through pain. He pushed through fear.

And he pushed through daily discouragement by keeping his eyes on the goal – walking.

Finally the day came when he was able to walk away from his wheelchair. Then he left his metal braces behind. Ray Ewry could walk!

Now that alone was an incredible victory, but his accomplishments only made him hunger for more.

He developed more exercises and worked out diligently. Soon he was running.

Then he was jumping. He jumped for the sheer joy of jumping. He jumped because he could.

He kept jumping...and jumping... and jumping...

Then he set his goals even higher, becoming a competitive athlete in track and field. He graduated from Purdue University in 1897 with many medals. Yet there was more to be accomplished. The Olympics had just restarted in 1896. Ray set his sights on competing in 3 events. You may not recognize them because they are no longer Olympic events: the standing high jump; the standing long jump; and the standing hop, step and jump.

Just think of our current "jump events" without the running start and you'll be able to envision what he did.

Ray prepared for them with the same determination and tenacity that got him out of his wheelchair. His trip to the Paris Olympics resulted in 3 gold medals. In the remaining 8 years of his Olympic competition he collected 7 more. That's right – 10 Gold Medals! Ray Ewry became known as the *Human Frog* because of the amazing power in his once shriveled legs. No other Olympian in history has won as many gold medals without losing a single competition. Even Carl Lewis silvered once. *But not Ray Ewry.*

His legacy is much greater than his ability to jump, however. What do you do when people tell you something can't be done? Do you give up and quit? Do you let them win over you? Do you let someone else determine your future? It is easy to do sometimes. But let Ray, the Human Frog, remind you of the power of persistence. He worked hard. He never quit. He sweated and cried and pushed. He decided as a boy that he was in charge of his future . . . and no one else was ever going to tell him what he could or could not do!

Ray believed in himself and saw himself walking and running and winning. He believed he could and he did. I hope that today you determine where your life goes. I want you to believe in yourself enough to keep on working for your goals and dreams!

"Hey, guess what I saw on Saturday?" Nicole squealed with delight. Her friends looked up from coloring their pictures and waited for her to answer.

"I went to an air show and saw a real fighter jet. It swooped through the sky and one day I am going to fly airplanes."

Nicole stopped talking then, stood and gazed out the school room window. Looking up to the sky, her imagination soared as the clouds wisped through the air. She could only imagine the feel of a real airplane beneath her hands. She dreamed and dreamed of soaring through the blue sky.

"Nicole? Nicole? Are you coming? We are going outside."

Her friends' call interrupted her dream, but only temporarily. She knew what she wanted. All she had to do was look up to the sun and she knew where she would be…*one day*.

United States Air Force Major Nicole Malachowski was only 5 years old when she knew what she wanted to be when she grew up. She attended an air show and the sight of an F-4 Phantom fighter jet roaring through the clouds captured her heart and dreams. And once she set her sights on the sky, her feet have rarely been on the ground.

Nicole appreciates her parents' belief in her – in her dreams -- encouraging her tenacity and offering her courage to follow those dreams. In an interview, Nicole remembers when she would ramble on about becoming a fighter pilot: *"They would often ask me rhetorical questions to get me thinking. Questions like, 'So you're going to be a fighter pilot? How does one become a fighter pilot?'"*

Nicole then figured out the answers… and instead of chasing boys through junior high, Nicole chased down pilot instructors, airplanes, flying lessons and cockpits. She starting flying at age 12. She few solo at age 16! After school she rode her bike to the airport until she got her driver's license. She was flying before she could drive!

Nicole is an amazing woman whose dreams have taken her literally to the top of the world.

After graduating from the Air Force Academy and working there as an instructor pilot, a conversation with her husband prompted her to land the wildest ride she had ever taken.

"Honey, you should try out. You're qualified. I think you might make it."

"Really? You really think I should apply? Really? Actually, I've not thought about that. But you really think I could?"

Her husband, Major Paul Malachowski, is no stranger to airplanes. As an F-15 weapons system officer evaluator, he was more than able to judge his wife's ability. With her husband's words of encouragement, and his deep belief in her ringing in her ears, Nicole applied for, and was granted, a position with the elite and selective U.S. Air Force Air Demonstration Squadron . . . or as they are better known, the Thunderbirds.

With that selection, she flies into history books. Major Nicole Malachowski is the very first woman ever in its history, to pilot an F-16 Fighting Falcon.

"*The Air Force has so many great opportunities out there, and all you have to do is apply,*" she said. "*It never hurts to try, does it?*"

WOW! This woman has inspired not only me, but thousands of people everywhere who watched her fly that screaming Falcon fighter jet across the noble blue skies. As a public relations organization for the Air Force, Nicole has spoken to hundreds of children across the globe. Her own words echo our mission here at SBIY: pursue your dreams because they can come true!

"*I hope (my) service in the Thunderbirds is an example to young girls and to all children that they can achieve their dreams . . . it's great to have a dream; it's great to have goals,*" she said. "*Pursue something that you are passionate about, and then pursue excellence in that. And surround yourself with a positive team. I hope that when they see the Air Force Thunderbirds, they realize they can achieve any dream. I think I am living proof that dreams do come true.*"

Today, you probably won't strap yourself into the cockpit of a Fighter jet and soar above the city. I know I won't. But I will step out into a world where my dreams of writing and photography can come true. I can begin today to take the steps needed to live out my heart's passion. And so can you!

We are no different than Major Nicole Malachowski. She may skyrocket through the skies at top speeds, but her life is lived one day at a time. One goal at a time. One dream at a time. You and I can take on things the same way she does . . . one step at a time. If we don't quit and don't give up, then we, too, will reach the heights of our dreams!

You're only limited by the size of your dreams, and the size of your determination to make them happen.

"This poor child will never amount to anything," thought his mother, *"and it's all my fault."*

Little Geronimo had everything going against him. Born to a single mother and living in extreme poverty, Geronimo was a sickly child. It amazed his mother that he even survived childhood - perhaps it would have been better for him to have died young.

Geronimo Cardano proved his mother wrong. His body might not be strong, but the strength of his spirit and his bright intelligence made up for it. He managed to attend the universities of Pavia and Padua, Italy and received his medical degree in 1524 at the age of 23. Because he was illegitimate, Geronimo was not allowed to practice medicine. His brilliant mind was appreciated by all, however, so he was appointed to the chair of mathematics in Milan, and later even served as the rector of the College of Physicians, and Professor at the University of Milan.

Geronimo was brilliant in math and discovered the general theory of cubic and quartic equations, the need for both negative and complex numbers, and the theory of probability. He also researched magnetism and was an astronomer. As a member of the medical profession he wrote on the causes of disease, treatment for typhus fever and developed a sign language for the deaf and blind.

Enter Juan Pablo Bonet . . . nearly 100 years later.

"This poor child -- there must be a way . . ."

Sadly watching the little deaf boy's frustration while being tutored, Juan knew there had to be a way to get through to him.

A Spanish priest serving as secretary to the second most powerful man in Spain, Juan felt his employer's pain and frustration. His son could only receive his inheritance if he was literate – but he was unable to communicate because of his deafness.

Juan knew of several wealthy families in the same predicament – they needed to educate their heirs, but were unable to teach them how to effectively communicate.

After much thought and prayer, Juan developed a plan . . .

He taught his new pupil breathing exercises -- how to form sounds, using his lips, tongue and teeth to pronounce each sound. Juan had created the forerunner of our modern speech therapy. Using Geronimo Cardano's sign language, Juan used both sound and the manual alphabet to teach his pupil how to communicate. Because of their success, in 1620 Juan published the very first book about phonetics and speech therapy. He also included the manual alphabet. By publishing his findings along with the alphabet, Juan made signing available to many and gave those who were without speech a voice.

It took a brilliant man like Geronimo Cardano, and a compassionate man like Juan Pablo Bonet, to create a way for the deaf and blind to communicate. And it was because of these men, that over 260 years later, Annie Sullivan was able to break through Helen Keller's dark isolation and give her the vital gift of communication.

You know, Cardano and Bonet never knew about the wild success Helen Keller experienced because of their work. Often we don't get to see the end result of something we are involved in. Instant gratification is not always available to us.

Does that mean we should abandon what we are doing? Of course not! In fact, it should fuel us to keep going! Who knows what good will come of the song you sing, the story or poem you write, the children you teach, the computer program you design?

Success is so many different things – we believe you will achieve yours!

She stood with her hands on the wall as her music teacher played notes on the kettledrum. Concentrating on the vibrations she was feeling, Evelyn knew what note she was playing by where she felt the vibration on her body. It felt good to be part of music again.

Evelyn remembers having perfect pitch and being able to sing a specific note without aid of an instrument playing it for her. She loved playing the piano and clarinet. She smiles, remembering when, at the age of 10, she performed on the piano in a local old folks home.

But with the loss of her hearing two years later, she now "heard" a note by associating where she felt it. Music is, as she points out, vibration, whether it's vibrating against your ear drum or another part of your body. *"The low sounds I feel mainly in my legs and feet, and high sounds might be particular places on my face, neck and chest."* She says that her feet, legs and tummy are her best ears.

Evelyn's passion for music was spurred on by one of her later music teachers who told her she could never pursue a career in music – *after all, how could she, she couldn't even hear*. Evelyn says that was one of the best things that ever happened to her because she became even more determined to make it happen. But Evelyn didn't want to be just a percussionist -- she wanted to be the featured artist – out in front and accompanied by the rest of the orchestra!

And she has done just that! After graduating from the Royal Academy of Music with honors, her career took flight. Helped by the press's love of the sentimental and emotional story of the plucky deaf teenager, Evelyn became a musical phenomenon. She produced six albums, performed concert tours in Asia, Europe and the U.S., and even became a TV talk show celebrity.

Evelyn may very possibly be the best percussionist in the world – she's definitely the first who has ever made a successful full-time career as a solo percussionist. She can play any kind of music – from classical to rock – and she is extremely innovative. When you watch and listen to Evelyn play, you have to leave all your preconceived ideas about deafness at the door. She doesn't *play* music – Evelyn *feels* and *becomes* the music. And her expressiveness pulls you right into the experience as well. About her music she says, *"That's me – that's my voice."*

Evelyn's won more than 80 international awards including a Grammy. She has been voted Scotswoman of the Decade and been awarded the Officer of the British Empire by Queen Elizabeth. That award has been extended to "Dame Commander" for her services to music. She can now be correctly called Dame Evelyn Glennie.

Evelyn's career has spanned more than 20 years and she has composed original works (as well as having original works composed specifically for her!). She has a grueling international touring schedule and often plays as many as 60 instruments during a single live performance.

Watching her makes you glad she didn't let her doctor or her music teacher steal her dream.

Have you ever experienced someone telling you something you felt strongly about, couldn't be done? Have you ever shared a fantastic idea or goal with a family member or best friend and their immediate reaction was -- "that's crazy"? With just two words spoken, your excitement comes crashing down around you and your idea, dream or goal lays at your feet, dashed into a thousand pieces.

Have you let others de-rail or limit you? Instead of following your dream, working on your idea or mapping out how to reach your goal, have you let someone else's opinion rob you of what's yours?

There are multitudes of people who were told they "couldn't do that" or "wouldn't succeed" but have ignored such comments and gone on to become wildly successful.

Some years ago Evelyn said: *"I have been a soloist for over ten years because I decided early on that just because my doctor made a diagnosis that I was profoundly deaf, it didn't mean that my passion couldn't be actualized. I would encourage people to not allow themselves to be defined or limited by others. Follow your passion; follow your heart. They will lead you to the place you want to go."*

The next time someone tells you "that's crazy" just smile and ignore them.

Follow your dream -- no one can steal it unless you let them!

★ *The Baltimore Bullet* ★

"The Baltimore Bullet" quickly pulled on his red, white and blue wind jacket and pants. As the United States National Anthem swelled loudly and stirred his spirit, Michael bowed his head to receive the Gold Medal.

His dreams ran through his head as the sweat ran down his back. The years of training toned his muscles and his mind. He focused on the crowds' applause and let the pride of being an American rise. This young man stood tall, head held high and waved back to the people as the Gold Medal glimmered in the sun. Michael let his thoughts wander back to when he was a young 7 year old boy...

"Michael! Michael! You have got to pay attention! Quit daydreaming! Can you tell me what I was talking about?" His teacher quizzed him yet again.

Michael hung his head that day. He couldn't keep still. He kept looking out the window and day dreaming. He tried to listen. He really wanted to do well. Every day he hoped he would be able to stay out of trouble. He willed his mind to pay attention to his teachers. He was sad when he couldn't follow their instructions.

When Michael was diagnosed with Attention-Deficit Hyperactivity Disorder (ADHD) he enrolled in a swimming class in hopes that he could work off some excess energy. He needed a physical outlet.

The rest, as they say, *is history.*

Swimming for Michael Phelps became his salvation . . . by age 10 he held a National Record, and by age 15 he qualified to compete in the 2000 Summer Olympics. He was the youngest swimmer to ever hold a world record. Now in 2008, he holds 38 National titles, 24 World records, and has been named "World Swimmer of the Year" four times!

Michael is simply the fastest swimmer to come around in a long, long time. Thus his nickname, "The Baltimore Bullet."

Incredible, right? I think so . . . yet as I read, I asked myself this question: *How did Michael get there? How did he go from disgraced little boy to World Champion athlete?*

Raised in a single parent household, Michael struggled growing up. He not only had sisters to contend with, he had his own uncontrollable impulses which kept him in a frenzy. However, by giving himself totally over to swimming, Michael found a way to succeed. Once he started serious training, Michael devoted himself to being the best. For five years solid he never missed, skipped or failed a day of practice. For five straight years he kept on... on through all the seasons regardless of the weather. He pushed himself and then pushed some more. His coach says he is the ***"Greatest Olympian ever."***

His work paid off because he didn't quit. Even now with many races won and lost, and with multiple titles to his credit, Michael continues to strive to be the best.

"I don't really think about what anyone else is doing and how they race their race or whatever. I know that if I train as hard as I can and I do things differently than other people do, I'm gonna be fine. I like to race the best, but I can (only) control what I do and if I'm the best prepared as I can be, then I'm gonna be happy, and that's all that matters."

Michael knows that part of his strength is giving back to others like others gave to him...a young distracted kid trying to keep his head "above the water." Along with 2 other swimmers, Michael has co-founded "Swims with the Stars," and is reaching out to kids of all ages and all abilities with swim clinics, swim programs, and instructional materials. He wants to take his knowledge, passion and energy to kids everywhere and help fuel their interest in the sport that he deeply loves.

Michael keeps the future in sight. He knows one day he will retire but for now he does what he has always done -- *"he writes his goals for the year down and keeps them next to his bed."* And he reads his goals, then plans how to get where he desires to go.

Follow Michael's lead and you, too, can have wild success!

POWER BOOSTERS

Who needs to know you believe in them?

_____

_____

_____

_____

_____

_____

_____

_____

_____

What opportunities are available that you've been afraid to take advantage of?

_____

_____

_____

_____

_____

_____

_____

_____

_____

_____

★ *Keep Walking!* ★

"Let's go guys...Ok...out the door...Time for your walk!"
"Easy...good girl...good boys!"

Victoria's enthusiasm always created excitement when she took the dogs out walking. As a professional dog walker in London, she had lots of onlookers. She usually literally had her hands full!

"Heel! Sit. Wait...wait...okay...go!" "Good dogs! Good dogs!" "Yeah!"

The sun shone brightly over the fragrant flower wall. The brightly colored blooms seem to turn their heads toward Victoria as she and her canine companions passed. She breathed in deeply... pondering whether or not she had discovered her niche in life. While the morning found her with three of her favorite dogs; three very well trained, obedient and joyous dogs, one of this afternoon's appointments was an entirely different story. A story that occasionally gave Victoria doubts about her passion.

3:00 p.m. and it was time to go get her... the large, very ill mannered dog she'd almost come to dread. Still she had hope that her training techniques would work. She didn't get to see this dog every day, so progress was hard to gauge.

"Ok...sit! SIT! Good girl! Let's get your leash on! SIT! DOWN! Good girl! Ok...out!"

"Hum," thought Victoria, *"that was easier than usual. Let's see how the walk past the neighbor's dogs goes. WOW! She ignored them both! The training was working -- it was working!"*

"Perfect! Good girl!" her praise of the dog interrupted her thoughts.

The year was 1990. Victoria Stilwell was then well on her way to becoming all she'd ever dreamed. A native of Wimbledon, England, Victoria now is one of the most recognized and respected dog trainers in the world.

Victoria started out her career walking dogs. When she saw her clients' need for help with their dog training problems, she sought further education and certification. Simply, she saw a need in her business and decided she could be the one to fill it. She pursued something that would help her business but at the same time help her customers.

Victoria already had a passion for animals, dogs in particular, and combined her sensitive personality and her care for the humans with the open opportunity she saw existed. Her background in theatre and stage was a plus as she found herself before the bright lights of television.

Today, Victoria's TV show, "It's Me or the Dog" is viewed in over 20 countries worldwide. She literally goes into family's homes where there is great conflict between the two legged and the four legged companions. With grace, and smarts, she is filmed interacting and redirecting behavior of both the human and the dog. Sometimes she amazes even herself at how obedient these dogs can truly become.

Victoria is also an accomplished author, and a very sought after animal educator and trainer. She has been featured in magazines and TV shows around the world. Her expertise is craved internationally. Her advice, when heeded, can change people's lives. **Her** life has certainly evolved from walking dogs in her neighborhood.

Victoria is a perfect example of someone who creatively found success doing what she loves! It was not an overnight phenomenon; but she believed in her interests and desires. **She believed in herself and would not give up.** I know it wasn't easy and I am sure it still isn't easy for her today, to always "retrain" both the humans and their dogs to respect each other.

I'd be willing to bet for every successful show we watch, there are several that didn't turn out quite as well. But you know - Victoria takes a few steps forward in giving, and learning and pursuing every time she ventures out into a new family's life.

You could do that too. Oh, maybe not retrain dogs in 2 countries, but you can take a few steps toward your goals. *And you can decide to not give up!* You can look at what you really love to do and find ways to make that a bigger part of your life. You can choose to believe in yourself!!

If you are enjoying these stories, you need to know about…

A beautiful personalized certificate!
A powerful Movie!
Powerful Emails - Created for Teenagers & Adults - Delivered Daily!

Someone Believes In You was created to...

Change the World - One Person At A Time!

Imagine... someone you believe in receives a special certificate in the Mail (you can be anonymous if you want to be); they are given the link to a powerful movie affirming someone believes in them, and then they are sent an email every single day - telling them someone believes in them, sharing encouragement, giving motivation, telling stories of amazing people, inspiring the courage to fulfill their dreams & move beyond their fears.

The world of more and more people revolves around the Internet - now **you have the power to turn it into a source of daily strength for them!**

Who do YOU want to give the Gift of Confidence to??

-   Your kids
-   Your spouse/partner
-   A family member
-   A friend
-   A neighbor
-   A co-worker

www.SomeoneBelievesInYou.com

Glancing at the baby sweetly sleeping in her stroller, Jo thought to herself, *I hope she sleeps awhile longer.* Strange -- the dips and turns life takes. She never thought she'd find herself on welfare, but here she was. Walking her daughter in the stroller so she'd fall asleep, Jo would then take refuge in a café to write.

When she closed her eyes, she saw her story's characters come to life. The trick now was capturing them and putting them on paper! She smiled, letting her mind drift and remembering the first story she'd ever written down . . . she was about 6 years old and the story was about a rabbit that caught the measles and was visited by his friends, including a giant bee.

Born in England, Jo basically grew up on the border of Wales. Although not a good student, she loved reading and writing. After graduating from college, she moved to London and worked for Amnesty International doing research on human rights abuse in Africa.

The baby stirred and Jo held her breath – ah, good, she went back to sleep...

Jo remembered the crowded train trip where the idea for her book came to her in its complete form. *"I really don't know where the idea came from... all these characters and situations came flooding into my head."* As soon as she got to her apartment, she started writing. The year was 1990.

In December of the same year, Jo's 40 year-old mother died after a ten-year battle with multiple sclerosis. She never knew Jo had started work on a novel. Deeply affected by her mother's death, nine months later Jo moved to Portugal where she taught English in a language institute. While there she married a Portuguese television journalist and their daughter, Jessica, was born in 1993. When they divorced the next year, Jo and Jessica moved to Edinburgh, Scotland to be near her sister.

This was a very difficult time for Jo. Choosing not to return to teaching full-time, she went on welfare so she could continue writing. She knew *"that unless I finished the book very soon, I might never finish it... and so I set to work in a kind of frenzy; determined to finish the book and at least try and get it published."* Unable to afford an electric typewriter (much less a computer), Jo first wrote in long hand and then typed the story on a manual typewriter.

Sitting in that café, watching her daughter sleep and writing her books, Jo had no idea what was to come...

Once the first book, the *Philosopher's Stone,* was completed and she found an agent, it took another year of rejection after rejection before finding a publisher. Finally, in August of 1996, her agent called to tell her he'd found a company to publish her book. *"After I hung up, I screamed and jumped into the air; Jessica, who was sitting in her high-chair... looked thoroughly scared."*

The world would soon become entranced with Harry Potter and his adventures. (It's interesting to note that against Jo's wishes, the U.S. publisher insisted on renaming the book the *Sorcerer's Stone.*)

J. K. Rowling (pronounced roll-ing) has been named by *Forbes* as the first person to become a U.S.-dollar billionaire by writing books, that she's the second-richest female entertainer, and the 1,062[nd] richest person in the world. Jo had no idea her Harry Potter books would become the worldwide phenomenon they are. She is uncomfortable in the limelight, and is much happier giving to others than she is speaking about herself. Jo is very involved in helping women and children around the world, combating poverty and supporting multiple sclerosis research.

J.K. Rowling is a success because she never gave up. For 6 long years she lived with very little in order to push her dream forward. It was when things were the worst that she clung to the belief the stories she was writing were meant to be read. And millions of readers around the world have proven her right.

You and I may never be famous. We may never be known beyond our family and friends. But each of us is important. And each of us has a dream. We can choose to be true to our dream, and like Jo Rowling, do whatever it takes to achieve it.

★ _Eyes Open_ ★

"I hate this dress! And I hate this fashion!" Ida yelled passionately to her husband as she dressed.

A buxom woman living in the 1920's, Ida had a hard time adjusting to the "flat chested" look of the day. She was a visionary and a self-made woman. Ida knew what she wanted and she began to go after it. She emigrated from Russia to marry her boyfriend who had immigrated a few years earlier. They started with no money. They had nothing but a dream of a better life in the USA, and they had Ida's irritation with American fashion.

Not fitting into the current fashion known as "Boyish form," Ida asked the question: _"Why fight nature?" Why couldn't we make something that actually FITS a woman's body?"_

Not only did she ask the question – she had the means to provide the answer. An avid Women's Rights Activist, she had long ago turned up her nose to the idea of working for someone else. Instead, she bought a Singer sewing machine on the installment plan and began her own seamstress business.

In 1921, when women were "wrapping their breasts," Ida started her own dress shop in Manhattan. She thought women could look better in their dresses and set about to do something about it. She and her husband, William, designed built-in bandeaux with cups that separated and supported the breasts. They were an instant hit.

The women's bra company Maiden Form was born.

Ida was the management and marketing genius behind their success. She bought ads, negotiated with Unions and introduced assembly-line production. She pushed the boundaries by running "racy" ads featuring photographs of women in bras.

Ida Rosenthal proved female executives could succeed at a time when working women rarely advanced further than factory worker or secretary. The bras she helped create liberated women with comfort, freedom and sensuality. They also made her and William multi-millionaires.

Ida is a shining light of what can be accomplished if you keep your eyes open, recognize a need, and set out to do something about it!

I don't care how long you live. I don't care how advanced society becomes. I don't care how many inventions are invented. There are always problems to solve; solutions to be presented; easier ways to do things. You just have to believe it. You just have to keep your eyes open for the opportunity that ignites your passion and purpose.

Next time you feel that wave of frustration about _"how things are done"_, look at the situation again. Do you see a better way? An easier way to accomplish that task? A more productive solution?

If so, then pursue getting things changed. Ida believed she had a better idea - a more comfortable way for women to live. And she simply lived out her dreams and passions.

Living out dreams and passions – what a sure-fire way to find success!

> _"Each one of us has a fire in our heart for something. It's our goal in life to find it and to keep it lit."_
>
> _~Mary Lou Retton_

★ *Deciding Ahead of Time* ★

Will this day ever end? agonized Nat as the sun started down.*"Will it ever be over?*

Discouraged and displeased, Nat walked home the long way. He walked slowly and painfully. The day had been the worst yet. He needed that job. But he had lost it.

His thoughts raged inside his head.

What are you going to tell Sophia? How will you live now? She won't love you anymore. His thoughts teased and taunted him as fear and depression broke his heart.

As he trudged up the stairs into his home, Sophia met him at the door with a hug and kiss. Nathaniel Hawthorne then announced to his wife that he was a failure because he'd just been fired from his job in the customs house. His wife's response completely took him by surprise.

"Now," she said triumphantly, *"you can write your book!"*

Hawthorne stared at her. *"What are we going to live on while I am writing this book?"*

Much to his surprise and delight, she opened a drawer and pulled out a substantial sum of money.

"I've always known you were a man of genius," she told him, *"and I knew that someday you would write a masterpiece. So every week - out of the money you gave me for housekeeping - I saved part of it. Here's enough to last us a whole year."*

Because of his wife's belief and confidence in him, Hawthorne was given the time needed to write one of the classics of American literature: *The Scarlet Letter.* From there, he went on to become one of the best 19th Century American authors, and is credited with being a central writer in the history of American literature.

Each of us plans on being successful. Few of us wake up in the morning and think *today I'm going to be a failure.* It's a fact that life will eventually throw us a curve-ball and muddy our clean slate. But it's how we live day-by-day, and moment-by-moment, that determines whether we wallow in that mire or rise above it.

Like Hawthorne's wife, Sophia, we can decide ahead of time how we will respond to adversity. We can practice every day by choosing to make small deposits of gratitude and positive thinking. This kind of attitude chooses to seek out the good in people and situations. It looks for new solutions to old problems. In fact, it doesn't see problems at all, but rather opportunities for growth and advancement. These small, daily decisions set us up for those larger, more difficult moments of decision.

Just as Sophia's belief in her husband influenced an entire culture of American literature, you enrich and enhance your world. You may not write the great American novel, but you will experience life in a more meaningful and more fulfilling way.

And isn't that what success is all about?

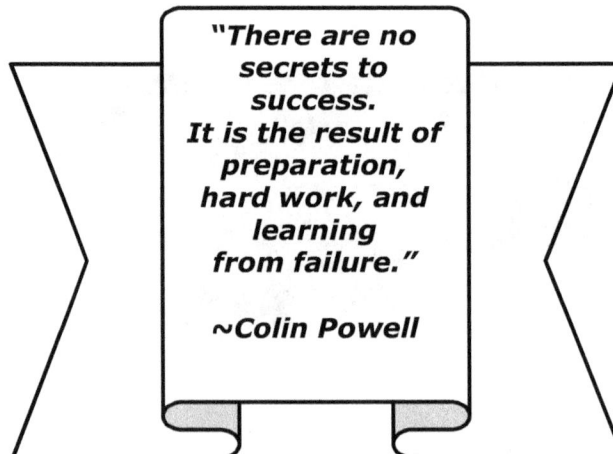

> **"There are no secrets to success.
> It is the result of preparation, hard work, and learning
> from failure."**
>
> **~Colin Powell**

★ She's Type A++ ★

Do you follow the Olympics?

Interested in trivia about sporting events?

Can you answer these questions then?

Who broke the world record in the women's 50 m freestyle swimming event THREE times in the early 1980's?

Who won five medals alone in the Sydney Olympics in 2000?

Who is the first swimmer to compete in five Olympics: 1984, 1988, 1992, 2000, and 2008?

Who will be the oldest female swimmer ever in its history, at 41 years of age to compete in the 2008 Bejing Olympics?

The answer to all these questions is Dara Torres - swimmer phenomenon.

Dara started swimming in Beverly Hills, California because her brothers swam at the local YMCA. The sibling rivalry turned competitive as Dara learned to win. At age 14, she broke the world record in the 50-meter freestyle, but wasn't too impressed with herself or her record. What impressed her was that she didn't lose. Coming in 2nd or 3rd is nearly unbearable to this tanned, tall woman with an easy laugh. Her friends know she doesn't necessarily play to win - she plays hard so as to not lose. Her biggest competition is not the girl on the next starting block, but the girl within. She likes to improve her time, her form and her body!

Even with a young daughter, Dara hasn't slowed down. She continues to win swim meets and pursue her passion of sports. As she takes time to intensify her workouts for the Olympics, she takes time off from her broadcasting job, modeling contracts, and television network announcer position.

Dara has simply pursued her first love with single determination and purpose. And she is still winning but it is not without pain or obstacles. Injuries, bone spurs, torn muscles, and even 10+ surgeries haven't deterred her path.

So how did she do in Beijing? She competed in the 50 meter freestyle, 4×100 medley relay, and 4×100 freestyle relay and won the silver medal in all three of these events!

You may not be able to keep up with her, her grueling schedule or her physical feats, but you can mimic her focus on pursing her passion. You can keep trying, keep going, and keep moving toward the goal!

We probably won't be on the starters' block of an Olympic event, but we are in the event of life and we have many life races to join.

You might lose some, but you'll eventually win if you just keep on keeping on!!

I encourage you today to remember Dara; the swimmer that has not allowed age to slow or stop her, but is turning up the speed and moving out!

Keep pursuing your goal and you will know success!

> **"You've got to say,
> I think that if I keep working at this and want it
> badly enough I can
> have it. It's called perseverance."
> ~Lee Iacocca**

★ *A Sweet Melody* ★

The sweet strains of the violinist wafted across the auditorium and the audience hushed.

Each note, perfectly pitched and in tune, caused the music to swell deep inside each listener. The violin seemed magical in his hands and he and the instrument melted into one precise movement.

The tuxedo clad professional, stood with the spotlight glowing around him and bowed to a thunderous applause. This open and welcome reception was shockingly different from the musician's afternoon experiment.

His thoughts flowed to the day's events as he continued to play his sold-out concert hall. Earlier that day, he stood on a dirty street corner and played the same melody. With his violin case open, he appeared to beg for money. The hustle and bustle of New York City overshadowed his expertise.

No one stopped to listen. No one clapped. No one noticed. Amazed and in disbelief, the violinist stood for hours and played… no one cared.

No one.

Fritz Kreisler was a maestro of music during the first 60 years of the 20th century. A child prodigy, he studied with the best of the best. His parents ensured he could do all he wanted within the music world. To read about him now, one reads of concerts, recordings, his brilliance, his operettas, and his art. His amazing contributions to the musical world runs long.

However, read again and you will see interruptions, failings and mistakes. He tried out for a Philharmonic orchestra and was rejected. Because of his discouragement, he abandoned music and tried painting. He grew tired of that just as World War I began and he joined as a soldier. Injured, he returned home. He tried music again. Giving concerts resulted in some serious negative critique and he stopped playing. After months of silence, he decided to try one more time. He chose to begin again and this time, he determined to keep playing.

He resolved to never quit.

The result of his decision? Fritz Kreisler became the leading young violin virtuoso of his day. Musical creations of new acclaim led to multiple recordings and the reputation of Master Violinist. He became one of the most famous and sought after musicians of his time. A car accident in 1941 left him severely wounded and fighting for his life. He recovered and continued to give concerts.

Fritz chose to start again… and again. He believed the music inside him deserved to be heard. He believed in himself and he believed in his listeners.

Return with me to that concert where he played before a sell-out crowd -- that crowd who paid high ticket prices to be allowed to see him -- those concert goers actually felt privileged to be able to see such a master. They were flattered to pay handsomely and walk into the hall.

Imagine Fritz's reaction to his street corner experiment.

"The reason I'm a bit weary tonight," he told his audience, *"is because I played on the streets of New York all day today dressed as a street musician with my violin case opened for donations. It does me good to play for the people. But not one person stopped to listen, or gave me a cent!"*

Interesting, isn't it, that this brilliant violinist would be ignored on the city streets because he was judged as a beggarly street musician, but at night in a concert hall, people would happily pay to hear him?

As our world changes every day around us, we need to learn to open our eyes and our ears in curiosity and openness instead of turning a blind eye or deaf ear. Just think of the beauty those folks in New York City missed that day. They were preoccupied or quick to judge. They dismissed a genius, thinking him a "loser." The great Kreisler was freely playing for them with the same brilliance and technique he offered the well-to-do of the city later that evening.

Be curious. Be aware. And NEVER QUIT!

POWER BOOSTERS

What are you willing to DO to make your dreams come true?

_____

_____

_____

_____

_____

_____

_____

_____

What fear is keeping you from following your passion?

_____

_____

_____

_____

_____

_____

_____

_____

_____

_____

The surf crashed onto the sandy beach and the sun seemed to halt in the middle of the sky. White wispy clouds framed the water and everyone was having fun. Relaxing with a boogie board, the beach was a favorite place for Chanda. Water has a calming effect and this California girl was no stranger to the waves. Yet the dilemma of Chanda's health tainted the day. Watching their children romping and rolling on the beach, her parents, though silent on the outside, thought the same thoughts...

What if she is in the water and she has a seizure?
What if no one sees her?
She could die!
She's only 9... why does she have to have epilepsy? I wonder if we should go home?
What if she can't tell us she needs help?

The splashing the kids created was matched by their boisterous laughter, and soon the parental worries ceased. However, they both knew they would have to talk about it soon. Chanda was still so young and many decisions would need to be made, but for now their greatest choice was which kid to toss into the wild waves rushing into shore.

Chanda Gunn and her parents decided it was in her best interest and safety to not pursue water sports. At that young age, she had multiple seizures daily. The water in its liquid form was simply too dangerous for her. As they dropped off her brother at hockey, they wondered if water in its frozen form could be their answer to Chanda's desire to play sports. It seemed with the protective helmet and gear, that she would be safe if a seizure did hit her.

It proved to be a perfect match. In fact, she is the first player to be a finalist for the nation's best women's college hockey player (The Patty Kazmaier Award) and an award as college hockey's finest citizen (The Humanitarian). She's also received the Honda Inspiration Award. In 2005, she was voted top goalie in the world championships. Her team won the gold! In 2006 at the Winter Olympics, she won a bronze medal. There she played around 250 minutes. She had 50 saves. This two-time All-America goaltender is as at home on the ice as she was in the waves.

"Chanda was an extremely shy, quiet child until she put on goalie pads. Then her entire personality changed. She grew tremendously confident and showed abilities I had no idea she had," Chanda's mother says about her daughter.

This tough gal has her epilepsy under control and uses her sports fame to speak to groups, especially kids, whenever she gets the chance.

Her advice to parents or kids themselves with any kind of challenge is steeped with experience. *"Of course, children with epilepsy may have a more difficult time, but if they are told they 'can't' or they 'shouldn't' they are going to grow up always feeling unsure, and may not try new things. By letting your child participate in a sport you are letting them be accountable for themselves and also enabling them to view the handicap they have as less of a handicap, and more as something they deal with."*

Her attitude is great. She certainly walks the walk of someone who should know. It is inspiring to know that Chanda lives her life with the conviction she can do anything she wants. She may have to try harder or handle some things differently, but she is able. She is definitely capable!

Chanda could have sulked when her parents took her out of swimming and set her down on frozen ground. But she didn't. She simply chose to be the best she could be and look at her go!! You don't have to pull on a goalie helmet to take on discouragement or disappointment. Today, just be like Chanda and choose to be your best!!

> **"Ability is what you're capable of doing. Motivation determines what you do.**
> **Attitude determines how well you do it."**
> **~Lou Holtz**

★ He Became a What?! ★

"Papa, here are the last of the sacks – I've got to go – I'll be late!"
"Ok, Son, thanks for the help – be careful -- see you later."

Alfredo plopped the last sacks of beans and potatoes into the trunk of his father's car, hopped on his bicycle and tore off to work. He really didn't like working at the taco stand, but it was money to help the family. He missed pumping gas at his father's station – but because the government had devalued the peso, they'd lost the business. He remembers the night he found his father crying at the back of the house.

"Son, don't be like me. You've got to go to school!"

Alfredo agreed – besides, he liked school. So between helping his father however he could and working at the taco stand, he kept up with his lessons. When he was 14, Alfredo qualified for an accelerated program that prepared students as elementary school teachers. He caught a bus every morning at 4:30 am, but had to walk home in the blistering sun. Graduating at the top of his class, but without any political connections, Alfredo was assigned to a school far down the Baja peninsula. He refused the assignment and decided to take his chances in the U.S.

One of Alfredo's cousins was a migrant worker and arranged to meet him at the border. Hopping the fence, Alfredo was met by the U.S. Border Patrol and promptly returned to Mexico. He decided the Patrol wouldn't be looking for the same person in the same place on the same day, so he hopped the fence again, this time at night – and his cousin was there to meet him. It was Alfredo's 19th birthday.

The rest of his story is nothing less than remarkable.

After spending months as a field worker, Alfredo advanced to working machinery, qualifying him for a temporary work permit. But he says, *"I had that hunger in my gut,"* and knew education was his ticket. He moved to Stockton, California and took a job at a rail yard so he could attend college. He worked full time during the day and continued to learn new skills. Within a year he was the foreman.

With his English skills improving, Alfredo switched to working the night shift so he could go to school during the day. He discovered that science and math had their "own language" and English wasn't as critical. He made straight A's. From there he attended the University of California at Berkeley, became a teacher's assistant in three departments and also worked at a men's clothing store. Alfredo was in his element. He excelled in his studies and was accepted to Harvard Medical School. When asked if he found Harvard tough, Alfredo said, *"Not really. Compared to working in the fields, it was easy."*

In 1997, ten years after becoming an illegal immigrant, Alfredo became a U.S. citizen. *"I'm sitting there, ten years after hopping the fence, and it hits me how fast I came up."*

But his amazing story doesn't end there!

After finishing his residency, Alfredo was hired at John Hopkins School of Medicine. He holds four positions there: teacher of oncology and neurosurgery, director of a neurosurgery clinic, head of a laboratory studying brain tumors, and also performs 230-240 brain tumor operations a year.

Why brain surgery? Because it is *"the most beautiful organ of our body, the one that we know the least about, the one that makes us who we are."*

Alfredo is a very unique surgeon in that he gets to know his patients. He says that performing surgery on someone's brain is the most *"intimate relationship"* a doctor can have with the patient who *"grants you the gift of trusting you with their lives, and there is no room for mistakes."* He is always found visiting with the patient on whom he's operating just prior to surgery.

Following hours-long surgery, Alfredo often goes to the research laboratory. Although it is serious work there, too, searching for the cause of recurring tumors helps him unwind.

Imagine – in just 21 years, Alfredo Quiñones went from an illegal immigrant who spoke no English to one of the world's most respected brain surgeons!

You may never face the degree of challenges Alfredo did, but each of us will face challenges. Be like him and turn a deaf ear to those who want you to quit before you reach your goal.

A Fun-Loving Tycoon

The phone rings and Butch Stewart looks at his watch – 7 p.m.

"Hello?"

"Hey, Butch, it's my wife's birthday and I forgot I promised her an air conditioner."

"No problem man, I'm on my way."

By punching out a wall and installing an air conditioner that evening, Butch turned yet another couple into happy, loyal customers. By midnight their home is cooled down on a hot, humid Jamaican night and in the morning they will be singing Butch's accolades.

Butch Stewart still owns that air conditioning company, but has expanded his business reach to a Honda dealership, a newspaper, an airline and a line of luxury hotels. What drives this Jamaican? His main motivations come from: loving to succeed – embracing creativity – humor – thinking outside-the-box – having a good time – and seeing others happy.

Butch wasn't happy working for others (and he did plenty of that, too). He saw things that needed to be done and was able to envision how to make it happen. He was already a successful businessman when a friend contacted him about buying a run-down hotel in Montego Bay. The two men nearly lost everything while struggling to making that hotel profitable.

"We just kept the focus, and after a while we got to understand how the hotel business worked. We made sure that we got better and better every day. And then it became easy."

That hotel was the beginning of the Sandals Empire and Butch is now worth more than $1 billion (U.S. dollars).

Butch loved growing up on the beaches and rivers of Jamaica and has created a line of luxury resorts throughout the Caribbean that reflect that happy-go-lucky feeling. Everything is included at a Sandals resort – from food to entertainment. They even have a resort with *"river suites where you can swim right up to your room."*

Butch has stuck to his business philosophy of always giving his customers more than they expect and making sure they are always happy. That's also how he treats his employees.

Don't you think that's a great way of looking at business and at the world? Give more than expected, make things better and better, keep your eyes open for opportunities, dream big, don't be afraid to try new things, and keep a healthy sense of humor. As Butch says, *"The more you laugh, the better things are."*

If you ask for his advice for success, Butch says: *"Keep your feet on the ground. Think smart. Pay attention. Make sure that the customer is never disappointed...Nothing happens by itself. Listen to people, and don't be afraid to roll the dice. I do that every day."*

And he laces it all together with laughter, family, friends, good food, fishing, and playing dominoes!

So, be like Butch -- think smart, stay focused, don't listen to those who say "it can't be done," enjoy life, and make people happy!

Success won't be far behind!

84

★ *A Big Idea* ★

"This is so disturbing!" Albina looked at the polluted river and vacant lots filled with trash and reeking of garbage.

"Hey, don't dump your garbage there!" The youngster shrugs as she throws the trash and runs.

Albina Ruiz became aware of the growing problem of the lack of effective waste management in her native Peru while studying industrial engineering. After receiving her masters in Ecological and Environmental Management, she came up with an idea. What if she could create a community-managed waste collection system?

Albina chose El Cono Norte in Lima as her neighborhood guinea pig. She knew the municipality's waste collection was able to process only half of the community's trash. Not only did people not use the service, when they did, they rarely paid their bills. It was a vicious cycle.

People were tossing their garbage in the streets, rivers and vacant lots. The result was not only a smelly, ugly environment – it was also causing serious health problems. People were not only getting sick from their groundwater being contaminated, they also were being negatively affected psychologically by the whole situation.

Her idea was fairly simple -- find entrepreneurs – small business people – who would take charge of collecting and processing the garbage. This would result in two things: more efficient waste management and reverse unemployment. Albina helped people (mostly women) set up their businesses. They arrived at the fee of $1.50 a month for the service. Next she came up with all kinds of creative marketing ideas – including gift baskets – to get families to use the service AND pay each month on time.

The new business owners go door-to-door collecting garbage and the fees while educating people about the importance of respecting and protecting their environment. Some of these entrepreneurs have even built profitable secondary businesses by creating products like organic fertilizer out of the trash they collect.

Albina started this project (Ciudad Saludable – Healthy City) nearly 20 years ago and now oversees projects in 20 cities across Peru. She employs more than 150 people, has over 4,000 small business owners, and serves over 4 million residents. Her model is so successful she has been asked to create a national plan for Peru. Other Latin American countries have also expressed interest in her program.

Albina stays in contact with the people within her organization. She still visits other cities overwhelmed by garbage, checks in on the neighborhoods involved in her program and meets with government officials.

Albina says, *"Where most people see a problem – I see a possibility."* And her ultimate goal is to change the way people think.

Do you see a problem you can turn into a possibility? You don't have to tackle it alone – ask for help! There are a lot of people who will come alongside you – and there are a lot of possibilities out there needing creative people to solve them!!

Be like Albina and create solutions every chance you get. It's often in working on a solution, that you'll end up making new friends – and learn a lot in the process! And isn't that what success is all about? Learning – relationships – and giving back!

85

★ *From End to Beginning* ★

"John, are you finished with your homework?"
"No."
"John, are you finished with your work?"
"No."
"John, how about now? You finished yet?"
"No, not yet."
"John?"
"Nope!"

John wanted to do his work faster, but he couldn't. The words just didn't make sense sometimes. He wanted a lot of things.

John wanted to know about his father about whom no one would speak.

He wanted to get stronger so he could win more at wrestling. He like wrestling and the people he came to know through that sport.

He wanted to be alone.

He wanted to write. His step-father was a teacher, so he thought he could teach like him.

But he truly desired to be a novelist.

He had always loved details...and more details. His imagination and desire for solitude gave him a reputation as "moody and aloof." He would grow tired of being around too many people and would seek out time and space where he could be alone with his thoughts.

John continued to wrestle and coach wrestling; write and teach writers.

John realized as he grew up he was searching for answers in his writing. He searched for his biological dad whom he never met. (He only knew about him after his dad's death and John himself was a middle-aged man.) And although he tried and tried to imagine what his absent father would say and do, all he had was his imagination. And so he and his imagination started writing.

John used the discipline of wrestling and wrestling drills to guide him in the lengthy process of writing novels. Because he was a slow, poor student he was used to doing things over and over and over again until he finally figured out a way to get it right. And so he does the same with his novels. He writes and rewrites; writes and rewrites again.

"The building of the architecture of the novel--the craft of it--is something I never tire of."

He starts at the end of the story and works his way back to the beginning.

"I spend about two to three months planning the path of the book in my head before I write the last sentence of the novel. From there I work back to the beginning. From the day I think of the last sentence to the book's publication date, not more than a semicolon has changed."

He worked at writing. He read. He studied about writing and this little boy's imagination and dream grew into first one novel and then another novel and then another.

John's desire to be a novelist has come true with 11 novels to his credit!

John Irving is a great American novelist and Academy Award-winning screenwriter, with well-known credits as The World According to Garp, The Cider House Rules, and A Prayer for Owen Meny.

He never gave up, my friends. He could have stayed alone, angry, and used his dyslexia as an excuse not to write. He could have chosen to be a bitter man and disregarded his family and children like his father did. However, he chose to pursue his dreams and his dreams pursued him.

The literary world is much richer because John Irving gave his heart to his works. The big screen is richer for his screenwriting. You can be like that. Choose to be successful in spite of the hard and lonely things that occur in life.

86

POWER BOOSTERS

How would your life change if you felt the fear – and did it anyway?

_____

_____

_____

_____

_____

_____

_____

_____

_____

What do you believe your purpose is?

_____

_____

_____

_____

_____

_____

_____

_____

_____

He hurriedly threw a few things in a bag, his heart pounding in his ears. Whispering to his mother he said his goodbyes, *"I love you, Mother; we'll see each other again soon."*

"Be careful, son. As soon as you can, let us know that you arrived so we know you're safe."

With that they embraced and he disappeared into the darkness.

One of 14 children living in Colombia, Gustavo had been involved in the student movement and organized labor unions. Life had become more difficult, with guerrilla troops everywhere. When a professor and a co-worker were killed, Gustavo fled for his life. Two months later his family joined him in El Salvador. One brother didn't make it - he was murdered by the paramilitary forces.

That was in 1987. In 1991, Gustavo arrived in Maryland, USA along with many other Central American immigrants and refugees. Thousands of day laborers gathered in the parking lots of Maryland's suburbs. If they were lucky enough to be chosen for work, they were paid cash, received no benefits, and continued to live in poverty.

Instead of letting anger run his life, Gustavo turned it into positive action. He started organizing – because that's what he did best.

Gustavo now sits at a desk in Maryland as Executive Director of a very successful organization. He understands the immigrants' hopes and fears. He's very aware of the obstacles these immigrants face – he was one of them. Assimilation is very difficult for these Latinos who are family-oriented and hard working. He sympathizes with their anger over the injustices they face even in the U.S., but he also knows that here there is hope.

Gustavo helped organize CASA of Maryland in an effort to help day laborers find work and hold employers accountable in their hiring and payroll practices. They also provide direct services such as food and clothing. CASA added programs one by one and worked with 20 different organizations to create the Center for Employment and Training (the largest center of its type in the Washington, D.C. metro area).

16 years later, CASA is the state's largest organization serving Latinos. Gustavo has served as Executive Director of CASA since 1993 and says, *"I see it as my duty and view it as a labor of love to assist others up the ladder."*

CASA now helps workers find both temporary and full-time work, operates job training programs, as well as programs for language and literacy. They offer tenant support, health education, legal assistance, community organizing and leadership training. Just one example of CASA's accomplishments is a partnership with one of the nation's largest construction companies resulting in the creation of 450 full-time, full-benefits jobs and 6,000 temporary jobs.

Gustavo's "Energizer Bunny" energy, technical expertise, passion and political savvy have been key to CASA's success. One of his future goals is to create a National Day Laborers Union that will set wage standards, provide health care, and organize immigrants.

Gustavo Torres understands that one person cannot accomplish such things alone. *"Without CASA's 23 staff members and 12 board members, it would be impossible to do any of this. They are the stars, the heroes, the leaders...I learned early on that the only way to effect lasting change is through collaboration."*

Did you catch that? No one expected Gustavo to manage all that CASA has accomplished alone. He wasn't afraid to pull in as many organizations, businesses and people as possible to make things happen.

You and I can learn a lot from Gustavo Torres. We aren't expected to do what we can't do – only what we can. Sometimes we think too little of ourselves; we don't think big enough – don't set big enough goals. CASA wasn't a huge organization when they started. They were a few determined people who started small and kept growing.

That's great advice for us -- start small, and keep growing. Regardless of what others may say, you *can* accomplish your goals!

★ *She's Unstoppable* ★

"But, Mom, I want to see the world and speak to millions. I want to travel and be a world changer."

"Cynthia, now, now, be realistic, dear. You're a girl from the Midwestern U.S. You need to play it safe and be practical. There's a job opening downtown for a secretary. Try that and don't be so dreamy. You need to know you can support yourself. Don't be so idealistic, sweetie. Just be realistic. You know I love you.

Cynthia got her first job as a secretary.

"Cynthia, I am sorry but we are going to have to let you go."

She got a second job as a secretary.

Cynthia, I'm sorry but we need to reorganize the business, so you will be moving down.

After finding a job with a little less demand for attention to "detail," Cynthia stayed for ten years as a National Account Manager for a large U.S. telephone service provider. She worked and went to school to get her degree. In addition, she grew weary of the corporate atmosphere.

Her desire grew to write a book. She desired to capture all the people she studied that did extraordinary things with horrific obstacles. Cynthia knew about hundreds of people who were "unstoppable." They never quit. They tried repeatedly. And eventually she saw where they were successful.

Had she ever written a book? No.

Did she know how to write a book? No.

Did she have a publisher? No.

However, the next phone call went something like this.

"You've done what? You quit your job and sold your house? Why? Cynthia, what are you thinking? Where are you going to live? You are going to do what? Your savings? You took out your savings? Oh my, Cynthia have you gone mad?"

Cynthia did just that, leased a home 1/2 the size of her original, and began writing.

"Why make such drastic changes? So that I could be unstoppable in creating something that was really meaningful for me."

Meet Cynthia Kersey, *best-selling author, coach, speaker, consultant and expert in the field of human potential **AND** CEO of Unstoppable Enterprises.*

Cynthia has an entire business of helping others reach their dreams. She understands risk, failure, mistakes, and challenges. She has faced them all. When you hear her speak, she speaks of trying over and then over again. Taking things slowly...one step at a time.

"I've interviewed enough unstoppable people over the last 10 years to say unequivocally that unstoppable people get frustrated, disappointed, discouraged, and even have moments of depression, and yet they don't quit. So, it's not that they're so different. They just don't say, when they have difficulties, it's 'game over.' They just don't say, 'I'm not good enough.' They might think it just for a moment, but they'll dispute it, and they'll continue to move forward."

You can be like Cynthia. "Unstoppable." You may not have all the answers or know exactly what your next step will look like. That is ok. Just as long as you keep making another step! Never quit! Never, ever!

> *"The difference between a big shot and a little shot is that a big shot's just a little shot that kept on shooting."*
>
> *~Zig Ziglar*

Overcoming Discouragement

Have you ever heard of Maxcy Filer? Probably not.

Maxcy Filer was married, with two young sons, when he decided to become an attorney. He'd been inspired by two attorneys who were making positive changes in the laws of his community and he wanted to be part of that change. Maxcy was 36 years old.

So he went to law school, graduated, and took the bar exam. Like many others before him he failed on the first try. So Maxcy took it again. Well, he continued to take it throughout his sons' undergraduate schooling. And he continued to take it while they attended and graduated from law school. And yes, he continued to take it after he was working for his sons as a law clerk in their offices!

Finally, after 25 years and 47 attempts, Maxcy Filer passed the bar exam at the age of 61. While most people were retiring, he began living his dream.

What do you do when you get discouraged? I hope the next time you face discouragement, you'll remember Maxcy Filer. "Keep on keepin' on" and you'll come out on the other side -- which is success!

"A pessimist is one who makes difficulties out of his opportunities and an optimist is one who makes opportunities of his difficulties."
~Harry S. Truman

★ _Pine Needle Bears_ ★

"Richard? It's Dad. I wondered if you'd move back to Idaho. I'm older now and not doing too well. I need you... to come home and take care of the place. Can you? Will you?

Richard looked up at the skyscrapers of California, heard the millions of cars, and knew he was tired too. Tired of city life. Unfulfilled and dissatisfied with where his life was headed. Not living out his dream.

The back and forth conversation that occurred inside Richard's head went something like this:
"_He's your dad._"
"_He's a stranger._ (His dad truly was a stranger. They had been apart and estranged for decades.)
"_You are his son. It's the right thing to do. He's sick._"
"_I've never known him. I was in the fourth grade when we really spent time together_"
"_You're a man now. It's time now to make a new start._"

Yes, he was his son. What should he do? Richard chose to move to Idaho and start anew. Fresh air, clear mountain streams, majestic pine trees and abundant wildlife became his backdrop. After his move to the country, the artist within Richard roused. He longed for a creative outlet.

At first, he was preoccupied with the task of taking care of an elderly sick man. Because Richard chose to reunite with his father, they spent a wonderful year refreshing their relationship with each other before his dad passed away. The artist within Richard awoke fully now -- and desired to create. But what would he use for materials? Money was already tight.

One day, as Richard walked the river bed enjoying the bright morning sun, he thought about the question his new friend, April had posed.

"What would you do Richard if you could do anything? What would you love to be doing?"

Deep inside he knew the answer. The same answer he'd given through every available art class he'd attended in junior and high school in California. He wanted to be an artist. He **was** an artist - he just wasn't living like one... YET!

From that new friendship, and the call of the wild, Richard and April Carpenter (Yes, April is now his wife) took his dream and are making it reality.

Richard has found a way to "sculpt" with pine needles... yes, the needles from a pine tree. He gathers pine needles from the ground and then sorts, washes, trims and hand weaves life size bears. The trick? It takes a couple hundred thousand pine needles and over 8 months to make a life-sized bear!

Richard and April have managed to carve out a living from the gifts of nature. He not only weaves pine needle bears, he carves antlers and creates handmade buttons, and jewelry. Richard uses antlers he finds after moose and deer have naturally shed them. His carvings are intricate and delicate, oftentimes humorous dioramas of life in the northwest United States.

(http://www.mountainmagicoriginals.com)

Richard and April take what is around them and use it with integrity and care. But more importantly they are fulfilling that desire within to be happy, satisfied and at peace.

What about you? Are you living the life you desire? Is there an artist, writer, teacher, social worker, police officer...aching to be freed? What would you do if you could? I hope you will look at these questions and give them some thought.

Are you like Richard and need to recreate your life? Maybe you need to be true to that inner calling you hear. Maybe you need to dig deep and search for what really fulfills your soul. It will be in the searching and the finding that you will also discover your success!

★ _A Writer Who Could Barely Read_ ★

"I'm sorry, Mrs. Cannell. Stephen just can't keep up. He will have to repeat the first grade and hopefully he'll have a better year next year. He tries hard and is a wonderful student, but unfortunately he's continued to have a hard time."

"Mrs. Cannell, I called you to let you know that Stephen isn't going to pass fourth grade. His work just isn't advancing fast enough. He truly tries to get it, but he has such difficulties learning. He's such a great kid."

"I hate to tell you this, but Stephen will have to repeat the 10th grade. I am afraid I can't pass him. I tell you though, he's not ever a problem and he is a caring young man. I am glad to have him in class but his work just isn't good enough."

Well, Stephen also got kicked out of two schools and flunked almost every English class he took. While he did finally graduate high school – it was at the bottom of his class. It wasn't that he wasn't interested or motivated; he just had an incredibly difficult time reading and writing down his ideas. Even though English was one of his most difficult classes, he wrote in one of his yearbooks that it was his ambition to be an author. It wasn't until much later that Stephen was diagnosed with severe dyslexia.

But that didn't stop him from pursuing his passion -- writing stories.

Do you think he should have? Would you have encouraged him? If it were you would you have kept trying? Or would you have quit?

After all, think about it... he had a legitimate reason for NOT writing! Words and letters didn't make sense in his brain. Trying to get those words to process was a daunting task and one that often failed him.

Only one problem with "not being able to write"... _Stephen's passion was writing stories._

While working at his father's design firm, he started writing television scripts and story ideas. After selling his first ideas of _Mission Impossible_ and _It takes a Thief_ in the late 1960's, he went on to create or co-create more than 40 television series. Those 40 series required more than 450 written episodes! He has produced or executive produced more than 1,500 episodes. To his credit are the American TV shows: _The Rockford Files_, _Greatest American Hero_, _The A-Team_, _Beretta_, _The Commish_ and _Hunter_. He has written 12 best-selling police novels including the critically acclaimed Shane Scully series, _Runaway Heart_, _The Devil's Workshop_, _Riding the Snake_, and _King Con_.

He has won an Emmy, two Writer's Guild awards, two Edgar Award nominations and has a star on the Hollywood Boulevard Walk of Fame.

Even with his success, his disability prevails. Yes even today, according to an interview, Stephen _"frequently has to dictate ideas or even complete scripts to a personal secretary."_ His brain still doesn't allow those wonderful scripts to come forth easily. So how is it that Stephen, who could hardly read or write, could become such a prolific producer of the written word? It all has to do with knowing his passion and never giving up.

Stephen believed in himself and his dreams.

What about you? Are you living your passion? Do you believe in your dreams?

If the answer is no, you aren't living your passion or can't even name it, spend a few minutes remembering what you dreamed of doing when you were a kid. What did you want to be when you grew up? These questions may help you rediscover what excites you -- what inspires you -- what challenges you. The next step is to decide how to begin reclaiming your passion. Do you need to take a class, visit a museum, take a trip?

It's never too late -- decide to step out and make it happen. Your life will take on new meaning, you'll experience enthusiasm and joy, and the pursuit of your passion will result in great happiness and tremendous success!

POWER BOOSTERS

Is not believing in yourself holding you back from success? How? Will you let it continue?

_____

_____

_____

_____

_____

_____

_____

_____

_____

_____

What step can you take TODAY toward your success?

_____

_____

_____

_____

_____

_____

_____

_____

_____

_____

"Katie? Can you hear me?"

No answer.

"Katie? Katie? How are you feeling?"

No answer.

"Katie? Squeeze my hand if you can hear me."

Nothing.

"Well, I guess she's still too sedated. Let's give her 5-10 minutes and try again."

The postoperative nurses finished writing in Katie's chart and let her rest. Soon however, she was slightly conscious and trying to smile.

"Katie! Glad to see you. Can you hear me now?"

"Yes..." Katie whispered. Her throat was dry from the anesthesia.

She was all too familiar with hospitals, surgeries and their required routines.

You see, Katie Prevas was born with _"epiphyseal dysplasia, a disease that causes your joints to overgrow and your bones to become immobile."_ Although it only effects her left side, she also had scoliosis (or curvature of the spine). A rod surgically placed in her spine corrected the curve. By the year 2002, Katie had endured 20 surgeries...and she was only 17 years old.

Having a medical condition that made it impossible to wear high heels, walk without limping, play contact sports, or even sit cross-legged during a school assembly, has not stopped Katie. She insists on doing things her way.

"Sometimes, I have to remind myself there are things I can't do--but still plenty I **can** do. I've figured out what my limits are and learned not to care about what other people expect my limits to be. I surprise a lot of people, even myself sometimes. The expectations people put on you really shouldn't matter--you need to set your own goals."

Katie is happy with her body and herself. Sure, she'd like to be "normal" (whatever that is), but she is not wasting time sitting around watching the world go by without her. She is involved with life and is definitely living it on her terms.

"Katie, how are you feeling?" The nurse looked into Katie's bright lively eyes, a smile playing across her lips.

"I'm fine...just fine," came Katie's reply. _"When do I get out of here? I'm ready to go home now."_

She says this of herself; _"Anyone who knows me knows I'm unstoppable and definitely unbreakable. And once I put my mind to something, you'd better watch out!"_

I hope you are like that. _"Unstoppable!"_

If not, I encourage you today to take some beginning steps to getting that way. Determine that you won't quit until you've chased down all your dreams and made them reality!

> _"All mankind is divided into three classes: those that are immovable, those that are movable, and those that move."_ ~Benjamin Franklin

From Coal to Diamonds ★

★

The sounds of laughter echoed in his ears as his face turned red and his ears burned. *"It's not my fault,"* he thinks to himself. *"It's not my fault."*

As mean as it was, the laughter and the jeering actually pushed him to learn the language of this strange, confusing country all the faster. Focusing all his attention on his studies, he was soon earning the top grades in math, science – and yes, even English – the language that was so strange to his ears.

Da-i and his brother grew up in Taiwan with their mother. Their father left them to pursue graduate studies in engineering in the United States. And though they knew very little of him as a day-to-day father, he served as a long-distance role model. The boys were under a great deal of pressure to do well in their studies and follow in their father's scholarly footsteps. They wrote letters back and forth every week and were required to report all that had happened that week in school. Every letter was laced with conversation about joining their father in the United States.

When he was finally able to send for his family, Da-i was 12, knew no English and very little about this new country. Not only did he come to everything foreign, his father also gave him a foreign name - David.

Wanting his children to learn the language from the people instead of the classroom, Mr. Ho had them wait until they arrived in the U.S. to begin learning English. As you can imagine, being 12 and unable to understand anything that is going on around you was pretty terrifying. David says, *"I had done fairly well in school in Taiwan. I came here and all of a sudden I couldn't communicate. It was a devastating period."*

David's first months of school were frustrating and bewildering as he struggled with the language and fought to learn his lessons. But within 6 short months, he had made great strides in learning English. David had a natural curiosity and was attracted to math and the sciences. He graduated not only from high school with honors, but from MIT and Cal Tech with a major in physics and then from UCLA in California as a medical doctor. It was in California that he came in contact with an illness that couldn't be explained – one of the very first documented cases of AIDS.

David Ho had found his passion . . .

Dr. Ho saw his first AIDS patient in Los Angeles in 1981, then moved to Boston to pursue research on viruses - convinced those viruses were the key to this unknown disease. While most researchers believed AIDS was dormant in the initial stages, Dr. Ho's research proved it actually multiplied and churned out vast amounts of virus each day - right from the very beginning of the infection. The immune system eventually wore itself out fighting, and that's when AIDS showed up.

Dr. Ho took his discovery to the next level by shifting his attention from treating patients at the end of their lives, to inventing "cocktails" of drugs to treat them from the onset of the illness.

He found that the virus could mutate to accommodate single drugs, but when given multiple drugs (or cocktails) at one time, the virus couldn't spread! The result was remarkable, providing quality of life to those infected and removing the death sentence for many.

At age 37, Dr. David Ho was appointed Director of the new Aaron Diamond AIDS Research Center in New York City where he continues his research for a vaccination which will eliminate the threat of AIDS altogether. *"We want to push the therapy from controlling the virus to curing the virus."*

Da-i Ho faced many difficulties and enormous pressure as a child and young adult. But even as coal needs intense pressure to form into diamonds, sometimes it takes massive pressure in our lives to turn us into the beautiful people we are to become. Da-i Ho never thought he would become Dr. David Ho - on the brink of discovering the cure for a deadly disease – but that's exactly who he is.

Are you are facing difficulties or pressure? Try thinking of yourself as a piece of coal and let what you are experiencing create you into something beautiful. Don't become bitter – become better! Watch for the opportunity that will be presenting itself to you, and be ready to grab a hold of it like David Ho did, and don't let go! You will become the success you want to be!

"Well little one, life isn't always fair – but love will prevail."

Her infant's big eyes looked into hers as if he knew exactly what she meant.

When Dina Abdel Wahab first saw her baby her heart sank – then it grew a size larger to encompass this child with special needs.

As little Ali grew, Dina knew there would be challenges – especially when it came to her son's education. Cairo, Egypt was not the best place to raise a child with Down syndrome, but it was home. So Dina decided to create what did not exist.

"I didn't want to change my son's lifestyle, so I decided to try to change society."

Dina felt that preschools in Egypt basically provided babysitting and that's not what Ali needed. She knew that special needs kids like him needed the stimulation of non-disabled children with whom they can interact. Since that wasn't an option, Dina opened The Baby Academy with Ali as her first student.

Dina offered her school to children 3 months to 5 years of age. The child-centered philosophy of the school is based on love, learning and play. Curriculum is tailored to the specific child's developmental needs and designed to challenge all children to achieve their potential.

The Baby Academy is thriving. Twenty percent of the children enrolled are special needs kids. Dina is opening additional schools and will eventually franchise the concept. She points out that according to the United Nations, less than 4% of Arab children have access to preschool education. The Baby Academy is becoming a leader in early childhood education throughout Egypt and the Middle East.

But Dina realized many people could not afford The Baby Academy, so she is working with the government to help them include special needs children in Egypt's mainstream educational system.

Isn't that amazing? Dina created an extremely high caliber school for preschoolers because nothing existed when she needed it for her son. She started out small, and it has grown and grown. What she created for Ali is now in great demand by other parents of preschoolers throughout Cairo.

You never need to worry that you can't do something as well as someone else – because no one else can do exactly what YOU can do as well as YOU can!

Dina used her gifts to help her son and other young children. You have gifts to share as well. They won't look like Dina's – hers won't look like yours.

Your success will be uniquely yours – so don't give up!

"The secret of making something work in your lives is first of all, the deep desire to make it work; then the faith and belief that it can work; then to hold that clear definite vision in your consciousness and see it working out step by step, without one thought of doubt or disbelief."
~Eileen Caddy

★ *An Amazing Come Back* ★

The dark hall seemed endless. He had to get to her. Her dim night light taunted. Josh stumbled. He fell. He was drenched in sweat, terrified, nearly paralyzed with fear. The demons of drug addiction ruled him. He had no future. His past victories were erased. His tattoo covered body testified to his rebellion. This nightmare tonight had literally warned him of his own death.

His life teased him. His brain failed him. And his addiction? It was killing him.

His grandmother lay sleeping. Her life was peaceful and serene. It didn't seem fair. She could rest in peace. She said she loved him and believed in him -- even when he woke her at 3 a.m. from a screeching drug high that almost cost him his sanity. The years of drug use, or rather abuse, had ravaged his mind and body so that clear thinking eluded him. Rational choice was impossible. He had to get to her. It was the only thing to do...he had to get to her.

He stood over his grandmother. Disbelief at what he was about to do wafted dimly through him. The thought, *"if they could see me now, those old friends of mine"* ran through the very black, dark corners of his mind.

Trembling, he lifted the covers and crawled into the secure, comforting presence of her bed. As if he were a small boy again, Josh snuggled deep into the covers and craved peace. Desperate and gasping for life, Josh let his grandmother's presence soothe his soul.

And he woke in the morning, a changed man.

- Today (2008) Josh Hamilton is a Major League Baseball player for the Texas Rangers.
- Today (2008) Josh is a member of the the American League All-Star team.
- Today (2008) Josh hit the most home runs in the Home Run Derby.
- Today (2008) Josh is the only player in American league history to be the American League Player of the Month the first two months of the season.
- Today (2008) Josh is living proof *"that hope is never lost."*

Josh had been a superior high school baseball player in North Carolina. The spotlight had been all his and he enjoyed the attention of being named North Carolina's Gatorade High School Player of the Year *twice!* After his senior year, voted High School Player of the Year by *Baseball America* **and** Amateur Player of the Year by USA Baseball, he entered the minor leagues. The boy was doing it right.

That was 1999.

Although he enjoyed his multi-million dollar sign-on bonus as he debuted in his professional career, his focus veered off course after a 2001 auto accident. His life detoured and drugs overcame this home run king. He slowly disappeared from baseball and then from life.

He betrayed his team, his family and his body. And from 2002 -2006, he didn't play baseball at all. He tried drug rehab 8 times! And failed. He became in his own words a *"living dead man."*

"I was so out of it I had lost consciousness, but my body had kept going, down the middle of the road, cars whizzing by on either side. I had run out of gas on my way to a drug dealer's house, and from there I left the truck and started walking. I had taken a prescription anti-anxiety drug, along with whatever else I was using at the time, and the combination had put me over the edge. It's the perfect example of what I was: a dead man walking."

How did this superstar come back to see life, love, hope and peace?

How did he find himself a Baseball superstar again?

The morning after crawling into the safety of his loving grandmother's bed, he awoke from what he calls a spiritual experience with God.

His words tell the story best: *"How am I here? I can only shrug and say, "It's a God thing." It's the only possible explanation. Addiction is a humbling experience. Getting it under control is even more humbling. I got better for one reason: I surrendered. Instead of asking to be bailed out, instead of making deals with God by saying, 'If you get me out of this mess, I'll stop doing what I'm doing,' I asked for help. I have a mission now. My mission is to be the ray of hope, the guy who stands out there on that beautiful field and owns up to his mistakes and lets people know it's never completely hopeless, no matter how bad it seems at the time. I have a platform and a message, and now I go to bed at night, sober and happy, praying I can be a good messenger."*

His sobriety is a daily challenge – just as it is for everyone who chooses sobriety over addiction. He had a one night relapse in 2009, but faced it with courage and is now stronger than ever. He is determined to live the life of his dreams. With his own courage, and the support of his family and friends, he is doing just that! I stand in awe of his comeback as do thousands of fans. There is more to his story, but you get the picture, don't you?

There is hope for you and your dreams. If Josh can make it back from the deep pit of drug addiction to the demands of major league sports, you can make it back from whatever challenges and decisions have stolen your dreams too!

It's not what you do IF you make a mistake.
You will.
It's not what you do IF you mess up.
You will.
It's not what you do IF you fail.
You will.
It's not what you do IF fear creates a bad decision.
It will.
You're human – not perfect.
It's not IF.
It's WHEN.
When your choices, or circumstances, kick you in the teeth,
You get back up.
You choose to start again.
You choose to do it right.
You choose to succeed.
Every time!

★ *The Last Great Race on Earth* ★

"Hike! Hike"! called out the musher. *"Mush! Hike! All Right! Let's Go!"* The beautiful dog team responded to her commands and sprang into action . . . the team moving as one. The musher prepared herself for the racing speed of her team. The lead lines grew taut in her hands as her dogs set their pace.

The adrenaline coursed through her veins as the dogs began picking up speed. It was her first time for the big race. Months of training, grueling exercises and many, many shorter races had her, and her dogs, in top physical and mental condition. She knew she was ready. She knew her dogs were too.

Nothing remained between her and the finish line except over 1,150 miles of the roughest, most beautiful terrain on the planet: jagged mountain ranges, frozen rivers, dense forests, desolate tundra and miles and miles of windswept coast. In addition, she knew temperatures would fall far below zero, winds could cause complete loss of visibility, there would be long hours of darkness and treacherous climbs.

It's known as the Last Great Race on Earth. It's a race run in Alaska by mushers and dogs. ***It's the Iditarod.*** Each team of 12 to 16 dogs and their musher will cover those 1150+ miles in 10 to 17 days.

The idea of the actual race was born in the mind of Dorothy G. Page, the "mother of the Iditarod."

The phone rang at Joe Redington's house one dark Alaskan evening. It was Dorothy.

"Joe, I have an idea. Why don't we start up the Iditarod trail again and make it a race? There's no excuse to let history die out. And don't you think mushers from around would come? I just can't sit back and watch that trail be lost anymore. We'll lose it forever if someone doesn't do something. Will you help me? You're a musher. You know people. They'll listen to you. We can bring it back and keep it alive, don't you think?"

Joe's answer was a resounding YES! He became known as the "Father of the Iditarod."

Mrs. Page was an Alaskan historian who didn't want the Iditarod Trail, which had once been the major "thoroughfare" through Alaska, to be lost. By the mid 1960's most people in Alaska didn't even know there was an Iditarod Trail, or that dog teams had played such an important part in Alaska's early settlement.

The Iditarod Trail has a rich history as a supply line from the coastal towns to the interior mining camps, and even beyond to the west coast communities of Alaska. Mail and supplies went in -- gold came out -- all by dog sled. Legends were born and heroes made. In 1925, part of that trail became a life-saving highway for Nome whose population was suffering from diphtheria. The serum was brought in by bravely determined mushers and their faithful life-saving, hard-driving dogs. Dorothy believed in the history of these people and their dogs, and desired to see their return.

Many believed it a crazy idea to send mushers into the vast uninhabited Alaskan wilderness. Many opposed this "race into death."

However, to date, over 400 finishers have come from Canada, Czechoslovakia, France, Great Britain, Germany, Norway, Switzerland, Italy, Japan, Austria, Australia, Sweden, the Soviet Union and from about 20 states in the U.S.

The list of participants, winning records and legends is pages long. Books have been written and movies made around the stories of trial and hardship, victory and success. Yet each person and his or her dogs have accomplished a feat few of us would even attempt. Each one of them has gone the distance and is part of the Iditarod legend. And these "legends" have Dorothy and Joe to thank – because they had a vision and put their passionate belief into action.

While most of us will never run such a grueling race, each of us faces challenges and difficulties. And each of us who attempts something new and different will be at the receiving end of comments like, "it'll never work," "you're crazy," and "give up before you make a fool of yourself."

But for those who decide to go the distance and never quit: pure satisfaction, boundless joy and a deep sense of fulfillment will be theirs.

You may have your own, personal Iditarod race to run. Don't give up! Give it your all and you, too can accomplish what you desire.

POWER BOOSTERS

What will you give back when you're successful?

_____

_____

_____

_____

_____

_____

_____

_____

_____

What are 3 good things that can happen because of the challenges in your life?

_____

_____

_____

_____

_____

_____

_____

_____

_____

_____

"You are good, Jennifer. I like your work. I think you'll go far in the cartoon world. I am putting your work out for display. Want to help?"

"Thanks, I would love to. But I have got to meet my mom. I have a doctor's appointment about my eyes. I'm nearly late now...can I do it tomorrow?"

The artist brushes and art paper jeered from the desk. Jennifer had just come from the doctor's office. She thought of all her dreams of being an artist, a cartoonist. She wondered if there were blind artists in the world.

She could not figure out what to do with herself. She was only 15 years old, yet she had dreamed many dreams. She was not quite blind yet. She had her whole life ahead. What would it be like to be blind? How would it feel? What would she do when her eyesight failed? How old would she be? How would her life turn out?

Several years later, and the scene is set like this. ...

Ladies and Gentleman, I would like to introduce you to award winning singer, best selling Christian author, public speaker, motivator, and inspirational writer: Jennifer Rothschild.

As the applause grows, the curtain draws back revealing a woman dressed in white, smiling a beautiful smile. She sings words familiar to some in the crowd, *"It is well, with my soul."*

Jennifer lives that truth...even as she struggled at first with her life; she has found peace within her soul with her blindness. She uses her unique position to offer hope to thousands at conferences and seminars across the USA.

"For me, blindness is a circumstance that opens the door to a host of other bewildering issues. One of the biggest daily realities I face is the stress of not being able to drive, read, or enjoy independence...Fear betrays; hope never does. Fear and despair make us quiver; hope makes us unshakable. Rather than giving into fear and despair, we tell our souls to hope. Hope will always be on your side, cheering you on and defending you."

Jennifer eventually set down her artist brushes, gave up the idea of becoming a commercial artist and picked up a microphone to speak and sing...inspiring the multitudes. She also picked up a pen to compose several bestselling books.

"Through her signature wit and poignant story-telling, audiences are prompted to look beyond their circumstances to find unique 'gifts,' in unusual packaging."

Jennifer didn't give up. Instead, she refocused her life.

I want to do that too. Refocus whenever I need to.

You and I may not be battling a blinding illness but we battle many things that paralyze us from pursuing our dreams. Discouragement, depression, disillusionment...and even other people who try to stop us from dreaming...we face those every day. Jennifer's advice?

"Steady, small actions will slowly reduce the big feeling that is paralyzing you. Just because you have failed at something does not mean you are a failure. If you quit, the world will be lacking what you alone bring to it."

This woman knows her stuff! She speaks wisdom when she says, *"If you quit, the world will be lacking what you alone bring to it."*

So don't quit. Stay at it for the long haul.

> **"There are no limitations to the mind except those we acknowledge;**
> **both poverty and riches are the offspring of thought."**
> **~Napoleon Hill**

It's been said that if Lance's story were written as a movie, it would be dismissed as "trite melodrama."

But here's the truth. A deadly disease struck a successful athlete. Despite desperately thin odds, he managed to not only beat the cancer, but return to the sport he loved, and win its most coveted prize. But the beauty of Lance's story is that it doesn't end on the finish line of the Tour de France. His life has taken on new meaning. His website says it this way, *"No matter what his path, he will travel it with sure knowledge that every day is precious and that every step matters."*

Lance was always athletic and competitive and his mother was one of his greatest supporters. At age 13, he won the Iron Kids Triathlon, and became a professional athlete when he was only 16 years old. Training with the U.S. Olympic cycling developmental team in Colorado Springs his senior year, nearly cost him his high school diploma.

Lance's rise in the amateur ranks was seemingly effortless and he qualified for the junior world championships in Moscow in 1989. By 1991, he was the U.S. National Amateur Champion, and soon afterward turned professional.

Once in the professional realm, Lance would become the number 1 ranked cyclist with a spot on the U.S. Olympic team. But seeming tragedy struck while at the top of his game. In excruciating pain, Lance was forced to stop riding. In early October of 1996, he was given the devastating news that he had cancer.

In that moment, Lance's life changed forever. Tests showed his advanced cancer had spread to his lungs and brain and his chances for recovery were far less than 50-50. Scared to death, but determined, Lance started an aggressive form of chemotherapy. It worked, and his thoughts slowly returned to racing.

Even though the cancer had left him scarred physically and emotionally, Lance says it *"...was the best thing that ever happened to me."* His new perspective on life pushed him beyond racing to embrace the cancer community. He started the Lance Armstrong Foundation within months of his diagnosis to help others with the struggles they would face with this devastating disease.

As you probably already know, Lance went on to win the Tour de France in 1999, and became an international hero to both the racing world and the cancer community! He went on to win six more Tour de France titles and has been awarded nearly every sports honor there is. Lance Armstrong has become a symbol of hope, determination and inspiration!

I hope it won't take a crisis like Lance Armstrong's for you to embrace life with a grateful heart. I hope that regardless of the struggles you may be facing today, in your heart-of-hearts, you too can say *"every day is precious and every step matters."*

"The reason most people never reach their goals is that they don't define them, learn about them or even seriously consider them as believable or achievable. Winners can tell you where they are going, what they plan to do along the way, and who will be sharing the adventure with them."

~Denis Waitley

★ *She Lost It Then Found It* ★

In 1931, Marguerite was only 3 when her daddy packed a suitcase and sent her and her 4 year old brother, Bailey, alone on the train to live with his mother.

"Daddy! I don't want to!"

"You have to. I can't take care of you right now! Granma Henderson will see after you. Now get on the train. Go with your brother!"

Four years later, with no notice, he returned to usher the kids back to his estranged wife.

"Daddy! I don't want to leave!"

"You have to. Your mom will take care of you. Now let's go!"

One year later at age 8, Marguerite suffered intimate abuse from mother's boyfriend. After confiding in Bailey what he had done to her, Bailey told the family how his sister had been violated. The boyfriend spent only one day in jail. However, he was found beaten to death just days after his release.

After that incident, when they were returned to Granma Henderson yet again, Marguerite didn't protest… she couldn't. Understandably traumatized, Marguerite internalized her pain and quit speaking. *"I thought if I spoke, my mouth would just issue out something that would kill people, randomly, so it was better not to talk."* Nearly five years would pass before she began speaking again.

A close friend and teacher, Bertha Flowers believed in Marguerite and simply loved her. Bertha introduced her to classic literature, and slowly coaxed her to speak again. The friendship stirred something within that young girl. That literature would birth a passionate desire for all the arts within her, and Marguerite would spend decades experimenting with dance, speaking, drama, theater, and writing.

Her successes were slow and steady in coming, occurring between tragedy and heartache. You see, Marguerite also had a baby though she wasn't married; had a lover who forced her to work as a prostitute; married and divorced multiple times; and lost her son to a kidnapping. Many things happened to her and around her that should have kept this woman from following her dreams. But she didn't let the obstacles stand in her way; she let them be stepping stones from which to learn.

You probably know her by her brother's nickname for Marguerite: Maya. *Maybe you've heard of her. Maya Angelou.*

Her life story is not always easy to hear, or as pretty as her acclaimed poetry. Tales of hardship, single motherhood, multiple marriages, and failed attempts at life interweave with tales of Broadway plays, foreign born husbands, exotic European and African homes, strong friendships with the likes of Martin Luther King, Malcolm X, James Baldwin and in later years, Roberta Flack, former U.S. President Bill Clinton, and Oprah Winfrey, among others.

Maya is a true Renaissance woman . . . billed as poet, dancer, producer, historian, playwright, director, best-selling author -- she still performs and speaks across the world. Now at age 80+, her public performances are billed at over $40,000 per engagement!!

Hard to believe that mute little girl has gone on to be the first African American woman to:

- operate a streetcar in San Francisco
- write an original script that was produced
- be featured in the *Poetry for Young People*
- write and recite her own work at a Presidential Inauguration

As an author and recording artist, she has over 40 books, plays, poetry compilations, and albums. Her television, radio, stage and theater credits, awards and national prizes are as numerous as her fifty honorary degrees from universities and colleges throughout the world. I'd say she is extremely successful! Wouldn't you?

Maya's life was far from easy – but it was out of the struggle and pain that she found her voice. It was slow in coming – but it came! There is no such thing as an "overnight success"! Hold on! Believe that you will find your voice and you will! Success is on the way if you will decide to never quit.

★ *From Farming to Saving Lives* ★

"I quit -- I'm quitting the farming business!"
"I understand, dear, but what will you do to support your family?"
"I'm going into the fabric business!"
Little did Kaj know where that statement would lead him and his future generations.

It was 1950 when Kaj Vestergaard Frandsen left farming to enter business with a friend who owned four looms. Life had been difficult on his small Denmark farm and the prospect of the new venture sent excitement coursing through his veins. Although his partner and he parted ways fairly quickly, Kaj kept the looms and began selling fabric for jacket linings and women's uniforms. In just 17 years he became a millionaire. But ill health forced him to turn the business over to his son, Torben.

Over the next couple of decades, the high-cost textiles industry in western Europe took a nosedive. Torben tried moving the business to Ireland, and then Poland. Things were very tough until a friend mentioned there was 1 million yards of extremely fine fabric tucked away in various locations around Sweden. The material was completely out of fashion – and Torben acquired it at very low cost. He found a process that allowed him to reconstitute the fabric into blankets. Enlisting his older entrepreneurial son Mikkel, they began selling the blankets to the Red Cross and Save The Children.

Prior to coming into his father's business, Mikkel was quite the businessman in his own right. After graduating from high school he traveled throughout the Middle East and Africa and started a business in Nigeria importing used trucks, buses and engines. But a military coup sent him home – that's when he joined the textile business, making deals with humanitarian aid groups for the blankets.

Eventually moving to Nairobi in order to improve the business' operations, Mikkel extended operations to 19 countries. They provided blankets to refugee camps in Tanzania, Sudan and Somalia.

Mikkel's portion of the business (humanitarian textiles) soon outstripped the rest of the company's business of selling women's uniforms. Uniforms were discontinued. As the business grew, so did textile competition in India, Pakistan and China – all vying for the same United Nations' contracts. So Mikkel narrowed his market into smaller niches with new inventions.

The first product was PermaNet® - a plain mesh netting impregnated with an insecticide that repels mosquitoes and lasts for years (as opposed to most netting that only withstands a few washings). The World Health Organization claims that PermaNet and similar products have reduced child mortality rates by 25%-30%.

Another new product was ZeroFly® - a plastic sheet that contains insecticide to protect against mosquito-borne malaria and diarrhea transmitted by houseflies. This sheeting is used as temporary shelter after large-scale disasters.

More recently is a new invention called the LifeStraw® -- a portable, reusable "straw" one inch in diameter and 10 inches long. An individual can use it to drink from any water. It removes bacteria such as salmonella and staphylococcus from surface water in rivers and lakes and even puddles. How well does it work? Torben appeared on a Danish TV news program to demonstrate the LifeStraw® by drinking out of a Copenhagen lake, a salt-water canal and a toilet. The LifeStraw® provides safe drinking water for people on-the-go where no potable water exists!

I'm sure Kaj never envisioned those four looms evolving into a business that would save tens of thousands of lives in the poorest of the poor countries around the world!

Like Kaj, you and I may never know the long-term results of decisions we make. Every decision has consequences – no matter how small we may think they are. Who knows, a choice you make today may eventually develop into something that changes the way people live, think, work or play!

Yes, you ARE that important! Yes, your choices DO make a difference! Yes, HOW you make your decisions will influence your future – and perhaps the future of other generations!

"Andrew, where's the Big Mac?[©]*"*

"Coming up!"

"Andrew, the customers are waiting."

"Andrew, they need their change."

"Coming up!"

"Andrew, come in my office please. I am not sure this job is for you. Keep trying, though I am not sure we can keep you."

"Yes sir. Sorry, sir. I am trying."

"I know, but you are slowing down the team."

15 years old, Andrew struggled with his inability to read. Not that he couldn't read, but when he read, the letters were jumbled...out of order. As an example, that previous phrase "out of order" might look like "tuo fo rdore" to Andrew.

Creative and talented, Andrew learns differently than the average guy. His mind simply processes words differently. Not a problem, unless you have to rely on the written word to succeed.

Even at 15, Andrew determined to find what he wanted to do with his life.

Originally a California boy, he quit McDonalds and fought forest fires for a while. After high school, he moved to Wyoming and cooked for a short stint at a well-known American hotel. Seemingly one for adventure, he roamed up to Alaska and endured the sour, scaly, mess and smell of a salmon fishery.

All the while, he enjoyed cooking at home, but the idea of taking his love of food into the culinary world never occurred to him.

Instead, he left the kitchen, the salmon and discovered sales. He sold high-end designer shoes at two very prestigious stores, Neimen Marcus and Saks Fifth Avenue. And then, Andrew decided to go to college.

"Review Andrew Dornenburg's work? Well first of all, I find his papers to be messy. He is lazy. I'm not sure he can make it."

"Andrew? He is simply unfocused, that's the best I can say."

"Andrew Dornenburg? I disagree with all of you. I think he is creative and his ideas unique. I also think he has dyslexia. I suggested he get tested at the student center. He'll be somebody special one day. I'd bet on it."

One teacher believed in him and encouraged him. Amazing how that simple fact changed Andrew's life and the culinary world. Moreover, that teacher was 100% correct.

Andrew Dornenburg has gone on to become THE leading Chef in America. In partnership with his wife, Karen Page, he has become a premier best-selling culinary writer *and* author!! He is still dyslexic...he just learned how to make it work *for* him instead of *against* him.

Andrew says *" cooking saved me, in that it is a skill that relies more on the senses than on the ability to spell, and allowed me to learn that seeing things differently can be a plus (such as when coming up with a new dish -- or an innovative concept for a new book!)"*

Andrew did not listen to the naysayers around him. He knew he loved to cook and he loved to write. He knew he loved to serve people with food and make them feel good. So how did this 'lazy unfocused' man who wasn't talented enough for a fast food chain go on to be a leading culinary artist?

"You don't have to be perfect to be great. Team up with others whose strengths complement your weaknesses, and vice versa."

I encourage you today to be like Andrew. Take your favorite things to do and make them your life. Even if you don't have all the skills, enhance what you do have and look for others who balance you.

POWER BOOSTERS

What are 10 things you are grateful for?

_____

_____

_____

_____

_____

_____

_____

_____

_____

_____

Why are you grateful for them?

_____

_____

_____

_____

_____

_____

_____

_____

_____

_____

"But, Tetê, what will you do?"
"I'm not exactly sure, yet – that's why I'm going with you."
"Are you sure this is where you want to go – what you want to do?"
"Yes, I'm sure."

Maria Teresa Leal (better known as Tetê) was on her way to the home of her family's housekeeper. They were going to Rocinha, the largest _favela_ (slum) in Rio de Janeiro. And she was on a mission.

Raised in a wealthy family in Rio de Janeiro, Brazil, Tetê was shown how to look beyond social and economic status and seek to serve others. She had been influenced by example. Her father, a leading physician, was one of the very first doctors to volunteer every Saturday in Rio's _favelas_. Her mother, a school teacher, encouraged her to expand her education to seek ways to give back to society. And her eldest sister started Rio's first Arts Education School to teach education and the arts to mixed classes of wealthy, middle-class **and** _favela_ children.

Now it was Tetê's turn. Armed with a degree in Social Science and a license to teach elementary school, she was ready to make a difference.

Tetê knew that many women left their homes to do domestic work in the wealthy neighborhoods or ended up in sweatshops, taking them away from their children and their own homes. She also knew these women were famous for their sewing. So Tetê started a co-op for the women in Rocinha. Now they could work at home and still bring in an income to help their families. They started by recycling fabric by creating quilts, pillows and rugs to sell at local fairs.

But Tetê wasn't satisfied. She knew these women were far more talented and skillful than what they were doing. When an international high-fashion show came to Rio de Janeiro, Tetê knew what she wanted to do. She wanted the women of Coopa-Roca (short for Women's Artisan and Seamstress Cooperative of Rocinha) to enter the world of high fashion. But there were a few hurdles to jump. First was the need for high quality fabric. So she secured donations of silk, linen and poplin – all fabrics unaffordable to her poor tailors.

Next she found fashion designers in Rio who donated their time and talent to teach the Coopa-Roca members the basics of clothing production. Reporters from _Elle_ and _Vogue_ magazines attended one of those training sessions. Tetê was encouraged.

Realizing they needed more exposure, she used fashion shows and national media to get the word out about Coopa-Roca's quality merchandise. They started participating in fashion shows and Tetê continued to get their products shown in the best fashion, lifestyle and home decorating magazines.

Knowing the skills (designing, cutting, sewing and finishing) is important, but Tetê has also made sure the women also learn about delivery, administration and publicity. Not only does the end result create a better paycheck, the women improve their math and language skills at the same time. Tetê has even created a program called, "The New Generation of Coopa-Roca" for young women aged 14-21 who receive special training in production techniques and management. New Generation is supported by UNESCO and the C&A Institute.

Life is still difficult in the _favelas_. But the women are working for themselves, building up their self-esteem, their sense of identity and pride. Can you imagine how wonderful it must be for these women to see their creations on super models and in international magazines?

I'm so impressed with Tetê – aren't you? Just going into the largest slum of Rio de Janeiro and helping the women was a big thing. But to move them from quilts and pillows to international high-fashion is phenomenal. She took advantage of every opportunity and made opportunities when there were none! She knew what her goal was, and she set about to make it happen!

That is what it takes to be successful!

★ *Bitter or Better?* ★

"I'm ready; I'm ready...quit yelling! I'm coming...hey wait for me."
"Quit pushing...come on, guys...we're gonna be late for practice!"
"Watch out up here...there's needles and condoms everywhere"
"What was that?"
"A gunshot, moron...you know that."
"Let's get to practice. Coach said he had to check our work before we can hit the field."
"I'm ready to play..."
"Race ya!"

The guys raced up the alley and through the streets to the practice field. They laughed and good naturedly teased and joked...the way people secure and comfortable with each other do. Pushing and shoving to be first, the testosterone driven young males vied for first place in their self-paced race to get to Coach Andre.

Down the street from their unlighted practice field, Andre Ford dropped his U.S. Mail carrier's bag and took off his badge. It was time to go home. His steady job with the U.S. Postal Service provided a decent life for his wife and their two girls and he was a thankful man for his opportunites.

"I'm home, gang," Andre called to his family as they came to greet him.

"Is it practice night, Daddy?" His youngest wanted to know.

"Yep, baby it is," responded Andre throwing his arms around his girls, kissing his wife.

"Well, have fun getting sweaty," giggled the little ones.

Smiling, Andre changed into shorts and a t-shirt, laced up his athletic shoes, and grabbed the sandwiches his wife had prepared for him. Turning his mind to the team, he walked out the door and into the darkening evening. He knew those boys would be at the field shortly and he eagerly looked forward to working with them.

The stars of the team knew Coach was a fair and a good man. It was also no secret that if they didn't pass their school classes or got into any trouble anywhere, he didn't let them play. The less athletic kids knew they got to play, as long as they, too, stayed out of trouble, made their grades, and kept up their work.

These young men had found a hero.

As co-founder of the Marshall Heights Youth Development Program, Coach Andre Ford is making a huge difference in the lives of hundreds of inner city youth in Washington, D.C. The program oversees five football teams for ages 7 through 15.

In an area of D.C. known for violence, gang, and drug abuse, this man and his organization are shining a light into that darkness. Although football isn't for everyone, Andre realizes it has power to give the kids purpose, direction, self-esteem and self-discipline.

Andre is not a big burly man, nor a trained football coach. He wasn't the high school star athlete and didn't play ball in college. Fact is, he barely made his junior varsity team in high school, but he excelled in playing CHESS - a game where brains rule over brawn! When his life was devastated over a dear friend's senseless death, his sadness and despair needed an outlet.

He chose the forgotten kids of the city and started funneling hope, joy and faith into football practice, school work and good citizenship. Andre takes it personally how his boys perform on and off the field.

"I have to know every child individually," he says, *"all 240 of them. Dreams alone won't get you out of Southeast D.C., which is why (we) stress schooling and life skills; for those that don't have the talent, hey, go out and be a decent citizen."*

The result?

The football teams have succeeded in winning numerous local and regional games...playing teams with money and lighted fields. They've competed in the Pop Warner National playoffs three times, and they won the Pop Warner SUPER Bowl Championship in 2006. These playoff competitions weren't held in a dimly lighted field in the inner city. The glorious sporting events happened in Orlando, Florida, next to DISNEYWORLD! Those boys from the ghetto made it big time!

Coach has been name Washingtonian of the Year and received numerous honors from the U.S. Postal service, and many other service organizations. Yet his true joy remains watching his boys turn into men.

His athletes graduate from high school, many going to colleges and technical schools. Many return to live and give back to the area. Now these former teen football players are real men of integrity who are slowly changing the neighborhood into a safe family area. They are giving back life lessons they received from football and Coach Andre.

Success has come to Washington D.C. in all realms because one man chose to believe in the positive life-changing power of character, compassion and concern.

I want to be like that.

You know, Andre could have let his depression kill his sprit. He could have let anger ruin his outlook. He could have said, *"I'm not an athlete, I can't do that."*

He had a choice to be bitter or become better.

So do I.

So do you.

Let's choose today to play it positive. Let's look for ways to affirm those around us and believe that life can be better than what it is right now. I have a favorite saying I snatched from a popular song years ago..."It takes a little time to turn the Titanic around!"

It may not happen overnight but the positive changes we desire will happen if we keep on practicing!

I hope you feel encouraged today and when you feel like giving up, think of Andre and those boys having fun at ball practice!

"Dreams pass into the reality of action. From the actions stems the dream again; and this interdependence produces the highest form of living."
~Anais Nin

★ *Three Basic Ingredients* ★

"So, little one, what do you want to be when you grow up?"

"I'm going to own my own business and sell things to rich people!"

Moses grinned from ear to ear as he looked into the child's beaming face, *"And you will; yes, I believe you will!"*

Moses Zulu reflected on the little boy's eager response. Last year the little boy's answer would have been very different -- because last year he was an orphan living on the street. His basic needs -- food and a place to live -- were out-of-reach luxuries. He was overwhelmed by chronic illness, lack of shelter and frequent abuse by adults. He had no childhood, no time or energy to play and no future. He was like 70,000 other AIDS orphans in Zambia's capital city of Lusaka.

But Moses is a dynamic man who has a dogged determination to serve and save orphaned children in his homeland of Zambia. Many of these kids have been directly affected by the devastating AIDS epidemic. In 1990, Moses Zulu started Children's Town to provide for these little ones. At first it was two children living in a tent shelter. Today he has a staff of 22 trained adults living in six different houses on the Children's Town compound which also includes a community center and primary school. Over 300 children are part of the program.

According to UNICEF, nearly one million children in Zambia are AIDS orphans. Many flee from rural areas to cities after their parents' deaths because there is no one to care for them in the smaller villages. They come where they believe there is a means of survival – even if it means working as street vendors, resorting to crime or prostitution.

Until now…

Children who are fortunate enough to enter Children's Town go through a five-year program which concludes with a state approved ninth-grade diploma and a Trade Tested Certificate as a result of their vocational training. During those five years they are taught: academic subjects (like reading and math); life skills (how to get along with others – socialization); responsibility; values and self-care. They will graduate with vocational training in agriculture or crafts, plus learn business management. The practical skills learned could be carpentry, or how to run a farm or a small business. For those children who have no one to return to, equipment and land near Children's Town will be secured for them.

Children's Town has trained hundreds of students in agriculture, business and agribusiness. In addition to their studies, the kids attend counseling sessions and play in a steel band. The children perform and interact with the local community at least once a week.

But education is only part of what Children's Town provides. The children are organized into family units which gives them a home environment. This is where they learn appropriate behavior and other social skills. A Social Worker conducts home visits on a regular basis with the ultimate goal of reuniting children with their families if circumstances there are healthy for the child.

Children's Town is an oasis of safety and hope in an otherwise bleak and depressing future for many African children. It presents a marvelous model for other countries with high numbers of orphans, as it provides a way to respond with humanity and compassion in the face of the devastating AIDS crisis.

"At our core," says Moses, *"we enable our children to have dreams, to believe in themselves and to take responsibility for their lives."*

Ahhhh – there are three of the basic ingredients for a successful life regardless of who you are or where you live: have dreams, believe in yourself and take responsibility for yourself.

I hope today you will take the steps necessary (even if they are baby steps!) toward making these ingredients part of your daily living. Don't be afraid to dream – and dream BIG! Believe that you can accomplish your dreams, and then take full responsibility (no excuses!) for making them happen.

The future is yours!

"Mama, I'm so bored!"
"Mama, is there anything I can help with?"
"Mama, please give me something to do!"
"Mama, I've decided to go back to school!"

Coco Mousa was born partially blind and lost all sight by the age of fifteen. The third of eight children, he struggled to function in public school. Because there were no special programs for the unsighted in Cameroon (Africa), Coco organized friends and family members to get the help he needed to not only survive but excel!

Once he lost his sight completely, Coco was forced to leave school. After spending 18 months at home with nothing to do, he decided to pursue the only option available to him – enroll in the Vocational Training Center for the Blind in Bulu.

Once at the Center, Coco discovered many of the other young men had never developed the art of listening and were having difficulty learning. He organized study groups in the dorms where the more successful boys helped the others with listening and study skills. It was during these sessions that Coco became aware that **all** the students were gaining self-confidence and respect for one another. It was clear that unsighted individuals needed each other to survive with dignity and to become contributing citizens.

Coco found that upon completing the program, graduates were completely on their own – no follow-up, no job placement, and no opportunity to use the skills learned at the Center. Coco refused to accept a future of begging or living completely dependent on family. But what could he do?

His time at the Bulu Center impressed upon Coco the idea of working with other blind people to provide encouragement, motivation, and ultimately, the opportunity to become contributors to society. He and another graduate pooled their small government stipends and started a cooperative enterprise that provided important learning for the unsighted, but not a steady income.

Finally, the idea was born – Coco would start an organization, *"as he puts it, 'of blind people, for blind people' – The Club of the Blind for Rehabilitation in Cameroon."* Knowing that the prevailing attitude toward the unsighted left no room except begging or the most repetitive work, the Club was established with two main goals. The first was to encourage, motivate and train its members to start and manage their own businesses (as a group). The very act of establishing a local Club was their first business enterprise -- each Club is member owned and operated.

The second goal was for The Club to educate their local community about the potential of their unsighted citizens and how the sighted community could interact with them in positive ways. Blindness prevention is also an important part of this goal as most blindness in Cameroon is preventable.

Coco leads the way! Not only has he organized and created opportunities for the blind in his country, he is a noted song writer, musician and singer. He uses his talents as an entertainer to raise public awareness for the unsighted citizens of their country.

Coco took a negative and made a positive out of it. Instead of feeling sorry for himself and doing nothing, he chose to do something for himself and others who have lost their sight. By creating The Club, he is giving others hope and a future for the first time in their lives. And his life is richer because of it.

Each of us has some kind of disability or obstacle to overcome. It may not be as drastic as Coco's – it may be worse. But the lesson we learn from this courageous young trail blazer is that we don't have to accept others' expectations and limitations of us. We can choose to conquer the negatives and turn them into positives. Along with our obstacles, there are also opportunities for us to use the gifts and talents we've been given as well!

No one ever promised life would be easy or fair! It isn't – but you and I can let the hard times make us better people. Every situation offers a lesson to be learned and applied to life.

Choose to be like Coco and make a difference for others as you progress toward success!

★ *A Phenomenal Team* ★

"Dad, Can we run in a race?" Rick typed the words slowly, using his head to click a switch on his wheelchair that activated the screen. Rick has spastic quadriplegic cerebral palsy and cannot speak or walk. *"Well, Dad, can we?"*

Dick Hoyt, Rick's dad, looked at his son and wondered how in the world he could say 'yes.' He'd been a lieutenant colonel in the Air National Guard, but was no longer in the best physical shape.

Rick, a sports fan, had learned of a local Lacrosse player who was injured. The race was a fundraiser to help the injured player. Rick wanted to "run" because it would help someone else.

Dick decided he could work out and get in shape. Get in shape is exactly what he did.

Since Rick could not walk, Dick ran *and* pushed his son's wheelchair. They competed as a team.

Dick wondered what the doctors who told him and his wife to "put Rick away" at birth would say at his son's generosity. The doctors had been so very wrong in their prognosis of Rick. They said he would always be a "vegetable" due to lack of oxygen at birth.

Rick proved them wrong.

He learned to communicate with his specially adapted computer and attended public schools. He graduated from Boston University with a degree in Special Education. He now works at Boston College!

Wait, I got ahead of myself. Back to that first 5 mile benefit run…

Dick trained and they came in next to last. However, that night Rick said for the first time he just didn't *"feel handicapped when we were competing."*

That was enough for TEAM HOYT to run again. And again. And again. According to their website, they have competed in 958 events. Those events include marathons, duathlons, triathlons, and IRONMAN competitions.

In the IRONMAN events, Dick must run 26.2 miles, bike 112 miles, and swim 2.4 miles. He has done this grueling competition six times...all the while pushing, pedaling and pulling his son. They have a specially equipped wheelchair for these events and a custom bike that enables Rick to sit in front. There's also an inflatable raft that Dick pulls behind him as he swims.

The father/son duo receives invitations to speak and so they travel together, addressing audiences around the nation. Their love and motivation are captivating. Their dedication to each other is inspiring.

"Most of all, perhaps, the Hoyts can see an impact from their efforts in the area of the handicapped, and on public attitudes toward the physically and mentally challenged. 'That's the big thing,' said Dick.' People just need to be educated. Rick is helping many other families coping with disabilities in their struggle to be included.' The message of Team Hoyt is that <u>everybody</u> *should be included in everyday life."*

I stand completely amazed by the dedication and love these two men have and show each other. In addition to these races, they biked and ran over 3,700 miles across the USA. That incredible event took them 45 days!!

An interviewer asked Rick what one thing he'd like to give his dad. *"The thing I'd most like is that my dad would sit in the chair and I would push him once."*

You know, we probably won't be asked to carry our grown son across 958 finish lines, but we *are* called to live out our dreams. Rick had dreams of competing. And even though he knew he could not do it on his own, he was courageous enough to ask his dad to help him live out his dreams.

Live like TEAM HOYT!

Ask for help when you need it and keep on keeping on.

Oh, by the way -- TEAM HOYT doesn't win the races. They aren't there for the winning. They are there strictly for the competition. They are there because they can be.

If they can continue on, then surely you can, too!

POWER BOOSTERS

How many times have you failed? What have you failed at?

_____

_____

_____

_____

_____

_____

_____

_____

_____

What have you learned from these experiences?

_____

_____

_____

_____

_____

_____

_____

_____

_____

★ *From Dreamer To Explorer* ★

He sucked in his breath and his pulse beat a little faster as he looked at the breath-taking beauty. The great Himalayans had stolen his heart long ago – he had spent many years in their sometimes terrifying embrace. But his passion had moved off the dizzying heights, and into the faces and lives of the gentle people who shared his love of these mountains.

He shook his head in disbelief as he reflected on how far he'd come. . .

Born in 1919, Ed grew up on a small farm near Auckland, New Zealand. He was a dreamer and loved the outdoors. He could often be found walking the countryside, his mind miles away dreaming of all sorts of heroic activities. He would dream of saving beautiful maidens in distress, or executing dashing sword fights. His love of reading only fueled his imaginary adventures.

After finishing his primary education in a small country school, Ed commuted to a large city school by train. He was two years younger, and therefore much smaller than his fellow students. He desperately missed the friends he was forced to leave behind. It was a very difficult and lonely time. But it was also a good time. Ed savored the four hours he spent each day on the train riding to and from school, because they gave him extra time to enjoy his reading and indulge in day dreaming.

Ed chuckled to himself as he remembered gaining nearly a foot in height in two years. Suddenly he was bigger and stronger than his classmates. His confidence grew as his physical competence increased. Although he enjoyed sports, Ed knew he was anything but a great athlete. His was more of a rugged, physical strength - not athletic prowess. While he was an average student, he was also a strongly motivated individual who usually accomplished whatever he set out to do.

Ed laughs at the next memory. He saw himself out-hiking all his friends. He always seemed to have more energy, and was a stronger walker and hiker than the others. He liked to push himself to travel quickly on very long hikes. He muses: *"Most young people were more interested in going to the movies or going to the beach or something or other. I really wasn't all that great on that sort of stuff. I just wanted to get out in the hills."*

Edmund's senses kick into high gear as he relived being 16 and experiencing snow for the first time. For ten glorious days he skied and climbed snow-covered hills.

His new found love for climbing led him to climb other mountains in New Zealand, then the Alps, and finally the Himalayas where he climbed 11 different peaks over 20,000 feet high.

His infatuation with climbing finally lead him to the greatest challenge of all – Mt. Everest. Between 1920 and 1952, seven major expeditions attempted the summit of Mt. Everest but all failed. Ed joined two reconnaissance expeditions in 1951 and 1952. This brought him to the attention of John Hunt, leader of the ninth expedition of 1953. Hunt invited Ed to join him. It was a dream come true. All the men reached the South Peak, but all but two were forced to turn back because of exhaustion and the high altitude. The two men who continued on were Edmund Hillary and a Nepalese climber by the name of Tenzing Norgay. On the 29th of May, Edmund (age 33) and Tenzing became the first men ever to reach the summit of Mt. Everest -- 29,028 feet above sea level – the highest spot on planet earth.

Their amazing feat was announced on British radio the same evening the young 25 year old Princess Elizabeth was crowned Queen of England. Edmund Hillary later went to Britain and was knighted by the young Queen.

114

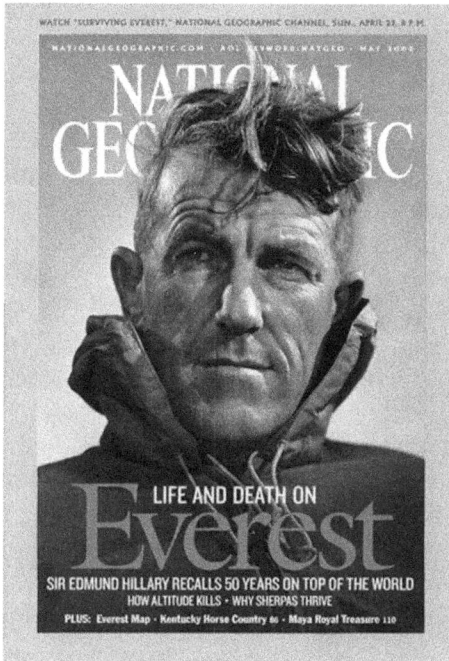

For the remainder of that decade, Sir Edmund led several expeditions to the Antarctic, the South Pole and other remote areas. But he returned often to his greatest love -- the great mountains of Nepal.

And now, here he was, determined to help those who had given him so much -- the Nepalese people.

Over the next decade, Sir Edmund helped build clinics, hospitals and 17 schools. He continued to work on behalf of Nepal's people and the Nepalese environment for the rest of his life. He died in New Zealand at the age of 88 on January 11, 2008.

To his dying day, Edmund Hillary never considered himself anything other than merely average. It was his motivation and love of the outdoors that caused him to do what no one else had.

He was a man of great humility and grace who believed everyone could be a success. *"I do think that virtually everybody that's born has the ability to be very competent at doing something. I think that, in itself, is worthy of aiming towards, just to be competent at doing anything you particularly wish to do."*

You, too, can be successful if you are relentless in pursuing your passion – that "something" which excites you. Let your dreams fuel your desire. Let your desire give birth to your motivation. And let your motivation create the pathway to your success.

Accomplishments are a wonderful thing, but to truly be successful, you have to make a DIFFERENCE!

★ *You Decide* ★

Kemmons Wilson had it tough growing up. His father died when he was nine months old. His young mother, only 18 years old, struggled to provide for her son. There were times there was so little money that they lived on a few pounds of dried butter beans for a week at a time.

What got him through those times was his mother's love. Every night she sat her little boy on her lap and said, *"You are designed for greatness and you can do anything in life if you're willing to work hard enough to get it."*

At 14 years old, Kemmons was hit by a car. The doctors said he would never walk again. He chose to believe differently. He could do anything if he was willing to work hard enough. One year later, he returned to school - walking on his own.

Then the Great Depression hit. His Mom lost her job, along with millions of others. He made the decision to quit school and provide for the woman who had done so much for him. The day he quit school, he made it his mission in life to succeed. He vowed to never be poor again.

Kemmons experienced varying levels of success over the years but he had not achieved his goal of financial success when he took his wife and kids on a vacation in 1951. He was frustrated by the shoddy accommodations available for families, and furious they dared to charge $2 extra per child. He knew it was too expensive.

His frustrating experience sparked an idea! He would offer an alternative - a hotel people could trust that would never charge extra for children. It was a completely new concept and most people predicted failure from the beginning.

Kemmons chose to believe differently. As with any business, he experienced enormous challenges. Money was short. Many times payment was an IOU. He had to overcome one obstacle after another - choosing to believe in his success every single day.

15 years later, Holiday Inn was the largest hotel system in the world, with one of the most recognizable names in the business. Kemmons had a belief that carried him through. *"You may not have started life in the best of circumstances. But if you can find a mission in life worth working for and believe in yourself, nothing can stop you from achieving success."*

Every generation believes all the great ideas have already been taken. There is nothing left to do. Ridiculous!

Your world is brimming with possibilities. Keep your mind and heart open. Find and identify that which fills a need and ignites your passion. Where you are in life today is not what is important. What's important is where you plan to be tomorrow -- next year -- 10 years from now.

"Think excitement, talk excitement, act out excitement, and you are bound to become an excited person. Life will take on a new zest, deeper interest and greater meaning. You can think, talk and act yourself into dullness or into monotony or into happiness. By the same process you can build up inspiration, excitement and surging depths of joy."
~Norman Vincent Peale

★ *Saving Lives* ★

His memories are so vivid that Willem can smell the pine trees, hear the birds and feel the soft earth beneath his feet. But it's his father's voice that captivates him. These were some of his most favorite times; walking with his father and listening to stories - stories that determined the course of his life.

Willem's father was a physician and director of a sanatorium for tuberculosis in Holland. They would walk in the woods around the sanatorium as his father told stories of life and death. Because of them Willem decided as a young child that he wanted to be a doctor to help keep people alive.

But the road was not an easy one. . .

"What does this say?" he would silently scream. *"All the letters are out of order and the words made no sense!"* Willem suffered with dyslexia, an unknown disorder in Holland in the early 1900's. In those days Dutch students were required to take 6 years of Latin, 5 years of Greek and be fluent in four modern languages. And he was having so much trouble with just one!

He was driven by his dream. Encouraged by those who believed in him, he worked harder than anyone else to make the jumbled words make sense. *People's lives depended on his success in passing the courses to get through school.* And pass he did… he entered medical school at age 19 with the intention of practicing medicine.

But his plans changed when, as a student medical assistant he had to care for a 22-year-old who died a slow and terrible death from kidney failure. Willem had to tell the young man's mother that her son was going to die and there was nothing they could do for him. *"… I began to think, if I could just every day remove as much urea as this boy creates - then the boy could live."*

The idea of an artificial kidney was born.

In addition to kidney treatments, Willem also became interested in blood transfusions which were being done in Europe and the U.S. Most transfusions were done directly from the donor to the recipient, but Willem read about a blood bank in Chicago and learned how to store blood so it could be used without the donor being present. Willem was in Hague the day World War II broke out and headed for the city's main hospital where he set up Holland's first blood bank. That blood bank is still in existence.

It turned out to be just one more piece in the complex puzzle that would make his dream a reality… Working with blood outside the human body, put his desire to create an artificial kidney into serious motion.

Because the Nazis took over the major hospital where he was working, Willem left and found work at a small hospital in a neighboring town and began creating. *Working with wooden drums, cellophane tubing and laundry tubs* (sounds scary!) Willem created a machine that drew the toxic blood, cleansed it of impurities, and pumped it back into the patient – the first kidney dialysis machine had been created.

Willem also perfected the artificial kidney and began performing successful kidney transplants. In 1955 he decided to make a disposable artificial kidney. *Because his idea was so new, he couldn't secure funding. Once again he used easily obtainable materials: a pressure cooker, coils of window screening, cellophane tubing and fruit juice cans!* It worked. With some refinements it made artificial kidneys available worldwide.

This is just a sampling of the amazing things this man accomplished. Willem Kolff lived through the difficulties of dyslexia, rejection of his medical ideas and inventions, Nazi occupation of his country, the scorn and ridicule of his colleagues, and the challenges of immigrating to a new country.

But through it all he kept his focus on what he knew he wanted and what he knew he could do even though others told him it was impossible.

Although they may seem overwhelming, don't let your circumstances (or people's opinions) dictate what you can or cannot do. Like Dr. Kolff, you can rise above your situation if you will keep your eyes focused on your goal, and turn a deaf ear to your critics.

"But it's just not right!"
"I agree, but the people don't know that."
"Someone needs to do something!"
"I believe I'm looking at that 'someone'!"

I imagine that conversation could have taken place between Nancy Kgengwenyane and her father.

Nancy was six months old when her parents divorced. She was raised by her father, a passionate man who loved Africa – all of Africa, not just their native Botswana. He taught Nancy that she had a responsibility to Africa to develop her mind and use it on Africa's behalf. The school she attended nurtured this belief and the headmistress, who was a strong feminist, encouraged Nancy in all areas of her academic studies. Because she was fortunate enough to attend a school for white Zimbabwean children, her father underscored the enormous privilege also carried heavy responsibilities.

Upon completion of her studies, Nancy attended the University of Botswana to pursue the study of medicine, but the advanced math caused her to shift her attention from medicine to law. In her fourth year she was required to write a research paper which involved interviewing people in local villages. After visiting many villages and getting to know the people, Nancy became aware of the deep chasm between the law and the reality of people's lives.

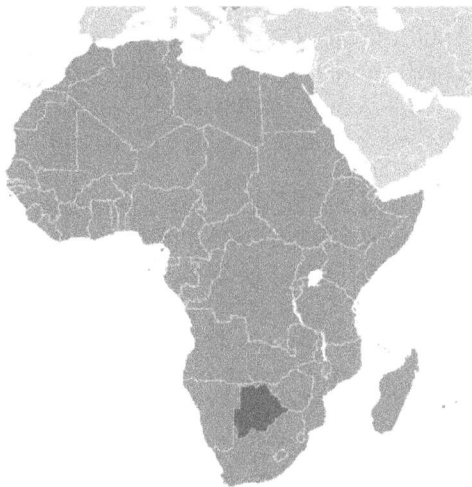

Because of this first-hand knowledge, Nancy's focus shifted into a passionate desire to represent the needs of Botswana's people – especially women and children. Her work to raise the government's awareness caught the attention of the Attorney General who offered her a position in his office. Because of her quick intellect, her education among whites, and her passion for Botswana and Africa as a whole, he transferred her to their New York City office. While there she met environmental activists and became aware of the huge disparity between international and trade laws and the realities of the people back home. Realizing how vital environmental issues are to Africa, she spent long hours volunteering after work. Her passion and commitment to this added dimension of her work became well known, and soon all pertinent environmental issues were referred to her.

Nancy resigned her post with the Attorney General's office and returned to Botswana. She started building grassroots support for legal reform and raising international awareness of the lopsided laws favoring multi-national corporations. She started a movement in Southern African that is the very first of its kind to challenge the industrialized world's definition of property and patent, and create an alternative that serves the developing world.

The issues are complex. For example -- there is a root which is native to Botswana and Namibia called Devil's Claw. It provides relief for a variety of medical issues, including arthritis and gout. The root has been used for thousands of years by the indigenous people and is now being harvested by multi-national pharmaceutical companies. In some areas, the demand is so high that the root is over-harvested, and nothing is left for the traditional communities themselves.

These multi-national pharmaceutical companies have a huge profit margin, but return an extremely tiny percentage back to the native communities. Sometimes local villagers are paid a very meager amount to harvest the roots. These people do not know how to profit from their own resources and the multi-national companies use this to their advantage.

Nancy's goal is to establish within Botswana an organization that provides expertise and lobbying clout on legal and policy issues in the area of trade, biological diversity and intellectual property systems. Because of her work in the Attorney General's office, she has a wide network into which she is tapping. And that networking web continues to grow throughout Africa, Malaysia, Latin America, the U.S. and Europe.

Nancy is becoming a force to be reckoned with – and she is leading the way to save Africa from continued depletion of its natural resources.

Nancy was raised by a very wise father. He understood that our intellect and abilities are not for our personal gain alone, but must always be used to help others along the way. His daughter is living proof that such a belief can make an enormous difference.

On your way to success, lift others and bring them along with you. The world will be a better place because you did – and so will you!

5 Million For Change

We have partnered with Together We Can Change The World, Inc. to mobilize 5 Million people who want to make a difference with their lives. We have discovered through our many years of working with people that most really do want to help – they just don't know what to do. We set to work to solve that problem – by creating every resource we can to empower people to make a difference with their lives. And it's all our gift to you!

Free E-books with over 1100 ideas for how you can make a difference. Free Movies. Free Songs. And so much more… All you have to do is raise your hand for change.

5 Million For Change Pledge

I raise my hand for 5 Million For Change
I will take time TODAY to make a difference in the world.
I will take time TODAY to do one thing – for one person.
I will take time TODAY to spread some love & caring into the world.
One thing – TODAY.
EVERYDAY!
Nothing is too small. Nothing is too big.
It is only important to take Action.
I will take time TODAY – to ACT – to create CHANGE!

www.5MillionForChange.com

www.5MillionStudentsForChange.com

★ *Weird Al* ★

Hearing the doorbell ring, Alfred ran to open the door of his California home. The year was 1966. It was a traveling salesman. What luck! Alfred liked these salesmen because his mom sometimes bought their products. And while the products never lasted, they were fun. Alfred scurried to get his mom.

"I am here to offer you or your son, maybe, a free lesson at the music school. Your choice of instrument! Guitar or accordion! Which will it be?"

And so it was that one day before his 7th birthday, Alfred walked through the music school doors and picked up the instrument that would one day become his trademark in the music world. Three years of accordion lessons stemmed from that one "chance" meeting.

What was his parent's rationale for choosing the accordion over the guitar? Remember this was California in the late 60's and guitars were everywhere. It was simple, his dad said, they *"'... figured there should be at least one more accordion-playing Yankovic (no relation) in the world...' referring to Frankie Yankovic: America's Polka King.*"

As an only child, Alfred's imagination was matched only by his intellect. Beginning school a year earlier than most kids and then skipping second grade, made him 2 years younger than his classmates. This proved to be no problem for the creative young man. In high school, he was valedictorian of his graduating class and created the "Volcano Worshippers Club" simply to get extra photos of himself in the school year book.

College is always a time of experimentation and Alfred experimented with radio. As a D.J. for the college radio station, Alfred's humor and song writing creativity began to find a stage...and as he pursued opportunity and fame, he carved out a solid place in music history.

His dad's philosophy regarding success proved so true for his son. He often told him: *"the key to success is doing for a living whatever makes you happy."* Making people laugh and not taking life or laughter so seriously - *that* made Alfred happy.

Even though the entertainer we know as Weird Al Yankovic didn't come from poverty or extreme situations, his story still resonates. He chose to do something he loved (performing music) and at which he excelled, despite the fact his musical presentations were not mainstream.

In case you are unfamiliar with Weird Al, his music consists of parody, satire and comedy. The nickname Weird Al is simply a leftover tag from college days. There is nothing weird about his musical ability to "rewrite" the messages of top hit popular songs into humorous renditions. The original recording artists feel honored to have their songs chosen for his satirical work. They laugh right along with Al and his audience.

For nearly 30 years, Al has been making us laugh and smile while he makes a difference in a sometimes bland and up-tight world. His shows are family friendly and he delivers them with his unique "tongue in cheek" style: "My Sharona" by The Knack became "My Bologna"; "Another One Bites the Dust" by Queen became "Another One Rides the Bus," and Michael Jackson's song "Beat It" turned into "Eat it."

You get the picture, right?

I encourage you to be like Weird Al.

Make the most of your gifts no matter how unusual they may be. From those days as a youngster on the accordion, Al carved out a niche for his talent. He has sold more than *"12 million albums which is better than any other comedy act ever! -- recorded in excess of 150 parody and original songs. He's performed more than 1,000 live shows. His works have earned him three Grammy Awards, four gold records, and six platinum records in the United States."*

And he still plays the accordion, too. Each of his albums has a song that, as Al sees it was *"intended to be a Polka."* And in his hands, that chosen song, indeed becomes one.

Your talents feed your success. So explore them well.

POWER BOOSTERS

Is what you're doing bringing you peace? Why, or why not?

_____

_____

_____

_____

_____

_____

_____

_____

_____

_____

What do you believe would give you inner peace?

_____

_____

_____

_____

_____

_____

_____

_____

_____

_____

★ _The Oldest Newspaper Boy_ ★

"Wings?" "Check!"
"Engine?" Check!"
"Newspapers?" "Check!"
Sound strange?

But to Hal Wright, West Coast cousin of the famous aviation Wright brothers, it made perfect sense.

Read his story and then guess how old Hal was when he quit flying (only because he got sick).

Hal Wright decided there was not enough to do in his life. He wanted more out of living. Being a long time resident of a small California town he decided the citizens needed a newspaper to stay connected. So Hal appointed himself founder, editor, reporter, photographer, columnist, and advertising specialist of the Sierra Booster Newspaper in Loyalton, California.

He and his wife Allene continued to live out his newspaper "harebrained idea" for years after most folks their age had quit living. Hal was also the "paperboy," delivering many papers by airplane.

Hal had been a gold miner in his younger years. A fall down a mining shaft had ended his days under the earth. He vowed to his wife to not go underground again. Obviously he never said anything about the sky.

"Hang on, here we go! Gotta swing down low so I get the paper by the house but not on top."

Swooping over the ranch houses, he would toss the papers out of the pilot's seat of his single engine 1949 airplane.

The subscribers to his newspaper are scattered over six hundred square miles so it made sense to deliver papers to the ranches in his airplane.

The pilot would carefully check the plane, but not being the newest of planes, Hal would occasionally call the town's tow truck driver to come and jump-start the engine. Even old planes need some help from time to time.

Hal survived 3 heart surgeries and even fought the FAA when they refused to renew his pilot's license due to age. He won the legal battle and for several years he was the oldest pilot in the USA.

Back in 1999, the townspeople and Hal celebrated the 50th anniversary of the _Sierra Booster Newspaper_. Hal was still flying his monthly paper route.

Have you guessed his age?

70? 80? or 90 years old?

Nope when Hal got sick he was still flying . . . and he was 96!

Hal was once asked when he was going to slow down. His answer, _"What for? I wouldn't know what to do with my time!"_

Our attitude and daily choices count. What you choose today will determine your future. For 96 years, Hal chose to have a full and rich life. He did what he loved and fought for his right to do so. He believed life was worth living and living well.

You can decide that for yourself, too!

Today is a great time to start. Decide today to do what you love. Maybe it will be a small treat or maybe even a life changing decision. But either way I hope you, like Hal, will choose health, happiness, and purpose – because living like that can only lead to success!

He peers into her eyes and asks, *"What do you see?"*
"It's a bit blurry."
"That's okay, be patient, it will clear up."
"Oh my! Oh my! I can see your face!"

The elderly woman reached out and touched the doctor's face as tears streamed down her own. She had lost her sight to cataracts and had no hope of ever seeing again. She missed watching her grandchildren play, watching her daughter rock the baby, watching the sunrises and sunsets. And then someone told her about the Aravind Eye Hospital where she could get cataract surgery for free.

Dr. Govindappa Venkataswamy (better known as Dr. V) decided as a young man that *"intelligence and capability are not enough. There must be the joy of doing something beautiful."* And that something beautiful happened when he mortgaged his home (instead of retiring) and opened a hospital in Madurai, India so he could perform free or low-cost cataract surgery for the poorest of India's poor. He performed 5,000 surgeries the very first year!

When social entrepreneur David Green learned about Dr. V, he was intrigued. When he found out the only reason Dr. V did 5,000 surgeries instead of more was because of the cost of the lenses ($150 a pair), he was hooked! And when David learned it only cost $10 to make the lenses, he became passionate about helping Dr. V and thousands of people who had lost their sight to cataracts. David managed to arrange for donations, but quickly decided making the lenses themselves was a better way to go. He calls it "compassionate capitalism" -- instead of focusing on getting the highest possible profit from every item sold, the focus is on a smaller profit from each item and greater sales volume.

David started Aurolab in India and now supplies Dr. V with affordable lenses for millions of people! More than 2 million surgeries are performed every year at Aravind Eye Hospital using the products made by Aurolab. Oh yes – they now produce 10% of the world supply of lenses at only $5 a pair! (In addition to intraocular lenses, they've added glasses lenses, optical lenses, suture needles, cataract kits and hearing aids.

Aurolab's products are used by eye care institutions and ophthalmologists in more than 120 countries. They produce millions of lenses each year and make a 30% profit. Using the profits from Aurolab, Dr. V has opened five new eye hospitals in southern India.

These two men believe that humans are put on Earth not to get rich, but to serve. And that is just what they are doing – performing "miracles" for elderly Indians living in remote villages by restoring their sight. They've now added hearing aids to the mix! These people are given back their dignity and their ability to contribute to their communities once again.

There is a very important lesson here for you and me today. Dr. V and David Green are both very successful in what they are doing. But as far as they are concerned, their success is measured in how much they are able to give back -- to help others while they do what they each do well. For Dr. V, that is performing cataract surgeries. For David, it is creating the tools to allow Dr. V to perform those surgeries.

Each of us needs to reflect on what we're doing. There's nothing wrong with being a successful business person – both Dr. V and David Green are! There's nothing wrong with making money – as long as you are not a slave to it! There is a saying that money makes a terrible master, but a wonderful servant.

Success is not measured by wealth – it is measured by contribution.

I challenge you to do some measuring. Measure your motives, your contribution and your definition of success today against Dr. V and David's. Compared to them, how do you measure up? If you like what you see – awesome! Keep up the great work! If you don't like what you see, decide what needs to change, and then start taking steps to make those changes.

Success is not measured by wealth – it is measured by contribution.

"Oh my, look – over there!"
"It's huge – it's so beautiful!"
"Great catch! Wow!! Fantastic catch!!"
"We'll have a great dinner tonight!"

Orri and his wife were fishing on the Laxa River in northern Iceland which was famous for its salmon runs. This was his first trip – but Orri was hooked! He revisited the river over the next 18 years to fish salmon. When he was elected chairman of the Laxa Fishing Club in 1984, Orri was painfully aware of a disturbing situation - the decline in numbers of wild salmon returning to the river.

Born to a poor family in northern Iceland, Orri's parents' fortune changed when their region became a major center for catching, processing and exporting herring. But their success was short-lived. _"We overfished. And while the people made a lot of money from herring, ultimately we had to stop."_ Young Orri learned a valuable lesson.

After graduating with a degree in international business, Orri was successful in everything he put his hand to. He established his country's first Toyota importing business. He worked with the Icelandic Manufacturers setting up cottage industries throughout Iceland. Then he brought the manufacture of high-quality woolen goods to his country.

But it was his "love affair" with salmon that changed his life – and the precarious plight of Atlantic salmon -- forever.

Orri's awareness of the disappearance of the salmon in the Laxa River started a personal, life-long passion. First, he encouraged commercial fishermen to stick to a quota of untagged fish. Under his direction, the Laxa Fishing Club tagged and released fish into their river so they would be released if caught at sea. But a strange thing happened -- none of the tagged fish returned to their river. The tags were coming though – from fish processing plants in Greenland and the Faeroe Islands. Realizing that successful salmon conservation had to involve more than one country, Orri founded the North Atlantic Salmon Fund (NASF).

Orri learned that the wild Atlantic salmon population was disappearing fast! Ninety percent of the fish had disappeared since the beginning of the 20th century. The World Wildlife Fund stated that salmon had disappeared from Germany, Switzerland, the Netherlands, Belgium, the Czech Republic and Slovakia. Salmon were just barely hanging on in Canada and the state of Maine.

Every salmon caught in the open ocean meant one less salmon in a local river was coming home to all North Atlantic countries. Orri realized it would take an international citizen-led program to make the difference. He knew there were already people throughout Europe, Scandinavia and North America trying to restore and protect wild salmon. So NASF started their conservation efforts with commercial buyouts of the fishing nets used for salmon fishing. His organization then expanded to work with river conservators, anglers' associations, landowners along rivers, and scientists.

Orri knew protecting the wild salmon was just the first step – a first step that is currently showing awesome results. The salmon are returning!

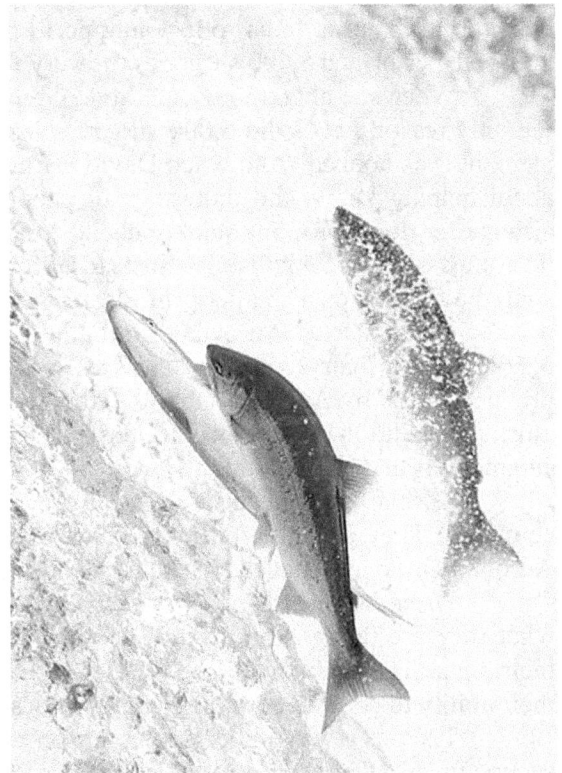

But there is a second step that is equally important – the survival of North Atlantic communities! Orri is networking with the citizen-base he'd been working with to protect the salmon, and is now reaching out to those who fish salmon as a sport and hobby. Orri's basic premise: a live salmon is worth more than a dead one.

Orri is helping communities realize that a wild salmon might fetch US$25, but the catch-and-release sport is much more lucrative for the local economy. Anglers need to hire guides, purchase permits, stay at lodges or hotels, buy provisions, rent equipment, etc. Catch-and-release is a much more sustainable income than commercial fishing, which kills the salmon. With catch-and-release, anglers return the salmon to the rivers to breed and continue the salmon life cycle – ensuring income for the communities.

It may take another 15-20 years, but Orri believes people and salmon *"can create a cooperative relationship that builds the health of both species."*

Orri Vigfusson took the expertise he learned growing up in the fishing industry, in international trade, and in networking with and helping others create sustainable economies within their villages, and applied it to a hobby he grew to love. As a result, he has been instrumental in saving the wild Atlantic salmon and helping countless communities create a new industry that saves the very fish they used to kill.

Sometimes life takes us along paths that seem to be disconnected, when in fact, they are all part of the same journey toward a single destination. When you find yourself on a side-road instead of the main path of your life-journey, consider where it may be taking you. No matter how difficult, be open to the important lessons or skills the side-road is teaching you. You will need them on down the road.

Here's to your success!

We do not inherit the earth from our ancestors, we borrow it from our children.
~Native American Proverb

"Alec, come and play."
"I will but first I gotta write something."
"Alec what are you doing?"
"Writing, Mom...be right there."
"Alec, are you finished?"
"Not yet, just have 3 more lists to write."
"Alec, are you talking to the girls?"
"Yeah, but I'm still writing."

Meet 9-year-old Alec Greven, 3rd grader from Colorado, published author, resident expert on girls and fundraisers.

At Alec's school in Colorado, he heard his teacher say he should be an "observer of the world," to focus on "small moments" and then write about them. So he did.

His writings have caught the attention of his teacher, principal, the news media, the publishing world and even landed him a segment on the *Ellen DeGeneres* television show. He compiled his writings into a book titled *How to Talk to Girls.*

While he is quick to point out his observations may not apply to the whole world, his truths regarding the interactions of boys and girls have a universal appeal. He based his information on his own observations from the classroom and playground.

- *Don't be a class clown. If you're the smartest boy in the class, girls will be prowling at your feet; and if a girl ditches you, move on, life is hard.*

- *Tip: How to get a girl to like you, talk to them and get to know them. Sometimes show off your skills, like playing soccer. Anything that you are good at.*

- *It is very hard to get a girl to like you. Sometimes it takes years to get a girl to like you. Girls can get crushes on boys.*

- *Pretty girls are the ones who wear earrings, fancy shoes and dresses nearly every day. Many boys get crushes on pretty girls, but sometimes you get a girl to like you and then she ditches you. Tip: about 73 percent of regular girls ditch boys, 93 percent of pretty girls ditch boys.*

His book was a "best seller" at the school at a fundraiser. Alec donated the profits, about $300, back to his school. He also thought it would be a great idea to have a creative writing contest, with winning entries becoming part of the annual book fair.

However, Alec will also "*encourage all the new authors to donate a portion or all of their proceeds to a charity of their* choice." Wow!

With his own book in print and now available for purchase, he is working on a sequel, *How to Talk to Girls Part 2.* ☺

Seems he's even inspired a classmate to write her own book. She titled it *"How to Get on a Boy's Nerves."* I love it, don't you?!

I encourage you to be like Alec -- confident and ready to meet the future. Today when you see your dreams do not be afraid. Go for it! Just take it one step at a time. Alec knows the way to be successful is paved with small steps.

Success knows no age limits – it can be yours, too!

★ *Embrace Your Passion* ★

She's a natural – a little mother hen!... Look at how the children flock to her... Fatou, I have a little boy who needs your help... Let's take you to Fatou, she can teach you about that.

Fatou was only five years old when a neighbor noticed she was a natural-born teacher. She brought children to Fatou one-by-one to learn from her. When she was 16 years old, Fatou attended a teacher-training institute and received a teaching certificate. She was the first girl in her family to attend school – education was not easy for anyone, particularly girls in The Gambia (Africa). This young woman grew up tutoring other children. Those early years planted important seeds.

During her teenage summer vacations, Fatou did volunteer work with groups of North American youth who came to The Gambia with Operation Crossroads Africa to work on rural development projects. The time she spent living and working with these young people deeply affected Fatou. The feelings were mutual. Two of the group's leaders went back to the U.S. and Canada and started raising money to bring Fatou to the U.S. to further her education.

In the meantime, Fatou did what she did best – teach. She had worked her way up to Assistant Principal in a private high school and had proof of what she'd known even as a child – students were not "stupid" or suffering from "lack of interest" as most parents and teachers believed. They were simply not being taught effectively. She developed a program and was greatly pleased when after a few months to a year of complete immersion in her program, students were proficient. It was time to take it to children in the public schools.

But first, the money had arrived from the U.S. and Canada to fund her graduate education in the United States. Fatou arrived in San Francisco in 1985. While completing her degree she became even more focused on her desire to help the kids back home in The Gambia. She slept on the floor so she could save money to purchase books for students back home. Her vision was very clear now – she would set up an independent tutoring center.

In 1998 Fatou did just that – she founded an after-school remedial program for middle and high school students and called it the ABC (A Better Chance) Learning Center. Located in the capital city of Banjul, the Center provides experienced teachers, reading and reference materials, a copying machine (because books are limited), and an environment conducive to learning.

Everything done at the Center is designed to strengthen the students' self-confidence, develop their intellectual curiosity and improve their general academic skills. ABC especially focuses on empowering girls to defy cultural stereotypes.

Fatou has taken it a step further and now offers ABC as an enrichment facility and resource center for teachers by offering workshops where methods and materials are shared. She has also moved beyond complete dependence on local and foreign donors and is including local citizen groups and community organizations around the country and the West Africa sub-region. Fatou has discovered that citizens are deeply concerned about the deteriorating national education system and are willing to contribute to her work.

It seems that Fatou Jobe was "hard-wired" from birth to be a teacher and a teacher of teachers. To those of us looking at what she's accomplished, she seems quite extraordinary. But Fatou would disagree – each step she took was a natural progression. From teaching kids her own age as a child to running a visionary Learning Center, Fatou has embraced her passion to help others learn.

Have you embraced your passion? Are you doing what you've been "hard-wired" to do? If so, you're experiencing fulfillment, challenge and joy. If you aren't, you're probably frustrated, restless and confused. What is it that you do well? What is it that excites you and you can "get lost in" for hours and not even realize that time is flying by? That is your passion! I encourage you to do whatever it takes to embrace it! In return, your life will be filled with satisfaction, growth, new experiences and excitement. That doesn't mean you won't have hard times and face great challenges – but it does mean you'll not be defeated or deflected by them!

POWER BOOSTERS

How do you want your life story to read. (Really think this one through…)

_____

_____

_____

_____

_____

_____

_____

_____

_____

What opportunities are waiting for you to take action?

_____

_____

_____

_____

_____

_____

_____

_____

_____

Joan says her father is *"fiercely independent. He cooks for himself and discourages all offers of help. You can't help him put his coat on. He tells me to take care of me."*

Her father is Mat Dawson -- a valued Ford employee and noted philanthropist. The man could live in a large house and drive a very nice car. Instead, he gets his enjoyment out of giving money away. It makes his job as a rigger at the Ford plant in Detroit, oh so fulfilling.

Paradoxically (Joan) who does not work for Ford Motor Company as her father does, but rather for competitor Chrysler Corporation, will be eligible for retirement in a few years. *"I'll probably retire before he does. He's living his dream to be able to help people."*

"I get joy, happiness out of this; I can go home and sleep good," Mat says.

Mat has donated money, now in the millions of dollars. All this from a man who has a 7th grade education, over 60 years at the same job, and no inheritance or lottery wins. His money is accumulated the old-fashioned way - by hard work and saving.

"I was raised like that, to help others. I have more than enough myself."

Mat chooses to drive an older car and stay in an older area of the city. Vacations are unknown to him because he likes to give away the money instead. He'd rather work overtime than treat himself. He is the first at work to take up a collection when hard times hit a colleague. He is especially moved by the plight of children. He always wants to make sure the kids are safe.

His recipients have been college-bound family members, Wayne State University, Louisiana State University, United Negro Fund, NAACP, varying churches and community colleges. His gifts range in the amounts of $10,000 to $1 million dollars.

Want to know his average annual salary? Guess!

$350,000? $750,000?

Nope, how about around $50,000!! He makes about $25 dollars an hour.

Mat's success may look very different from what you envision. But here's the key for him -- he has found the way to live the life he loves, the life of a giver.

You can live life the way you love, too!

Don't be discouraged and surely don't quit.

You can make it.

> *"Do all the good you can. By all the means you can. In all the ways you can. In all the places you can. At all the times you can. To all the people you can. As long as ever you can."*
> ~John Wesley

"I can't believe he's doing that!"
"Me, either! He turned down a full scholarship to the University."
"My parents would kill me!"
"Tell me about it!"

Marc's stomach was in knots – knots of excitement and anticipation -- when he decided what he was going to do. He just wasn't ready to attend the University – not yet (he would later graduate from Harvard University magna cum laude, and Oxford as a Rhodes Scholar).

But right now there was a burning need in him to understand and learn firsthand how others lived – what challenges they had to face in their day-to-day living.

So at the age of 18, Marc Kielburger not only turned down a full scholarship to the University of Ottawa, he left his job as a parliamentary page in the Canadian House of Commons. He booked a flight to Bangkok and spent eight months as a volunteer in a slum called Klong Toey. There he worked with HIV-positive mothers and infants and taught English in a primary school. Next, Marc headed for Africa where he spent another eight months living and working with a tribe that lives in a remote region of Kenya.

As you can imagine, these experiences changed Marc's life. They increased his determination and gave him the insights and skills he needed to begin making changes when he returned home.

In 1995, Marc's brother, Craig, gathered six school friends (all 12-year-olds) to begin fighting child labor. This led Craig to start *Free The Children*, a worldwide network of youth helping other youth through education. When Marc returned home, he joined Craig's endeavor.

Four years later, the organization topped 100,000 members. Teens who were involved with *Free The Children* started asking for hands-on tools for creating change. They wanted more skills and more training. They wanted to make a difference *now* – not later!

Marc and Craig pulled together a group of young people and spent an intense time finding out exactly what was wanted and needed. Then these two incredible young men developed curriculum and programs to provide what the youth wanted. The goal was to help teenagers achieve *"great things – today, not tomorrow."* They named the organization: *Leaders Today.*

Marc started by developing seminars where teens were taught about public speaking, negotiation techniques and fundraising. The brothers planned trips to Africa, Asia and Latin America so young people could experience how the rest of the world lives. Today this organization of young people reaches out annually to more than 350,000 youth to help them learn how to make a difference in their world – NOW!

Marc is dedicated to teaching young people how to realize and embrace our human interconnectedness throughout the world. He wants them to understand that each choice they make influences – in some way – problems, solutions, and lives somewhere else on the planet.

The idea is making volunteerism part of their lives so they see themselves as change-makers.

In 2004 Marc and Craig wrote the book *Me to We* which offers their philosophy on life: *"we can all build a better life – and our ideal world – through reaching out to others. In practice, it involves focusing less on 'Me,' and more on 'We' – our communities, our nation and our world as a whole."* That book became a manual that has sparked a youth movement to find meaning in life and in our world by reaching out to help others.

Marc is an amazing young man who sees himself as a world citizen. He understands that how each of us lives is very important. And he has taken it upon himself to make sure as many young people as possible gain that same understanding, and then do something about it.

I want you to know living this way isn't a terrible burden – it's a joy to be able to help others (directly and indirectly) by the way you live. You will make your life rich and full as you learn to think in terms of "we" instead of "me."

I hope you will discover the fun and enjoyment of reaching out to others as you move through life. You are never too young or too old to make a difference!

★ *Unfairly Imprisoned* ★

6-year-old Elvira looked up from her work in the fields. She was working beside her mother on her father's farm in Bolivia. *"Mama, why is Daddy so mean to those people?"*

"Don't look at them, Elvira, just do your work."

"Look, Mama! Look!"

Elvira watched as one of the field hands escaped. She later learned that her father hunted him down, whipped him and hung him by chains in their basement. Later that night, Elvira found her father's keys, slipped in quietly and invisibly into that dark, dank basement and freed the man. Young Elvira witnessed an atrocity that would never leave her. Those memories would carry her passion and zeal to right the wrongs of her society. Her courage came at a high price. Even though she was only a young girl, her father never spoke to her again – in fact, she was banished from her family and sent away.

Undaunted, Elvira Alvarez Ala grew up to carve a life as a staunch advocate for human rights and social justice.

Elvira didn't just see the injustices, she acted.

When her youngest child died because the local doctors refused to care for her family because they couldn't pay, she developed affordable public health care clinics so others wouldn't experience the same tragedy she had.

When she and her husband were working in an area where local miners sold their gold to an international mining company, she learned there was serious pollution of the drinking water because of the mining techniques. Elvira went to work publicizing what the mining company was doing. As you can imagine, this upset the mining company. It also made local doctors angry because their patients (who paid them in gold) were choosing to visit the new health care center Elvira's group was providing.

Elvira and her husband were accused of being subversive to the government and put into prison. Finally, after transferring to a woman's prison, a lawyer and a Human Rights group quickly proved her innocence. During the seven months it took for her release, she organized the other women in the prison to demand visits to their spouses in the men's prison. Their demand was granted.

After her release, Elvira worked on getting her husband and newly made friends out of prison. At that time, justice in Bolivia was delayed with serious violations of human rights. In order to obtain bail, a prisoner had to put up a valuable piece of property such as a car or even their house. Most people simply did not have the resources to do that.

The law also required a rehabilitation program be in place *before* a prisoner would be released. Ironically, no such programs existed and people could spend months, even years in prison – waiting and forgotten.

Again, Elvira acted. She developed a process to help these abandoned prisoners. Her system included the prisoner, family members, friends and a sponsor pulling together to work through the necessary requirements so the prisoner could be released. She put together the steps a prisoner's advocate must take, how to create and propose a rehabilitation program and carry it out, how to develop a support system for the prisoner upon his or her release, and how the prisoner could get work once out of prison.

What an amazing life! From abandoned child, to health care activist, to prison reform advocate, Elvira Alvarez Ala has boldly stepped into the gap on the behalf of others. Her life has been all about helping those whose freedoms or rights have been taken.

Elvira chose to use what life handed her and successfully turn it around to make a difference in the lives of others. She is a prime example of one who found success because of determination and perseverance.

Like Elvira's, we hope your success will make a huge difference for others.

"If we all did the things we are really capable of doing, we would literally astound ourselves." ~Thomas Edison

---

"Barry, you did what? You quit college? You barely started. You'd only been going, what, one semester? Great, so now what will you do?"

"Hey Barry, yeah, I asked around and we've got an opening -- in the mailroom. Since you don't have a degree, you'll fit in down there. Come to ABC TV studio on Monday and I'll meet you."

"Barry, I think you are right. Let's make those weekly movies...what shall we call it? If we are doing it more than once a month, we gotta name it something..."

"Barry, signing on that sitcom was brilliant. It's at the top of the ratings. You did it again."

"Barry, I am so sorry to tell you...but your brother didn't make it. He was shot. I'm sorry."

"Barry, we did it! The reality program is a hit. We are the top rated show again this week."

"Barry, sign here and the yacht EOS is all yours. Man, I'd love to know how it feels to own the largest private sailing yacht in the world."

You probably don't recognize this man's name unless you are a true American TV trivia buff. Barry Diller is the guy responsible for bringing many entertaining shows and movies to the big screen, as well as the TV screen. In the 1970's and 1980's we watched such shows as "*Laverne & Shirley, Taxi, Cheers;* and movies *Saturday Night Fever, Grease, Raiders of the Lost Ark, Indiana Jones and the Temple of Doom, Terms of Endearment* and *Beverly Hills Cop.*" In the 1990's, he developed reality TV with programming such as *Cops, America's Most Wanted* and unconventional shows like *In Living Color, Married...with Children*, and *The Simpsons*. He is also the inventor of the weekly 90-minute "made for TV" movies that have intrigued us for generations. He discovered that inexpensive to produce weekly TV movies brought in big revenue in high ratings.

In real life, media mogul Barry Diller has been a major player in the American entertainment industry for decades. He has bought and sold networks, invested millions of dollars in risky ventures, been taken to court and forced to reinvent himself, as well as his media empire.

Barry has done all this without a college degree.

Not to say he has gotten it easily. Even though he is a powerhouse in a mega dollar industry, he knows heartache. His brother's death is a little known fact.

However, that fact has influenced his life profoundly. His business endeavors have not always been successful.

Failure is common to those who succeed.

Since he started in the mailroom of the first television studio, he has worked his way up the ladder. He learned how to do his job well and then looked for ways to transfer his skills upwards to better paying jobs with more responsibility. Then he repeated that process. He increased his knowledge and his prowess to such a degree that in 2006, he was named the highest-paid executive with a yearly salary of nearly $3 million! WOW!

As Barry worked his way up, he worked with people along the way. He mentored many men and women whom the media calls the "Killer Dillers." Most of his protégés have become media executives in their own right. His "Killer Dillers" include the President & COO of Paramount Pictures, the Chairman & CEO of The Walt Disney Company, the head of Columbia Pictures, a leading executive of PDI/DreamWorks Animation, a principal of DreamWorks SKG, a former head of Walt Disney Studios, the President of BBC America, and the President of Production at Paramount.

Not bad for a guy with no formal training!

Today remember Barry as you flip on your TV or head to the movies. Chances are he and his visions are entertaining you.

And as you work toward YOUR dreams, never, never give up!!

"Hey Mom – listen to this! 'The best way to predict the future is to create it.'"
"Oh, I like that."
"Listen to this one: 'The most important thing in communication is hearing what isn't said.'"
"That's for sure – how many times have I said that to you?"
"I love this one: 'Trying to predict the future is like trying to drive down a country road at night with no lights while looking out the back window.'"
"That's a good one, too. Who are you quoting?"
"His name is Peter Drucker."

Peter Drucker was born in 1909 in a small village just outside Vienna, Austria. His mother had studied medicine, his father was an attorney, and their house was often filled with intellectuals, high government officials and scientists. Peter was exposed to all kinds of new ideas and ideals – one of which settled deeply into his mind – the importance of innovation and entrepreneurship. He was also affected by his kindergarten teacher who taught him "the concept of management" and his 4th grade religious instructor who asked, *"What do you want to be remembered for?"*

After graduation, Peter was unable to find work in Vienna, and eventually moved to Frankfurt, Germany. He got a job writing for the largest daily paper while working on his doctorate in international law and public law. It was during this time that he realized *all the brilliant economic students in the room were interested in the behavior of commodities, while I was interested in the behavior of people."*

Over the remainder of his years, that understanding was the core principle propelling him to focus on relationships instead of numbers. Peter was a prolific writer. In the early 1930's he wrote a piece entitled, *"The Jewish Question in Germany."* As you can imagine, it wasn't well received! It was burned and banned by the Nazis. In 1933, he wisely left Germany for England. He married Doris and then moved to the United States, where Peter served as correspondent for several British newspapers. He began his life-long teaching career and in 1943, Peter became a U.S. citizen.

Over the next *six decades*, Peter Drucker became the "guru" of organizational management with his introduction of management by objectives. (He actually disliked the term "guru." He once said, *"I have been saying for many years that we are using the word 'guru' only because 'charlatan' is too long to fit into a headline."*) He not only continued teaching at the university level, he also wrote and did consulting work with some of the largest U.S. companies: General Electric, Coca-Cola, Citicorp, IBM and Intel.

In 1971, Peter and Doris settled in California where he taught at the Claremont Graduate School, consulted and wrote until his death in 2005 at the age of 95. The last class he taught was in late 2002 when he was 93!

Peter Drucker changed the landscape of organizational management by introducing the human element – not only in how businesses and non-profit organizations are run, but how they market and serve their clientele. He stressed respect for the worker, teaching that employees are assets and not liabilities. He taught the need for "planned abandonment" – needing to leave behind what is no longer working. He reminded companies that their primary responsibility is to serve the customer, not make a profit -- for without the customer they cease to exist.

But Peter's insights extended far beyond the business world. He consulted for many government agencies in the U.S., Canada and Japan, helping them become more successful. Some of the organizations he helped were the Salvation Army, Girl Scouts, C.A.R.E., the American Red Cross and the Navajo Indian Tribal Council.

Did you catch that phrase "planned abandonment"? This is a key to success – we have to leave behind what no longer works and move on to something else. That reminds me of the definition of insanity -- doing the same thing over and over and expecting different results.

Incorporate "planned abandonment" in your life and serve others and success will surely follow!

POWER BOOSTERS

If failure was not possible, what would you do?

_____

_____

_____

_____

_____

_____

_____

_____

What makes your heart race with excitement?

_____

_____

_____

_____

_____

_____

_____

_____

"Ma'am, would you buy a newspaper? They are 5 cents."

The 7-year-old waited somewhat impatiently. The need for a bathroom was pressing. Hopefully, she would buy a paper and he could move on. It was hard here in rural Idaho. However, little Jon's family needed the money he made from his newspaper sales. When fortunate, he profited $2.00 in a week.

As a teenager, Jon worked hard to provide his family with necessities...the family automobile, paying doctor bills and even paying *his dad's* way through college. Eventually his dad graduated from college and became a teacher. But for most of his life, Jon was poor.

Poverty robbed him of feeling secure as a boy.

When asked what he learned from his first jobs, Jon quickly replied, *"I think we learn most things about business when we're 7 or 8 years old. So much of it is about people and relationships. I learned that I did not want to put my children in the same position I had been in -- putting money into a family pot to pay the bills. It is too heavy a load for a young man. It had a profound effect on my entire life."*

Who is Jon? In addition, why should you know him?

Well, if you have bought a dozen eggs or eaten a Big Mac© then you have utilized two of Jon Huntsman's inventions: Styrofoam egg cartons and the Big Mac© hinged box. After those profitable inventions, he founded his own company. With a long list of impressive business acquisitions and mergers, Jon is now a billionaire.

With his generosity, Jon is also a giver.

In addition, Jon applied the lessons he learned growing up poor. While eight of his nine children work within his businesses, (the youngest is mentally disabled) all his kids own their own position. They didn't have to support their dad. And Dad has made it an example to live by his belief that it is a joy and a privilege, as well as an absolute duty in life, to *'give money away.'* Charitable giving is part of his company's mission statement.

Jon is the founder and former CEO, now chairman, of Huntsman, one of the largest chemical companies in the world. Forbes magazine calculates Huntsman's personal wealth at $3.2 billion. That is an incredible amount of money. Yet in 2007, he gave away $750 million in contributions and donations!

Mind-blowing! To hear others speak of him, you learn he is courteous, honest, kind and simply a nice guy. When asked about his success, he eagerly credits others, *"I had men and women surrounding me who were smarter than I was and who really get the credit for many of these early innovations and productions that have changed literally the world in which we live."*

He knows that giving is better than receiving.

Even cancer didn't change Jon. He lost his mother, father and stepfather to cancer. He battled his own cancer diagnosis. Combating his own illness, he founded and helps fund a prominent cancer research center. His goal: *"find a cure for cancer and end human suffering."* His scientists are well on the way.

Even though Jon knows life is not fair, he advocates to all his employees and board members, *"...we must be fair in our dealings. That's the one thing I think that transcends everything we do in life."*

From a little boy selling newspapers to a kind billionaire grandfather, Jon offers much to emulate. His keys to success are generosity, looking for ways to make life better, and making fairness a character trait.

Make his keys your keys and enjoy your success!

"The three things that are most essential to achievement are common sense, hard work and stick-to-it-iv-ness."

~Thomas Edison

★ *Life Without Mom* ★

The 14 years since Warrick got word that his mother was murdered flashed before him like it had happened just seconds ago. Looking at the penitentiary where her murderer lived caused memories of his past life with his mother to flood his mind. He was 18 again...the eldest of six kids living a typical American life -- school, sports, home, girls -- until that evening -- until the horrible, violent, senseless, evening of his mother's death.

The sounds and smells of that teenager's home drifted back to him as he remembered a common conversation he and his mother shared... "Mom, I've got practice after school. I won't be home 'til late," Warrick yelled down the hall of the house his mom rented.

His mother, Betty, loved her kids fiercely. Like all single mothers, she worked hard. Her long hours ensured she could make ends meet in their Louisiana town. As a police officer, she took off-duty jobs to provide for her family. The dream of owning her own home was ever before her. She so desired to give the kids their own home...not another rental. However, clothes, school, and bills took precedence.

"Ok, Warrick! Your brothers and sisters will be here. I have to work at the grocery store tonight until after the night money drop at the bank. Y'all get all your homework done. Dinner is in the fridge. Be good to each other. I love you!" Betty called after the kids as they left for school.

"Love you too!" came the echoing replies as the door slammed behind them.

That night, Betty escorted the grocery store manager to the bank to deposit the store's money. It would be her last duty. Gunmen accosted her and the manager, shooting Betty. The wound was fatal. The robbers? Sentenced to death row while the driver of their car served a lengthy prison sentence.

Today, Warrick faced the doors that led him inside to a face-to-face conversation with the man who killed his mother. As Warrick matured and took his place as head of the family, he grew stronger. He grew stronger in his mind and his body. What he was doing was not something he wanted to do, but something he *needed* to do. He needed peace and the resolve to move fully beyond that dreadful night.

The hour-long conversation and its details are private -- known only to Warrick, the man, their attorneys and two men of Warrick's choosing. Security guards hovered nearby, just out of earshot but not out of sight.

In an interview afterwards, Warrick said, *"I don't hate him anymore. I've moved on. I'm in a better place."*

Who is Warrick Dunn? If you are an American football fan, you'll know his accomplishments...

- Associated Press National Football League Offensive Rookie of the Year -1997
- 3 times Pro Bowl selection - 1997, 2000, 2005
- Walter Payton Man of the Year Award - 2004

If you are a single mother living in Atlanta, Georgia; Tampa, Florida; Baton Rouge, Louisiana or Tallahassee, Florida you've probably heard of "Home for the Holidays." It's a program developed by Warrick, helping provide home ownership to disadvantaged mothers and their children. More than 75 parents and 250 kids have been assisted in making their dream home a reality.

According to his foundation's website, Warrick says,*"... I did not grow up with many material things, but I was surrounded by the love of my family, friends and coaches. My mother worked overtime to put food on the table and a roof over our heads. Although we did not have much, she taught me how to give of myself and to be generous to those in need...each of us can do our part to help in some small way to make our community a better place to live. As a result of growing up in a single-parent household, I have focused my charitable efforts on helping single parent families obtain first-time homeownership."*

WOW!! This young man does what he does because he is not afraid to love. He loved his mother, and he honors her life and her memory by choosing to be the better man. He chose integrity.

Success is meaningless without integrity. As you strive toward your dreams, remember Warrick and measure success as he does.

"It's none of your business, Carolina!"
"But why not? If it affects my neighborhood, it affects me and it IS my business!"
"You don't understand, dear. It's just not how things are done – just don't get involved."
"That's not an option, Mother. I have to do something!"

Carolina Biquard's parents were raised in a country where the State took care of people. She understood their hands-off mindset came from living under Argentinean dictators. But their passive mentality disturbed Carolina and fueled her desire to get involved and do something for her community.

After receiving her law degree, Carolina got involved with a project in Buenos Aires working with street children. The group's desire to build a better community, not just provide charity, impressed Carolina. She volunteered with the project for three years and then decided to abandon her career as a lawyer. Instead, she decided to *"become a human bridge between this project and the community."*

This head-strong, and compassionate woman became a pioneer in Argentina where non-profit organizations (NPOs) were basically ignored by the government and private sector. They were on their own. There was no organization, no networking, no collaboration between them, and no recognition or support. Carolina truly became a "human bridge" for NPOs throughout Argentina.

Carolina's quest took her to the United States to learn more about non-profit organizations – how they work, how to raise funds, and how to raise community awareness about their services.

In 1992, Carolina was ready…

She began teaching courses in NPO management and fundraising at the local university. At the same time, she worked on her Master's Degree. In 1994, Carolina created Fundación Compromiso ("Commitment Foundation") to help Argentinean NPOs organize, grow, and reach their potential as agents of social change. Her timing couldn't have been better.

This was the missing key for the people of Argentina. The government had drastically cut back on services to the people. In response to the dire needs of the populace, a group of diverse NPOs stepped up to the plate to provide what the government had withdrawn. They were known as the "third sector."

But there was a problem – these NPOs were disorganized and struggling. Carolina's Fundación Compromiso filled the void by providing training for staff members and much-needed networking between the organizations. And the people of Argentina benefited because of her labor of love.

It's interesting, isn't it, that Carolina was raised in a family that taught her not to get involved in other people's lives? But her heart and head didn't accept what she was taught. Deep inside she knew she had to do something. Carolina saw a huge void that needed filling. It took her several years before the idea of what she needed to do took shape. But when it did, she learned what she could, adapted it to her culture, and worked until her vision became reality.

What a great role model for you and me! I want to be like Carolina – don't you? When I see a hole in society that I know I can help fill, I want to have the same strength, courage, and conviction that she had to do something about it, regardless of what people say. Carolina learned to be creative and "think outside the box," to adapt other people's ideas to her situation, and to come up with new and fresh methods to help people help others.

I hope you will think about Carolina today and decide to make a difference in your world. Don't be afraid to "think outside the box." Don't let others keep you from doing what you know in your heart-of-hearts you need to do.

Hold fast to your dreams and your determination and you will know success!

★ *He Still Boogies at Age 95!* ★

The woman was upset and had a knife. He should have known better. Joe Willie didn't need this argument. However, as altercations sometimes go, the fight got way out of hand. He was a guitar player -- at least he had been.

Now, with his arm stabbed and seriously injured, his future loomed bleak.

That woman had done more than hurt his pride...she'd managed to disable not only his guitar playing, but his future as well.

What could he do? Playing music was his livelihood, his love and passion. Born in Mississippi in 1913, he had left school in the 3rd grade. Education certainly couldn't help him now.

He had nothing to "fall back on" and he was too hurt to play.

How would he live? The outcome of that silly argument now threatened to change his life.

Joe Willie reasoned with himself - if he couldn't keep playing the guitar, he'd switch instruments. Piano was just as good -- definitely easier on his arm. So he chose to be creative and not quit. He chose to play the piano.

We should be glad he did. This piano man also acquired a nickname as the years passed. You may be familiar with him if you listen to "boogie-woogie" music or "rhythm and blues." I am talking about Pinetop Perkins, one of "America's most powerful octogenarians" and the "yardstick by which great blues pianists are measured."

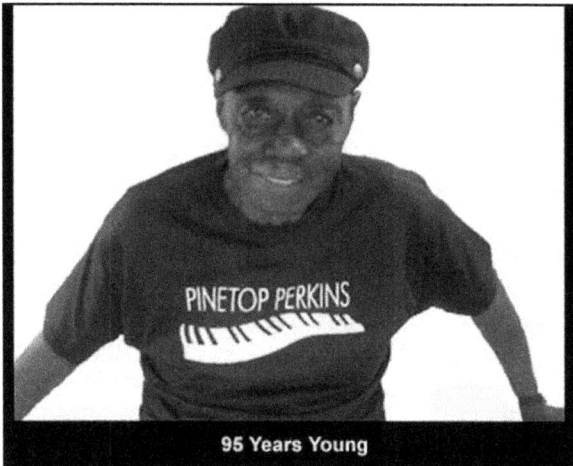

95 Years Young

For most of the EIGHT DECADES that he has played, he's played as the accompanist -- the 2nd guy -- the background guy. Not the headliner. Not the main feature. Therefore, to fulfill a life dream, at 80 years of age, Pinetop soloed. He recorded HIS album. Then he did it again -- 15 times. Yep, 15 more records in 15 years, many of them award winning

And he hasn't stopped there. In 2010, at 96 years old, he is still boogieing!

At 96, Pinetop still performs several nights a week in Texas

At 96, Pinetop still tours around the country several days every month!!!

At 96, Pinetop is a living music legend influencing great musicians around the world.

Pinetop has a reputation for being "*friendly charming and a gentleman. He says yes to everything and is quick to joke. He loves people and makes everyone feel good around him.*"

Isn't that cool? Never too old! NEVER!

Did you notice the choice he made early in his life...when his arm was injured? He had *to choose to do something different. He learned to play the piano by watching others, and still can't read sheet music! Once he had conquered this new skill, he happily returned to the pursuit of his dream – MUSIC.*

I did not say it was easy, just that he did what he had to do to make his beloved music.

We, too, have choices to make every day, small and large. I want to be like Pinetop and choose to adjust when I have to and never give up.

Don't you give up either! You can make the most of your life, starting today.

> *"I am tomorrow, or some future day, what I establish today. I am today what I established yesterday or some previous day." ~James Joyce*

"But why do we have to move again, Mama?"

"Why don't they like us, Papa?"

The little guy kicked at the dirt in frustration and confusion. It seemed just as soon as he started to make friends and get settled into a new school, he was uprooted and moved again.

Rinto's family moved often when he was young because neighbors didn't accept his parents' mixed religious and ethnic marriage. Consequently, he attended many different schools and lived in many different villages and communities.

However, at one of his schools, an elementary teacher encouraged "hands-on" learning outside the classroom. As a result he was introduced to working on projects in poor communities and public hospitals.

These experiences directly affected the difference he would make as an adult.

"The people need to know how their money is being spent!"

"The village leaders are taking advantage of their people and need to be accountable to their villagers!"

Rinto Adiono was verbal and determined.

As a college student in the late 1990s, Rinto had the freedom to develop his interest in economics and public policy. Java was undergoing political change and he became active in the anti-corruption movement of the time. He got involved in citizen initiatives and contributed research to "pro-poor budgets." But he was frustrated with simply writing books or training legislators on the subject of fiscally responsible community budgets because it reached such a limited audience. It also didn't ensure the needed changes would happen.

Rinto understood that for the needed changes to be made in the local communities, he was going to have roll up his sleeves and work directly with the people. And, he did.

The first thing Rinto and the community leaders did was analyze the local budget. Discrepancies and poor management was the norm.

For instance, one village's budget had 900 million rupiah ($96,000) allocated to cover the cost of lunches for the 45 regional legislators while children were going hungry. Rinto helped the village request 1.4 million ($150) for a children's nutritional food program. Another village had a high incidence of women dying in childbirth. Rinto found the problem was transportation to the nearest hospital was slow and grueling. He helped the village get funds earmarked to build a health clinic and pay a health care worker to live in their village. With his help other villagers obtained funds for supplemental food for young children, and hired teachers for village schools.

Knowing the needs were widespread and he was only one man, Rinto created the School for Budget Analysis and Advocacy (LADANG) and started teaching local community workers how to do what he was doing. He designed materials easily adaptable to each community, as well as to the needs of networking groups such as farmers' unions, the women's movement, and children's rights organizations.

Wow!! Rinto is one amazing man! He had a very difficult childhood, but because of an imaginative school teacher he experienced helping others first-hand. As a result, Rinto is successfully changing the world for many people in his country of Java.

Sometimes it takes just one childhood experience to cause the direction of a person's life. Who knows who you are influencing? As you reach for your dreams, remember that others are watching.

> "If you always put limits on everything you do, physical or anything else, it will spread into your work and into your life. There are no limits. There are only plateaus, and you must not stay there, you must go beyond them."
> ~Bruce Lee

POWER BOOSTERS

What do you need to learn to achieve your dreams? How can you make that happen?

_____

_____

_____

_____

_____

_____

_____

_____

Who can you partner with to achieve your dreams? Who can you ask to help you?

_____

_____

_____

_____

_____

_____

_____

_____

Consistent, Stubborn and Diligent

Are you one of the nearly 22 million Americans who click on the TV each week to watch Dancing with the Stars? 2008 saw a special celebrity competing.

Want to guess how old she was? Try 82!

Dancing With The Stars is an American reality show. A celebrity teams up with a professional ballroom dancer and learns how to dance such dances as the foxtrot, cha-cha, waltz, samba and tango. They then perform live, and three professional dance judges score their performance. Program viewers also vote electronically or over the phone. The lowest scoring team is asked to leave.

Hours and hours of work learning, practicing, and performing are required. Muscle tone and fitness are required as well as agility and flexibility. Most contestants are young. They have to be.

Or do they?

Who is her competition on this dancing show? How about Olympic sports stars, professional football players, and actors *decades* younger. **Octogenarian** (someone in their 80s) Cloris Leachman dances her way across the stage with lights glaring and music swelling. Looking and acting decades younger, this woman recently completed work on three – yes – three films. In addition to the dance program, and those three films, she currently tours the U.S. with her one-woman show *CLORIS!* **and** is writing her memoirs.

Her schedule makes *me* tired!!

Cloris started out with a dream to be an actress. She began pursuing it in high school. She competed in the Miss America pageant (she was Miss Chicago) and won a scholarship that she used to study acting in New York City. Her undergraduate college degree was in drama.

Cloris is one who knew what she wanted to do early. She simply put herself in the line of success by working her dreams. She's worked hard and often. She has taken the roles offered, and been available to try various genres and characters. She's been on Broadway, radio, TV programs, TV sitcoms, Hollywood movies, and a voice on animation films.

From the credits in her life, I counted over 60 films, 60 TV roles or appearances, and over 25 Emmys, Oscars, or Golden Globe awards. Actually, she's won over eight Emmys – more than any other female performer! That's a record! How awesome to be awarded for doing what you love.

Cloris created a niche for her talents and never swayed. Even at an age where many folks are fading, she is picking up speed!

Here's a key about dreaming – be consistent, stubborn and diligent.

Focus on the future and never let go of your dreams!

> *"I believe in the power of desire backed by faith because I have seen this power lift people from lowly beginnings to places of power and wealth; I have seen it rob the grave of victims; and I have seen it serve as the medium by which people staged a comeback after having been defeated in a hundred different ways."*
> *~Napoleon Hill*

★ _Coming to America_ ★

"Welcome home, Papa! What was America like? Did they know you were on a diplomatic mission? Did they know who you were? How did you find it? Was it like they say, Papa? Was it?"

Curious and intelligent beyond his years, Jacques wanted to learn more.

"Well, I must say, I am impressed with the American education at the university level. There are some good prep schools there as well. But Jacques -- you are still young, you know."

" Papa, are you serious? I can go?"

"Do you truly want to move to America? You can stay here and go to Cambridge...but yes, if you want to study there as you grow, you can!."

"Oh yes, Papa, I do!"

"Then it is settled. To America, we will go."

To America! Jacques Barzun was only 12!

Jacques' father was a member of the _Abbaye de Créteil_ (a group of artists and writers) and worked in the French Ministry of Labor. Many "modernist" people frequented his home as he was growing up. He associated with the poet Apollinaire, the Cubist painters Albert Gleizes and Marcel Duchamp, the composer Edgard Varèse, and the writers Richard Aldington and Stefan Zweig. He has this to say about his parents: _"I grew up a child of a bourgeois family, with emancipated parents who surrounded themselves with people who talked about ideas."_

With his sights set on the United States, Jacques couldn't dream of anything better. After arriving there, he attended a preparatory high school and then made his home, literally and figuratively, at Columbia University. Columbia is an Ivy League school in the New York City neighborhood of Manhattan. It was founded by Great Britain's King George II and prides itself as the originator of the Pulitzer Prize. (The Pulitzer awards outstanding achievements in journalism, literature and music and has for over a century.)

After graduating as valedictorian of his 1927 class, Jacques stayed at Columbia from 1927-1975 as Professor of Cultural History, Dean of the Graduate School, Dean of Faculties as well as Provost. After retiring from Columbia, his _second_ career spanned another decade as an editorial consultant at Scribners (a well-know New York publishing and research company).

As a French-born American historian of _"ideas and culture,"_ Jacques had great interest in _"French and German literature, music, education, ghost stories, detective fiction, language, and etymology."_ Over his lifetime he would write _over 40 books_ (not counting his reviews, analyses and editorials) on a wide array of topics, including science, medicine, psychiatry, art, and classical music. He even _likes_ baseball and detective fiction!

I use the present tense "likes" because as of this writing (June 2010), Jacques is still alive at 102!

You know, growing older did not dissuade this "Renaissance man" from pursuing his dreams.

Jacques, _when 84 years old_, wrote an 850+ page non-fiction novel titled _From Dawn to Decadence:500 Years of Western Cultural Life, 1500 to the Present._ He calls it his "swan song." The novel became a New York Times Best Seller.

Jacques' life and accomplishments are long but he doesn't dwell on them. At 100 years of age, he is _"usually out of bed by 6 A.M. He brews coffee, reads, exercises for forty minutes, and heads down the hall to his study...dips into the manuscripts and books that people send him, answers letters, and takes calls...he likes to read in the sunroom..."_

Jacques' feelings about aging? _"Old age is like learning a new profession,"_ he quips. _"And not one you chose."_

Getting older is an adventure and one that can be enjoyed! Be like Jacques Barzun and face all of life with an adventuresome spirit! _Who knows -- if you do it right, you too might be fulfilling your dreams when you are 100!_

★ *Your Special Genius* ★

The infant's first cries were strangely out of place. Not in a hospital, not in her parent's home, little Gabrielle was born in the French poorhouse where her mother worked. She didn't remember that of course, but six years later she did remember the fear and bewilderment when her father abandoned her and her four siblings at her mother's death.

"Where did Daddy go? Where's Mama?"

"I don't want to go there – I want to go home!"

*"The orphanage **is** your new home, Gabrielle. I'm sorry, but you have no other place to go."*

At 6 years of age, Gabrielle's world tumbled down around her. With no family to take her in, she became a ward of the state and was placed in a Catholic orphanage. This would be home for the next 9 years.

When Gabrielle turned 17 she was moved to another convent school. The nuns there found work for her as a seamstress. But Gabrielle left that job for a brief career as a cabaret (café) and concert singer and adopted the name Coco.

The year was 1910, and it didn't take long for Coco to make the move to the big city of Paris and secure financing for her first business – making women's hats. She expanded from hats to clothing, and moved to the French sea coast resort towns. Her radical clothing designs were eagerly adopted.

Coco's free lifestyle was reflected in her rejection of the women's clothing of the time that included tight-fitting corsets, long dresses, and petticoats. She threw all that out and moved to a relaxed, comfortable, simple fashion, with short skirts and a casual look. She introduced a simple daytime suit for women, and pioneered "costume" jewelry by wearing multiple strands of pearls or gold chains. She also introduced heavily sequined evening attire.

Always seeking comfort in her styles, Coco took the soft Jersey fabric (then used for men's underwear), and created the first relaxed, sports clothing for women. She also used this fabric for her suits.

But it was her signature perfume that made her a millionaire – Chanel No. 5 was the first-ever scent that carried the name of its designer. Of her perfume, Chanel said, *"This perfume is not just beautiful and fragrant. It contains my blood and sweat and a million broken dreams."*

Out of a sad, tragic beginning, Gabrielle "Coco" Chanel carved out her unique one-of-a-kind genius and created a revolution in women's clothing. Her simple, elegant designs transcend the decades and remain the basics of good taste, fashion and design.

Like Coco, you are unique and have your own special genius – you just need to discover and embrace it! Don't be afraid to look at things differently. Think outside the box.

Encourage "the child" within you, and embrace the spontaneity and specialness that is exclusively YOU!

Let **your** special genius shrine through!

> *"Thoughts lead on to purposes;*
> *purposes go forth in action;*
> *actions form habits;*
> *habits decide character;*
> *and character fixes our destiny."*
> *~Tyron Edwards*

★ *A Purple Envelope* ★

She took her place at the table. It was another Friday night concert somewhere in the middle of the United States. Thousands of people were streaming to their seats. Concert time was more than an hour away, but crowded was the only word to describe the walkway between the entrances.

"T-shirts! T-shirts! Garth Brooks T-shirts! Get 'em and wear 'em to the show!"

"Garth Brooks hats! Wear 'em like he does!"

At the end of the night, a weary Martina met up with her husband, John. She smiled as she watched him stride up the stairs. He had worked the concert too, 'mixing' sound. In fact, she had taken this job to be with John. She had grown so tired of staying home alone when he travelled. The one semester of college she had attended, staying behind at home, hadn't suited her at all.

Now she was hawking fan gear for a major country star.

Selling t-shirts had been the only job vacancy. She enjoyed the contact with his fans. Her own dreams however, would take her to the stage as well. At least she hoped they would.

This show over, she exhaled. Sitting in the corner chair of their hotel room, she dialed her parents. Wanting to connect with her roots, she reminisced. Years of family bands, family concerts, and local dance stages drifted back to her. She came from a small town in the middle of nowhere Kansas. The "local" venues where she sang were *very* far from the starlight of the capital of country music -- Nashville, Tennessee. Her small but appreciative audiences were usually made up of many family and friends.

Hanging up from chatting with her folks, she turned to John as he readied for bed.

"Hey, honey, I heard from a friend tonight that RCA is looking to add another female voice to its roster. Know anyone over there?

"No, babe, I don't. They won't listen to unrequested material, either. That I do know. It's only a small obstacle. We'll figure out something. We gotta get your voice heard down there. You should be singing...."

"Well, what do you have in mind?"

John and Martina creatively placed her photos, biography, and 2 demo tapes in a large purple envelope addressed to RCA records with the **bogus** words "Requested Material." It worked!

Just a few short weeks later, she had both a record deal with RCA and a new job with country music super-star, Garth Brooks, as *his opening act!*

This, my friends, is Martina McBride. Her gorgeous voice went from nowhere, to being awarded *Top Female Vocalist, Favorite Female Country Artist, Female Video of the Year or Female Vocalist of the Year* ten different times between the years of 1999 and 2004!

Her creativity in drawing attention to her voice created the venue in which her dreams materialized. The stage became her home. Her husband, John, created and owns one of the top concert sound companies in the music industry.

Did she have a college degree in music? *Nope.*

Did she have the 'right' family? *Nope.*

She simply contented herself with selling shirts as she *waited* for her time to come. Never giving up. Never quitting. Always looking ahead to what could be.

Then Martina pushed just a bit with that purple envelope edging out her competition. By believing in her dreams she knew she had nothing to lose and everything to gain by being different.

Today may you be encouraged by Martina's story, her life, and her belief in her dreams.

I encourage you to dream today, and everyday. One day you may see those dreams come true! (The opposite is true as well. If you don't have dreams, they sure can't come true, now can they?)

So dream them and work them – anyway!

★ *He's A Hero to Me!* ★

Jorge angrily slammed his way into the house. *"I'm not going back, Mama, I'm NOT!"*

"What is it, son?"

"The teacher was laughing as loud as the kids at me today in class just because I'm Mayan. I'm not going back – ever!"

"Jorge, come here." His mother pulled him onto her lap and gave him a big bear hug. Then she lifted his chin until he was looking her straight in the eyes. *"Jorge, when you get a little older you can get work like your Papa. You don't have to stay in school, in fact, it's better for you, and us, if you don't."*

Those weren't exactly the words Jorge expected to hear, and something changed within him. He climbed off his mother's lap.

"It's not right, Mama!"

"No, Jorge, it isn't. But that's how it is."

Jorge's father was a brick layer and both he and Jorge's mother tried to shield their eight children from discrimination because of their Mayan ancestry. They refused to teach them k'iche, their native language, or anything else about their culture.

But as Jorge watched his parents and thought about what lay ahead of him, he decided he wanted something different. Deep inside he knew he was as good as the other kids. And he was going to prove it to them – and to his parents.

Jorge remained in school and dug in. He listened more carefully, paid closer attention in class, learned the material, and earned top grades. He also bore the brunt of many cruel jokes and laughter.

Resisting his parents' wishes, Jorge remained in school and did not drop out to go to work. He became president of the student council and vice president of a national student group. And he went on to the university.

While at the university, Jorge became a student leader and activist, speaking out in favor of social change. When Guatemalan politics worsened, Jorge received threats on his life. In 1982 fled the country. Over the next ten years, he returned to Guatemala, but had to flee two more times. But he never gave up on his commitment to social change for his homeland.

Finally, in 1993, Jorge returned to Guatemala and started working in a government primary school. He was amazed and concerned that many of the teachers simply didn't show up. At the same time, he began working on educational initiatives both within, and outside, the public school system. He joined "teacher-practitioners" working with students who couldn't attend school. He also began teaching poor adults in rural areas.

It was his experiences teaching outside the public school system that gave Jorge his idea…

Rather than fighting a losing battle of changing the school system from within, he decided to create an alternative school system. He realized the best way to get the Guatemalan schools to improve, was to give them some major competition.

Social equality is the curriculum's guiding principle at Jorge's schools. Wealth and poverty, cultural diversity, and gender equality, are all part of the studies. Each month has a theme: community, family, environment, the Mayan nation, human rights, health, and democracy, are just a few. The students vote on the topics to study. They not only read and do class work around the month's theme, students and teachers hold

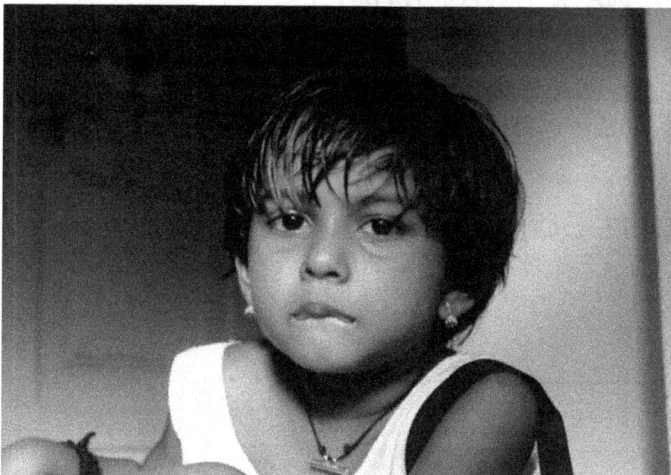

discussions on how the theme relates to their personal lives. The goal is to offer children a better understanding of social realities, their individual talents, and their ability to change society for the better.

Student fees help finance the schools, but Jorge is very sensitive about making education available to everyone. Some of his creative funding includes: foreign sponsors for individual students, a Spanish-speaking language institute, and corporate sponsorships for each school. There is also a parent board that manages small enterprises (such as handicraft production) to help raise funds. Parents also sit on the school board and are invited to join their children in the classroom.

Jorge's parallel school system has one overarching goal and that is to challenge the pace of education reform in his country, while offering a rigorous educational experience that engages and empowers *all* students for future leadership.

From bearing the scars of ridicule and prejudice because of his indigenous roots, Jorge Marciano Chojolán Pacajoj has risen to leadership within his country. He is a hero in my book!

Instead of leaving his country, Jorge chose to make it better. Rather than living down to others' expectations, he rose to the challenge, and is making a difference in a very difficult situation.

Regardless of what others think about you or how they treat you, you can be like Jorge and rise above the negativity.

I hope you will think about Jorge's story today and choose to live as a victor and not a victim. You can overcome whatever challenges come your way. You can rise above those who would try to bring you down, and even offer them encouragement along the way.

You are a remarkable person!

"I will! I am! I can!
I will actualize my dream.
I will press ahead.
I will settle down and see
it through.
I will solve the problems.
I will pay the price.
I will never walk away from
my dream until I see my
dream walk away;
Alert! Alive! Achieved!

~Robert Schuller

POWER BOOSTERS

What problems do you need solutions for? Write them down and let the answers flow...

_____

_____

_____

_____

_____

_____

_____

_____

_____

_____

Do you see a problem you can turn into a possibility? What is it?

_____

_____

_____

_____

_____

_____

_____

_____

_____

_____

_____

★ *He's Got Spunk and Ingenuity* ★

The teacher called out the daily attendance. When he got to Simon's name, he marked him absent. *Again.* Seems that kid was never in class. Looking at Simon's record, he'd spent almost as much time being kicked out of schools as he did in school.

"I need to withdraw from college. I am not finishing."

"Well, I am sorry to hear that. First name, please."

"Simon"

"Simon, you are fired."

"Simon, I have the records for this morning's meeting. You are going to have to declare bankruptcy."

"Mom, it's Simon, the chart is out. We did it...it's a hit. The song is number one! It's a success...What? What? What did you say? Dad died...a heart attack?."

"We can't do this anymore. Simon, we are going to have to declare bankruptcy."

"Mom, it's Simon. I know I'm 30 years old, but I don't have a place to live. Can I move home for a bit? Just till I get back on my feet again?"

This guy has had a hard time, huh?

Think someone who quit school *and* hit bankruptcy for hundreds of thousands of dollars **twice** in a few years would ever be successful? Think again. This same man knows the secret to success. That secret is to never quit. Never. Keep trying. That is exactly what Simon did. Today, he pulls in about $200 million a year. Not bad for a guy who never finished college.

Full of spunk and ingenuity, Simon has definitely seen his fair share of hard times. Along with his dad's premature death, Simon knows the harsh realities of life. While he now makes millions of dollars a year, it has taken deep failure to produce the business success he enjoys. Simon Cowell faces his future as an artist-and-repertoire executive, television personality, and producer. We know him best as a judge on *American Idol* and his home country of England recognizes him from *Pop Idol* and *The X Factor.*

Controversy is his middle name. His trademark phrase is *"I don't mean to be rude but..."* Simon is brash and outspoken. Many days however, you will find him visiting different children's hospices. He has the kids come visit him on the set of *The X Factor* and brings them backstage. His work with these sick kids shows his true heart.

While Simon is a man of many faces, I think his tenacity and resilience are quite admirable.

Many would have quit and simply holed up in despair and declared life too hard. You and I both know men (and woman) who have done just that. I am glad he didn't. While you may or may not like his TV productions, you can learn a valuable lesson from his life.

You may see a millionaire on the outside, but a closer look reveals a determined dreamer who worked until his dreams were reality.

I hope you'll be a determined dreamer, too.

> *"Desire is the key to motivation, but it's determination and commitment to an unrelenting pursuit of your goal – a commitment to excellence – that will enable you to attain the success you seek."*
> ~Mario Andretti

"Lola, you've got to stop this insanity!"
"I'm sorry you feel that way."
"You're embarrassing your husband and family – you MUST stop!"
"I will never stop. Please give my love to Father."

I can only imagine that such a conversation took place between this courageous woman and a well-meaning friend or family member. Movies are made from stories like Lola's!

Born into a wealthy Ecuadorian family, Lola Samaniego Idrovo had every advantage. But desire for the finer things in life took a backseat for her because of the teachings of her doctor-grandfather who was deeply involved in issues of social justice and poverty. Her empathy for those who suffered resulted in her majoring in anthropology at the university. Intense pressure and criticism from family, her ex-husband, and wealthy peers, only fueled her passion to help the poorest of the poor.

After graduating, Lola worked in Chile, Brazil, and Ecuador, promoting human rights. She observed first-hand the dire situation of women who had been deserted by their husbands. Men were leaving their families in growing numbers every year - seeking employment in different regions of the country, or leaving Ecuador altogether, and never coming back. Women were left with little or no income or resources to help put their lives back together.

In rural areas, women were often forced to leave their land and move to cities in search of work so they could provide for their families. They usually ended up living in slums and finding themselves in even worse predicaments. Families lived in dark, one-room cement block homes (about 90 square feet) with no access to basic services or a yard. The block houses created a cold cement world which forced them into a vicious cycle of bitterness, shame, inability to provide for their families, and further desperation.

When eight women with whom Lola was working approached her about their particular situations, her work experience and creativity kicked in. What if they could band together and create their own village? Lola contacted 178 of the poorest families in the area with her idea – she called it an urban village.

The families formed an association, and under Lola's guidance started planning. Their village would be near a large city for access to services, markets, and schools. They would pool their incomes to purchase land so they would be true land owners and not just another group receiving government handouts. Unlike the typical concrete block structures, houses would be attractive, comfortable, and sit on a small plot of land for private gardens. There would also be a community orchard. Members would help each other build their homes, and they would construct a public center for education, community meetings, and recreation. Care would be taken to maintain the ecology of the land.

Within five months of the association's establishment, the members purchased five acres.

Lola has also developed a leadership team of 25 women whom she trains and works alongside. Not only is the urban village changing the quality of people's lives, the process is changing individual lives as well. She is determined to extend this urban village model throughout Ecuador, as well as other countries around the world. She envisions an entire global network of urban villages working together to share best practices and lessons learned.

You know what's really amazing about Lola? She so believes in her model that she has actually left her family and moved into the urban village. Her wealthy family and friends can't understand her.

It's important to surround yourself with people who are positive and supportive – people who will encourage you to reach your full potential. These will be people who sometimes challenge you and make you evaluate where you are with where you want to be. They will hold you accountable for your actions. They will help you move forward - not allow you to stand still and get stagnant, complacent, or apathetic.

Be like Lola, and go after your dreams regardless of what others think or say. Be true to your heart. Embrace your passion. Live without regret or compromise.

Andreas was very nervous. He had just been assigned the job of managing a new journalist at the radio station where he worked. That wasn't the problem. The problem lay in the fact that this young 24-year-old had just lost his sight in an accident.

"Poor kid – life sure isn't fair."

"I wonder what it's like to not be able to see."

"Gosh -- what am I supposed to do with him?"

Andreas Heinecke had never had direct contact with an unsighted person before. Sure, he'd seen them around town, but more as a curiosity than anything else. Now he was expected to integrate such a person into the daily workings of the radio station. He was at a loss.

"A blind journalist? How's he going to do his work?"

"I've heard they develop heightened senses. Wonder if he has? Or is that just a myth?"

When the young man arrived on the scene, Andreas was startled to realize he couldn't look up information in dictionaries or encyclopedias (this was before the Internet). How was he going to get around that? Journalists had to verify and document their work!

Andreas's pity for the young man was quickly replaced with admiration. He respected the young journalist's keen sense of hearing, ability to listen, and put pieces together.

"Don't be afraid to ask me questions, Andreas, I won't be offended."

DIALOG IN THE DARK

YOUR SENSES WILL NEVER BE THE SAME

Andreas' life was completely changed.

Fascinated with the world of the unsighted, Andreas was shocked at the discrimination shown against them. While it was true the German government provided well for the disabled, Andreas discovered that fewer than 15% held jobs.

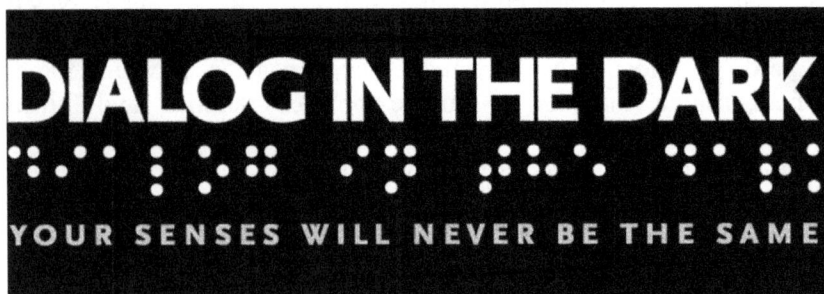

Two years later, Andreas changed jobs and started work at the Home for the Blind Foundation in Frankfurt, Germany. He wanted to be able to share the experience he had gained about unsighted people with other broadcasting corporations. He searched for ways to engage both sighted and unsighted people in conversations where they wouldn't be influenced by pity, insecurity or prejudice. He realized the barriers that needed breaking down were sighted people's fear and misunderstanding of the unsighted world.

The solution became obvious – reverse the roles and let them meet in complete darkness.

In 1996, Andreas left the Home for the Blind Foundation and started ***Dialogue in the Dark*** where sighted people *experience* what it is to be blind. Such interactions had been done before, but it was sighted people leading blindfolded people. Instead, Andreas asked unsighted people to do the leading.

When visitors come to ***Dialogue in the Dark***, they join a small group (usually 8 people). Before beginning the 60 minute journey, they are shown how to use a long cane and are made aware of what they will be experiencing. Upon passing through an entrance area, light levels are progressively reduced until they reach complete darkness. At this point they are met by a Guide who takes over – the guests not knowing they are being led by an unsighted staff member.

The Guide takes them to a room that appears to be a park complete with bushes, trees, a fountain, bridges, benches, and different types of ground such as grass, gravel, and mud. Wind blows from all directions; scents are created while the sound of birds, and a rushing of a stream complete the invisible landscape. The group explores the room for 15 minutes, and then moves on to the next exhibition room.

This room features a city theme dominated by the noise of traffic, honking cars, and market and construction sounds. The noise makes it difficult to gain orientation. This room is considered very stressful, but thanks to the Guide's ability to lead the group, everybody finds their way out of the chaos.

In order to relax, the next stop is a boat trip. The visitors board the boat, take their seats, and experience a little sea voyage with wind, spray, waves, the sounds of seagulls, and passing ships.

Depending on the exhibition there may be more rooms such as a supermarket, art gallery with sculptures to feel, or a sound room where music can be sampled as a whole-body experience through high-performance loudspeakers.

At the end of the exhibit, visitors reach an eating establishment where they are welcomed by music and a waiter who asks for their order. Eating and visiting with invisible people helps to deepen the sightless experience.

Dialogue in the Darkness is a very flexible program that can be taken to businesses, trade fairs, and museums – even the Olympics! When the Winter Olympics were in Turin, Italy, *Dialogue in the Darkness* provided an exhibition which included a fast ride in a bobsled instead of the usual boat trip.

This program is much more than "entertainment" – it dissolves old mind-sets and patterns, and allows the visitor to experience another world.

Since 1989 more than 5,000 blind and partially sighted people worldwide have gained income and recognition through this remarkable program. Employers who experience *Dialogue in the Dark* are filling vacancies with disabled individuals. In fact, 40% of the staff members of *Dialogue in the Dark* find employment within 18 months.

Since 1988 there have been exhibitions in over 20 countries and more than 150 cities in Asia, the United States, and Europe. There are also numerous permanent exhibitions in Germany, Austria, Italy, Israel, Mexico and Brazil, to name just a few. Over 6 million visitors worldwide have experienced what it means to hear, smell, taste and touch things without being able to see them.

Andreas has now expanded the idea to create *Scenes of Silence* where deaf and mute Guides lead visitors through a completely silent world. Further plans include creating the experience of old age, migration, exile, crime, and punishment.

What an amazing man – what a wonderful idea! Andreas has helped over 6 million people overcome their preconceived ideas, fear, and prejudice, toward disabled people. He's helped over 5,000 people secure jobs and become contributing members of their communities. But just as importantly, Andreas' whole intent is to break down barriers and create bridges of understanding, acceptance, and respect, between people who are different.

May you also build bridges as your build your dreams!

"I believe that you cannot go any further than you can think. I certainly believe if you don't desire a thing, you will never get it."

~Mother Charleszetta Waddles

★ *Tenacious Dreamer* ★

This woman's life reads like one of her novels. These fact-based excerpts represent her real life, and after you've read them, you'll discover who she is and why you probably have read her works.

Ready? Let's read on!

"Come to dinner honey!"

"Be right there...in a minute," the 7 year old called to her mom. *"Just gotta finish writing in my journal."* She turned back to her writing. *"Nothing much happened today."* Satisfied, she flung her notebook under her bed, hidden from her siblings, and scurried to dinner.

"Mama, what is a 'depression'? Why are those people standing in line for food?"

"Mama, why did Daddy die? He was just sleeping. I don't understand."

"Mama, I don't care if they pay us. I don't like them. I don't like the boarders that live with us. I want my room back!"

"Mama, my brother is not dead! Joseph will get better. You'll see, he is not dead. Quit saying tha - he is not dead!"

"It's another rejection notice. They don't want my writing."

"It's another rejection notice...they don't want my writing."

"It's another rejection notice...they still don't want my writing."

"It's been 6 years and 40 rejection slips! But I am not quitting. One day, they will publish my works."

A grown woman now with five children of her own, the aspiring author had worked as a secretary, a switchboard operator, a catalogue model, and airline flight attendant. She continued her education and her writing through all the tough events of her life. Yet, the hardest times were still ahead. She lost both her husband and her mother on the same night. Suddenly she was widowed, and her children fatherless.

With those deaths, there was much to overcome. Still she wrote. She never quit.

She wrote short stories, radio programs, and catalogue copy. She worked hard to see her dreams come true. Finally, after many attempts to publish, she received word in April 1974 that her novel, *Where Are The Children* had been accepted for publication! Success! Her payment of $3000 was quite a meager sum for a novel.

Nevertheless, it was a start. Best of all -- no rejection notice!

Then 3 months later, the paperback rights to that book sold and her payment soared to $100,000!!! WOW! What an increase, huh?

It gets better. In 1976, just two short years later, her second novel sold for $1.5 million!

The rest as they say *"is history."*

The woman I am talking about is Mary Higgins Clark. She has published 24 suspense novels. EACH book is a bestseller in the U.S. and in Europe.

Did you catch that? After 6 years and 40 rejections, every suspense novel she has written became a best seller!

Phenomenal!

Moreover, even today, *all of her novels remain in print*. Her debut suspense novel, *Where Are The Children*, is in its seventy-fifth printing! That is an amazing feat!

She has written children's books, co-authored books with her daughter, and done non-fiction works. Numerous books became television films, and four were made into full screen movies. She is, at 80+ years of age, the Number One best selling fiction author in France, and recently began working on yet another book.

I hope I am that stubborn and tenacious with my own dreams. I hope you are, too. Keep trying. Keep at it!

I can imagine the conversation…

"Mr. and Mrs. Pistorius, I don't quite know how to tell you this."

The doctor waited as the new parents prepared themselves for the bad news. *"Your baby is not right. He has a very serious congenital leg and foot defect."*

The doctor waited and watched the parents' faces blanch. They looked at each other and then back to him. He could feel their fear. *"He is missing one of the calf bones in each leg and has no ankles."*

He handed the newborn to the parents who were trying to take it all in. They pulled back the blanket to see their son had only two toes on each deformed leg.

"Will he be able to walk?" The severity of the problem hadn't quite sunk in.

"Well, he could undergo a series of major operations and walk with a painful limp all his life. But I would recommend amputation of both legs."

After consulting with the best orthopedic surgeons in the world, and seeing happy, well-adjusted children with double amputations, Oscar's parents made the agonizing decision to amputate both of his legs. His father remembers how much Oscar loved having his feet tickled, *"He used to curl up laughing when you tickled them."*

Oscar's legs were removed halfway between the knees and the ankles when he was 11 months old – just one month shy of his first birthday.

That was 22 years ago (in 1986).

Today, of Johannesburg, South Africa is known as the Blade Runner, and ***"the fastest man on no legs."***

Not at all offended by that moniker, Oscar just smiles. He says, *"I'm not disabled, I just don't have any legs."*

Within six months of having his legs amputated, Oscar was walking with prosthetic stumps. His father says that by the time he was 2 years old, he was already racing 20 yards to a fence and back *"and was frighteningly fast. He always beat his friends."*

Oscar has been running and winning Paralympic events for years. But his dream is to race able-bodied runners in the Olympics. That desire caused a huge ruckus in the sports world because of the legs he wears for running.

Known as Cheetahs, they are high-tech carbon-fiber legs they look like backwards question marks. Some claim his artificial legs give him an unfair advantage. Oscar denies those claims: he has poor traction on wet tracks; maintaining balance is difficult (especially when cornering); wind pushes the legs sideways; and it takes him longer to get started and into his running stride.

In 2007, the IAAF (International Association of Athletics Federations) banned use of *"any technical device that incorporates springs, wheels or any other element that provides a user with an advantage over another athlete not using such a device."* They claimed the amendment to the competition rules was not aimed at Oscar.

Not surprisingly, Oscar appealed the decision and scientists began monitoring his track performances and carrying out various tests.

Their decision – Oscar had considerable advantage over athletes without prosthetic limbs. With these findings, the IAAF ruled him ineligible for competition in able-bodied athletic events.

Oscar refuted the findings and appealed to the Court of Arbitration for Sport. This Court ruled that the IAAF had not provided sufficient evidence proving Oscar's prostheses gave him an advantage over able-bodied athletes, and cleared him for able-bodied competition.

Oscar's sights were on the 2008 Summer Olympic Games in Beijing, China but he missed making the South African team by a little less than 3/4ths of a second. 45.55 seconds was the Olympic qualifying time, and he ran a 46.25 second race.

At the 2008 Summer Paralympics, Oscar took gold medals in the 100, 200 and 400 meter sprints.

"I have full respect for the Paralympics," said Oscar. *"But I tell people this all the time. You'll never progress if your mind is on your disability...I'd really like to dominate the Paralympics until the end of my career...But in able-bodied racing, I'd really like to be a known name for a long time."*

Is Oscar discouraged? Are you kidding?! His next goal is to qualify for the world championships next year (2009) in Berlin where he will face able-bodied runners. ***I have no doubt we'll be watching Oscar Pistorius in the 2012 Olympics in London!***

Did you catch what Oscar said about making progress? *"You'll never progress if your mind is on your disability."*

How many times do you concentrate on why you can't do something? That kind of thinking will keep you exactly where you are!

Decide to be like Oscar and choose to overcome whatever is holding you back. Concentrate on what you CAN do and decide to become better and better at it. Push through the pain, the naysayers, and work hard to become a victor like Oscar.

Keep your mind on your ability!

"Gratitude unlocks the fullness of life. It turns what we have into enough, and more. It turns denial into acceptance, chaos to order, confusion to clarity. It can turn a meal into a feast, a house into a home, a stranger into a friend. Gratitude makes sense of our past, brings peace for today, and creates a vision for tomorrow."

~Melody Beattie

POWER BOOSTERS

Are you an optimist or a pessimist? Which would you like to be? What are 2 things you can choose to be more optimistic about right now? How would that change things?

_____

_____

_____

_____

_____

_____

_____

_____

_____

What skills do you need to hone to make your dreams come true?

_____

_____

_____

_____

_____

_____

_____

_____

Cut In Half!

Truman never dreamed he would almost die at age 36. Never thought about not walking again. Certainly never considered he would lose both his legs.

A young father, and a strong man, Truman looked the burly muscular part of a railroader.

Working at a Texas train yard on a warm summer day, Truman Duncan slipped and fell under a moving railroad car. He had been trying to connect it to another moving car. Normally just a routine job, that day it ended tragically. The accident severed Truman's body diagonally from his side though his pelvis and down across both legs. Literally cut in two by a 20,000-pound hunk of steel, Truman knew he needed help.

He needed it fast.

As he fought the numbing effects of shock, he pulled out his cell phone and dialed the USA emergency number, 911. As all such calls are recorded in the States, the public can hear his actual call.

Asking for help, you can hear him calmly say, *"I think I've been cut in two. I'm going into shock. Hurry up, ma'am, because I'm about to pass out."*

Reports say as the emergency workers tried to free him, he managed to stay conscious long enough to talk to his family. Eventually he would pass out and remember nothing of the helicopter ambulance that transported him to the hospital. He remembers none of the next 3 weeks. With his beloved family by his side, he lay in a coma for 3 1/2 weeks and then went through 23 surgeries in 4 months. But the most amazing thing? *Truman lived.*

His strong will to live centered on his intense desire see his kids grow up. That was the thought that kept him going during those first intense moments of pain. He wanted to see his kids grow up. He wanted to see the future.

And how is his future?

Truman is living proof that life goes on. To listen to him speak from his electric wheelchair is to hear a joyous man, full of gratefulness, and life. He has had countless opportunities to give up, to be angry, and to become bitter. However, he is none of those things. He is confident, laughs often, smiles graciously, and believes that *"life is good."* He has returned to the same job at the same place. He says his life is *"just as full now as it was before the accident."*

In a recent American television interview, it is said of Truman, *"he's speaking out now to let others, including soldiers who have suffered traumatic injuries like his, know that life is still very much worth living."*

Truman himself says, *"Life is good. It may take me a little longer to do some things but I still do everything I used to do."*

Those activities include swimming, playing with his kids, playing ball, and mowing his own yard. He drives himself in a car equipped with hand controls. Since coming home from the hospital, he has barely stopped. He still has more to overcome. It has been 2 years since he lost his legs, and now he wants to use prosthetic legs. I am sure he will do that, too!

I want to be like Truman. I think if I could capture his strong and gentle will to live fully, I would bottle it and give it to everyone I met. On the days I feel like giving up and quitting, I will think about Truman. As he lives his life, he does so encouraging everyone he meets with a quiet confidence that they too can go on. I want to be like that as well.

If you are discouraged today, think about the truth inside today's story. Think about Truman and the train.

And never ever quit trying!

★ _At the Bottom of Society_ ★

The nine brothers and sisters huddled together.

"Ok, it's decided then. When one of us gets to the university, he or she will help the next one get there."

In many countries this idea wouldn't have been as big a deal as it was for Antonieta and her eight sisters and brothers. Born into a rural Mayan-Kaqchiukel family in Guatemala, it was rare enough for males to get an education – unheard of for females!

Life is anything but easy for the indigenous people of Central America. In Guatemala more than 50% of the poor, rural, primarily indigenous population lacks even the most basic of services (including schools) and only 7% of their homes have access to telephones, radios, or other communication.

Indigenous women in particular live on the outside edge of society. They do not have the same opportunities as men to study, learn Spanish, leave their communities, and improve themselves, much less serve in public office. They are mistreated within their own communities by being forced into servitude to their husbands. In addition, because they often live in extreme poverty, women must concentrate on feeding their families with little or no thought to their own needs or rights.

But with the help and support of her family, Antonieta Castro Abaj pushed her way out of this marginalized existence. Her parents encouraged all their children to study. And because of the pact the siblings made of helping each other get a college education, each one did attend university. From extreme poverty to economic success, the Abaj family now has a veterinarian, doctor, teacher, pilot, and Antonieta - who is championing the cause of indigenous women in Guatemala and throughout Central America!

Antonieta knew all too well that the poorest of the poor didn't have time to think about human rights – they were too busy trying to stay alive. So how could she help these people, especially the women who were at the very bottom rung of society? She knew she couldn't get them excited about their rights and possible escape from their dire situations with promises of freedom. It had to be something tangible, and it had to positively affect their husbands as well. What did they need the most? They needed money.

She came up with a plan. She offered women small, no-interest loans, and help them advance, **IF** they attended one of her study groups. Antonieta went door-to-door recruiting women with the promise of financial help, if they would attend a special group she was offering just for them. It worked!

The study groups discuss pertinent issues ranging from local community issues, to national and even international politics. Through their discussions the women not only learn about their rights, but also develop interest in the politics of their local community and region. And, as the women begin to bring in an additional income, their husbands and families encourage them to continue attending the study group.

Equipped with new knowledge and confidence, they are ready to get involved at the community level. She teaches them about the importance of having personal identification cards, and then helps them obtain them and register to vote. She encourages them to attend community meetings, helps them contact the correct officials about their particular concerns, and encourages them to run for elected office.

While none of the first women who courageously sought political office were elected, they fostered hope, and set the precedence for others to follow.

Knowing she is only one woman who can do just so much, Antonieta trains the women who are members of the study groups how to recruit, start new groups, educate, and train even more women. Her simple approach is spreading throughout Guatemala and Central America.

Talk about a success story! Not only is Antonieta a public woman to be reckoned with, she is making a huge difference for marginalized people in her country, and throughout Central America. She is one who speaks with knowledge and authority, because she has already accomplished what she teaches others to do.

Wisdom comes from experience and is an integral part of success.

Remember Antonieta as you pursue your dreams!

★ *Meet Joe the "Grafter"* ★

"What's he got?" asked the woman to her friend as they walked to the coffee shop.

The glittering sidewalk held no space around the old man demonstrating something, but they just couldn't make it out. The women wanted coffee, but curiosity made them slow their pace. The desire to know more about this corner vendor peaked as the mocha tinged aroma wafted around their noses.

"I can't see it for sure," answered her friend, *"I think it's a gadget of some sort. He was here yesterday when I went to the gym. Had a big crowd around him then, too. Maybe after we get our coffee, we can get close enough to see what the fuss is."*

With coffee in hand, the women secured a prize position right next to the older man.

Dressed impeccably, his soft voice barely registered above a whisper. Not "barking" like a carnival vendor, this man presented an air of wealth and dignity. Next to his feet, several white plastic tubs held both peeled and unpeeled potatoes and carrots, as well as scores of silver vegetable peelers. Sitting on his stool, he gestured to the fold-out copy of a recent magazine feature article...about him.

His goal? To give a whimsical, polite demonstration and afterwards to sell those imported stainless steel peelers.

His price? $5.00 for each peeler

His patrons? Adults and kids alike, business professionals, construction workers, and the average New York tourist.

His name? Joe Ades

Where? Various locations in New York City, USA.

When? Six days a week, 10 hours a day.

His motivation? "I want the kids (his grandkids) *to go to the best colleges that it's possible to go to. And I want to pay for it."*

His age? In 2008, 74 years old! He passed away in 2009 but his legend lives on...

Meet Joe Ades, a.k.a. *"the gentleman peeler."*

Joe has a wonderful, eclectic life story. This street corner "act" has been his only job...ever. Not endeared to the term *salesman*, Joe strongly prefers the British term "grafter." Grafting means *pitching goods in the street, or at gatherings like fairs or marketplaces.*

Joe has lived in New York for decades, and he doesn't just live in the shadows of New York City. He (and his wife before she died) enjoyed a lavish up-scale apartment in Park Avenue...in one of the richest zip codes in the USA. He spoiled her, he says, to rare wines and rich food at the city's nicest restaurants. He stored his surplus peelers stand in the former "maid's" quarters. Joe's classy tweed suits are a thousand dollars a pop. He wholeheartedly enjoys the bantering and camaraderie his sales produce. He sells every day because he wants to remain active, engaged, and vital.

His outlook on life bears repeating.

"That's the secret of happiness. Not doing what you like, but liking what you do."

When asked in a recent interview, *"Do (you) ever take a vacation?"*

Joe simply laughed. *"Life is a vacation! Every day is a vacation. And I love it. I just love it. I look forward to getting up every morning. It's not simply a way of getting a living. It never has been. It's the excitement; it's the challenge - the glorious uncertainty. Every day is fresh. The only time I'm really happy is when I'm set on that stool."*

Be like Joe -- willing to enjoy what you are doing, as well as bringing laughter and pure zeal for life.

Today as you choose your actions, be encouraged that there are many "Joe's" out there; living proof that you can be happy and successful at the same time.

★ *For Little Sister* ★

"Mama, why do we have to leave Little Sister here – why can't she stay at home...Papa, I don't like this place – let's bring Little Sister home... Mama, I miss Little Sister. It's not right that she had to stay in the public shelter. I'm going to make it so other kids don't have to live and die in places like that ever again!"

Raúl's mother hugged her son and assured him everything would be all right. But her heart was breaking and her soul cried out at the injustice of their situation and their inability to make a difference for her daughter. ***Little did she know that as an adult her son would indeed make a difference for children and families living marginal lives throughout Chile.***

Raúl grew up in a poor family and attended public school where the education was less than adequate. His community provided few opportunities for people, especially young people. Raúl's sister suffered from severe brain damage and died in a public shelter because his family couldn't afford the care she needed. After her death, Raúl vowed to work for those like his own family who lived under such poor conditions.

"Raúl, you are such a great listener – you'd be a natural in counseling!" Even with the difficulties of his situation, Raúl knew an education was his ticket for making the difference he desired. He persevered through his schooling and went on to study psychology at the university. As part of his studies, he worked with Chilean women who had been tortured during the military dictatorship. He drove a bus to support himself, and developed community activities in the poorest neighborhoods of Santiago.

Based on his life and educational experiences, Raúl Abásolo developed activities for young adults. He focused on drug prevention and countering the outcast lifestyle that hopeless youth adopt. In 1996, he launched Tour Marginal as a drug prevention program. It has widely expanded its services and influence throughout Chile. Everything he does revolves around building supportive communities for social outsiders. Instead of trying to change youth, he provides a safe and accepting environment where these street-wise, but vulnerable kids can channel their creative energy and find acceptance and respect.

Once these ostracized youth realize their own potential, he hooks them up with programs that will take them to the next level. It might be training in trade skills or business skills – or any of the programs within the five areas of Tour Marginal's vast network: culture, health, gender, grassroots, and research.

As these young adults move into the family atmosphere of Tour Marginal where they are accepted and heard, they gain self-worth and become accountable and credible in the eyes of their neighbors. As of 2003, Tour Marginal had reached more than 10,000 young adults and worked with over 200 organizations within Santiago, plus another 50 organizations in other regions in the country.

Because of this unprecedented networking with both governmental and non-governmental organizations, Tour Marginal is positively influencing how Chilean society views and works with marginal youth. He has been so successful in fact, that Raúl is teaching his model around the world.

I can imagine how very proud Raúl's parents must be of his amazing accomplishments, especially since he has done it all to honor the memory of his little sister. Like Raúl, you will find that major events you experience will influence the direction of your life. He could have grown up bitter and angry. He could have joined a gang and lashed out at society. No one would have blamed him for taking the violent way out. But that's not what Raúl chose.

When it comes right down to it, life is about choices, isn't it? Raúl was a young boy and couldn't do anything about his sister's or family's situation. None of it was his fault – he was born into it. But he made some important choices along the way.

Yes, it's all about choices. I hope you will be like Raúl and choose to take the higher, positive way. If life comes at you fast and furious with high mountains of pain to climb, or deep rivers of grief to swim, I hope you will choose to climb to the top or swim to the other side, no matter how difficult or impossible it may seem.

What did she feel? What did she want to do? She wanted to exclaim to the universe, to shout from the highest mountain, to proclaim to the ebbing ocean: *"The doctors were wrong! The doctors were wrong! Look at her now! There is no stopping her!"* How fantastically good to know that being wrong sometimes feels so right!

Tracy Turner watched as her baby girl packed her belongings for college. *"College!"* she thought to herself. *"Simply amazing, my baby is old enough to go to college!"* Tracy knew Katelyn's dreams were becoming reality. It was incredible that Katelyn had even survived infancy. Tracy let her memory float back to Katelyn's birth and early childhood, and temporarily forgot the packing task in front of her.

As clothes flew out of the closet, Katelyn's excited chatter misted inside Tracy's mind as the memories of the horrifying diagnosis rose up.

Tracy remembered and silently rehearsed the telling of Katelyn's story: *The doctors said she would die. Her spine didn't close during my pregnancy. It is called 'spina bifida.' Spina bifida means split spine. 'Bring her home and prepare for her death,' was the doctor's advice. Twice, they told her Katelyn would die. However, she didn't die - she thrived. She learned to walk - then she hurt her toe. That infection first caused them to amputate five of her toes, then her foot and finally her leg. But Katelyn lived. She lived....Her dad, though, couldn't handle the thought of a 'less than perfect' baby...he took one look at her and left all 4 of us just 3 months after her birth. He only looked at her beautiful face one time. All the surgeries that she endured...If I count them, it is 56! 56 surgeries! How can one woman go through so much and still laugh and smile and care and dream? But look at her now!! How glorious that the doctors were so wrong!"*

"MOM!" Katelyn raised her voice to seize her mother's attention. *"MOM! You are sitting on my new jeans...can you hand them to me, please?"* Katelyn smiled and placed her hand on her mom's shoulder.

Katelyn Wilbanks is a dreamer and doesn't know the word "quit." When an infection forced the amputation of her leg, she learned to do more than just walk with her prosthetic leg. She learned to do back flips! She has such a contagious smile, and an overwhelmingly positive attitude, people are drawn to her as if she were magnetized.

A chance meeting with Mary Ann Zoellner, a producer of the TODAY show (an American TV show), led to a deep friendship between the two women. That friendship altered Katelyn's life. When Mary Ann realized that due to medical bills Katelyn's family could not afford her "dream school" (the University of Oklahoma), Mary Ann stepped in to help find a way. She believed in Katelyn's future.

Meetings and phone calls ensued between Mary Ann and the University of Oklahoma. As details finalized, the TODAY show flew Katelyn to a filming of the program under the pretext of "telling the world about spinal bifida." Much to her shocked surprise, the president of the university presented her with a full scholarship -- tuition, books, room, and board.

The grateful young woman inspired so much attention, the OU alumni association raised over $130 MILLION so others like her could attend the school! As of 2008, Katelyn Wilbanks continues to attend the University of Oklahoma. Living in the athlete's dorm and working as a manager for the football team, she majors in journalism with a musical production minor.

What started out as a common friendship has created tremendous success for one young woman and one large university. *"I chose Katelyn because there are certain people you meet in life that are angelic and take your breath away. Katelyn was one of those people for me,"* says Mary Ann.

OU President, David Boren says, the university *"is going to be changed forever because she's here."*

Katelyn influences people everywhere with her gentle, positive spirit and her trademark smile. Never having had an easy time, she is passionate about life, and believes in her future against all odds.

You can make the same choice!

POWER BOOSTERS

What is something you have failed at many times, but really want to succeed at? What can you do to change the outcome? (By now you should be ready to go in depth with your answer...)

_____

_____

_____

_____

_____

_____

_____

_____

_____

_____

_____

_____

_____

_____

_____

_____

_____

_____

★ _She Was a Mahout_ ★

"Mom, Dad, I've decided to become a mahout."
"Well dear, we have no doubt you'll become anything you want. You're going to be a what?"
"A mahout – an elephant driver."

Caroline Casey is an achiever, actually most people would call her an over-achiever. Whatever she puts her Irish mind to, she accomplishes. Caroline was always a top student and excelled in college. She traveled extensively, founded a horticulture and landscape architecture business at the age of 22, and eventually became a successful business consultant to an international company.

But at the age of 28 she hit a corporate wall, and was unable to achieve at the high levels she was accustomed to. She quit work and decided to live out a life-long dream – riding an elephant across India. In fact, Caroline became the first western woman to achieve the status of elephant mahout. In 2000, she made the physically and mentally demanding 1000 kilometer trek (about 622 miles) across India.

But Caroline's story is not about being a celebrated elephant mahout. Her story is about the prejudice and difficulties she suffered (and overcame) as a result of being legally blind.

Growing up in Dublin, Caroline's friends laughed and joked about the clumsy kids who wore glasses. She didn't realize she had a vision problem until her parents bought her driving lessons. She couldn't pass the eye exam. At 17 she was labeled visually impaired and legally blind. Caroline and her parents hid her disability until she was 28 when she hit the corporate-world wall that changed her life.

Deciding to use her trip across India as a fundraiser and awareness raising venture, Caroline established The Aisling Foundation. She set the goal of raising EUR$250,000 (about $352,000 US) to support her trip **and** raise funding for various disability groups. A few weeks before the trip she had raised only had EUR$67,000. She managed to get a prime-time appearance on a national television talk show which enabled her to nearly double her goal -- EUR$480,000 (about $676,000 US)!

Caroline returned from her trip as an inspirational figure with a high media profile, and she took full advantage of it. She knew that almost 10 percent of Ireland's population lived with disabilities. 90 percent were unemployed and 38 percent lived in poverty. (By the way, these statistics are not particular just to Ireland, but hold true worldwide.)

While disability and rights groups had campaigned successfully for progressive legislation throughout Europe, businesses still resisted hiring employees with disabilities. Caroline knew first hand that like society in general, businesses see these people for what they cannot do instead of what they can. They also don't realize the spending power these individuals have.

Caroline decided to change how businesses look at, and deal with people with disabilities.

She organized her first "ability conference" for business and political leaders in 2001. Since then she has created The Ability Awards to recognize and reward businesses and public-sector organizations that strive to meet the needs of people with disabilities. These awards endeavor to make businesses and organizations "ability confident" as they meet the needs of employees **and** consumers.

She envisions spreading these programs around the world by funding "ability agents" who will create a network of communities supporting one another. The Aisling Foundation will also help by providing financial, network, and best practice support.

Now that's one enterprising, energetic, young woman! She's gone from a 17-year-old hiding a disability, to a highly successful business consultant and business owner, to an elephant mahout trekking across India, to a CEO changing the world of business for people with disabilities. Amazing!

Caroline is a wonderful example of someone who refuses to let what others perceive as her limitations define who she is and what she can do. How often have you let someone's negative comment stop you from pursuing a great idea? Have you ever shared a dream with someone who told you to stop dreaming and face reality?

I encourage you to stay true to your dreams and turn a deaf ear to those who would try to talk you out of pursuing them.

★ _Only One Arm and One Finger_ ★

As Stacy watched Nick race out the front door today with his new skateboard in tow, she remembered her son several years earlier. The cool fall breeze wafted over her as her memories focused in her mind.

"Nick, time for therapy."

No answer came from the young boy's room.

"Nick, we need to leave."

No answer.

"Nick, get your prosthesis. Time for therapy."

Silence overshadowed.

"Nick, you need your prosthesis. Let's go."

Knowing her son had been dressed and about ready to travel, she went to check on him.

As she opened the door, she found Nick furiously competing with his brother on a video game. Nick wasn't ignoring her; she knew he had simply been too focused on winning.

"Nick, game over!" Smiling sweetly, she turned off the T.V.

"Aw, Mom! I was so close to beating him! I hate those prostheses. They just slow me down. I am faster without those stupid legs. And the arm gets in my way. I don't want them. I don't like them. I can do more stuff without those fake things!"

Stacy remembers sighing, again. That had been such a familiar discussion at their house. This child of hers! What was she going to do with him?

"Mom! I do not want the prostheses on me again. Not those legs or that arm. I want to do it my way, it is better for me. Don't you understand? PLEASE! Get rid of them. I hate 'em."

With those words, Nick had scooted out the front door with his very first skateboard under his arm. On the way he bumped his wheelchair and scowled.

"Stupid chair, move."

Although she and her husband were largely responsible for his terrific "can do" attitude, Stacy used to wonder if they had instilled a bit TOO much confidence in Nick. He seemed oblivious to the fact he needed help. Born with one arm and one finger, Nick started life with a challenge. No legs, only a stump where his right arm should be and one finger on his left arm, he obviously required assistance.

She had so worried that day as she picked up the legs and the arm and simply stuck them in the corner of the storage closet. Nick shared a genetic disorder called Hanhart Syndrome Type II, with only 11 other people. The doctors had told her he would be born "fragile." _FRAGILE!_ Well, the doctors were wrong. Nick was far from fragile!

Meet Nick Santonastasso, a 14-year-old dynamo from New Jersey.

This young man is a ball of positive energy, enthusiasm, and triumph. He has compromised to use a wheelchair at school, but at home and everywhere else - drawing and writing, playing on the baseball field, the skateboard park, the football field, on the keyboards, or his beloved drums, he is "limb-less."

Nick's family decided early on to raise Nick exactly as his able-bodied siblings. The boy knows no limits and no bounds. His "can do" attitude keenly reflects his parents'.

"I know anything's possible. My parents just keep encouraging me to do stuff — like, don't give up and keep trying. If you fall down, get back up...It builds self-confidence in yourself to try it again. And you'll be happy and succeed and not fail."

By cupping a pen, pencil, or paintbrush, under his chin and stump, Nick even figured out a way to draw. Always ready to compete, he won a New Jersey statewide "family values" art contest. The contest was not for the "disabled," it was a regular art show. No one knew of his limitations until he accepted his award from the governor.

Hearing the front door slam, Stacy smiled. Back in reality, she hugged her arms to her chest feeling the peace that comes with making the right decision.

Nick had been right, of course. He could do more without the prosthesis.

"MOM! MOM! I did it! I did it! I finally did! This new skateboard is great. It's the right size! FINALLY! WOW! Did you see me? Did you? I figured it out! I figured out how to do it! MOM! I did it! I rode down the street on my skateboard doing a headstand! I got it! I did my headstand! I can do anything!"

You know, it is true. When you watch a young man with no legs and only one finger do a headstand on his skateboard, you know he will go far in life.

Fast forward to 2010, age 14… Nick decided it was time to learn to walk with prosthetics. It should have taken weeks and weeks of lessons. Instead, during only the second session he was walking without support, even allowing himself to fall so he could learn how to get back up. He amazed even people who had learned not to be amazed at what it could do.

Boy, I have no worries about Nick. I just hope the world is big enough to contain him!

Amazing! You can have that attitude. You can choose to believe that you, too, can do it all!

Look differently at what you are able to do, not what you cannot do! Think of Nick each time you are tempted to give up.

He would say *"…you can do it! Get up and try again! Anything's possible. You can."*

> *"People are always blaming their circumstances for what they are. I don't believe in circumstances. The people who get on in the world are the people who get up and look for the circumstances they want, and if they can't find them, make them."*
>
> ~George Bernard Shaw

POWER BOOSTERS

What are the most important things you have learned from this book? What will you start taking action on TODAY?

_____

_____

_____

_____

_____

_____

_____

_____

_____

_____

_____

_____

_____

_____

_____

_____

_____

_____

If you enjoyed these stories, and want to continue having their power in your life (we have hundreds) or you want to change someone else's life, you need to know about…

A beautiful personalized certificate!
A powerful Movie!
Powerful Emails - Created for Teenagers & Adults - Delivered <u>Daily</u>!

Someone Believes In You was created to...

Change the World - One Person At A Time!

Imagine... someone you believe in receives a special certificate in the Mail (you can be anonymous if you want to be); they are given the link to a powerful movie affirming someone believes in them, and then they are sent an email every single day - telling them someone believes in them, sharing encouragement, giving motivation, telling stories of amazing people, inspiring the courage to fulfill their dreams & move beyond their fears.

The world of more and more people revolves around the Internet - now **you have the power to turn it into a source of daily strength for them!**

Who do YOU want to give the Gift of Confidence to??

- Your kids
- Your spouse/partner
- A family member
- A friend
- A neighbor
- A co-worker
- YOURSELF!

www.SomeoneBelievesInYou.com

We have a FREE Gift for you!

Many times you just need a bright flash of light into your days to keep you inspired & motivated, and to give you hope. That's why we created **Daily Fireflies For The Heart**. You'll receive a powerful quote and then one of us will share a brief story or thought with you.

You'll also receive first notice of all new books and any specials we are having.

But here's the real deal… We want to stay in touch with you. We want you to be on our email list. It's really that simple. If you want to hear from us in the future, please go to the page below and sign up. If not, then don't. ☺

At least go check out the website, though. We paid big bucks to have the special landing page created – a memory of a special evening Ginny spent on the banks of the James River in Richmond, VA. You'll love it!

www.FirefliesForTheHeart.com

About the Authors

Who is Ginny Dye?

More about me... "I love all people, but have a special place in my heart for teenagers - I adore them! The magical years of 12-19 are my favorite.

I am also an author, with 16 books published under a variety of pen names: 5 novels for teens, 4 historical novels for adults, and 7 non-fiction. I have a great appreciation for the power of the written word in affecting change. It has been a passion of mine for the last 14 years to collect stories and experiences that will empower people to live their dreams.

For the last 10 years I have worked as a Trainer and Motivator for men and women of all ages. I have created entire Training Programs - learning as I went how to help adults move beyond their fears and doubts in order to achieve the dreams they have. I have learned with them - realizing how much easier people's lives would be if they could just believe in themselves and have a strong support system.

I am also the Founder & CEO of Together We Can Change The World – the parent company of 5 Million For Change, 5 Million Students For Change, Together We Can Change The World Day & Together We Can Change The World Publishing, and Someone Believes In You. Our vision is to empower people with all the resources they need to create an impact on the world, and also generate funding for non-profit organizations - empowering them to fulfill their mission without constantly worrying about money.

Someone Believes in You is an extension of our vision to impact the world.

I have learned that a single moment of Epiphany will not create lasting change. It is the daily impact, the daily lessons, and the daily applications that change patterns and habits in order to achieve your goal. When I dreamed of creating **Someone Believes in You**, I knew it had to have a daily impact - hence the 365 emails delivered daily for a year.

Fireflies For The Heart, Volume 1 is our response to people's demand to have a compilation of the stories. More volumes will follow...

When I first created **Someone Believes in You in** 2004, I wanted to be anonymous - not wanting it to be about me. Many voices convinced me that people would want to know the person behind the emails. I am human. I fail. I laugh. I cry. I simply want to make a difference.

My joy comes from knowing lives will be changed.

Thank you for joining me in my mission.

Ginny Dye

Who is Sandi Valentine?

Sandi, in addition to her role with **Someone Believes In You**, is also the **Director of Commmunication** for *Together We Can Change The World, Inc.* She is the editor of the ***BE the Difference*** Newsletter and has written many of the 101 Ways To Change The World Series published through *Together We Can Change The World Publishing.*

More about her... "I grew up in a family of people-helping-people and it has been a way of life for me. My kindergarten teacher referred to me as a 'mother hen' because I was always trying to help my classmates. As a teen, I was pulled into all different kinds of situations to help others.

Throughout my adult years (starting at age 18 and for over 36 years) I taught and worked with youngsters from preschool through college aged young adults. I've written curriculum, plays and skits, created learning situations and environments, and taken young people on local and international mission trips.

If I had to pick a favorite age, it would be adolescent middle-schoolers. These young people are at such a crucial point in life, and their creativity, wonder, inhibitions, and experimentation are still unspoiled and at their peak. There is never a dull moment!

Even while I was working with young people, I was responsible for adult learning as well. I found it exceedingly fulfilling to help others look beyond themselves and in the process discover the beauty that dwells within. I have always tried to move people beyond what they consider their limitations with encouragement and empowerment to reveal their unique strengths and purpose.

It is a true honor to be able to share stories and inspiration with you through Someone Believes In You! I sincerely hope our writings will help you grow and move beyond where you are now, into deeper and richer experiences of life."

Sandi Valentine

Who is Suess Karlsson?

Susan (Suess) Karlsson is a professional writer, speaker and photographer. She is also the owner of Reflections Studio.

More about her... "For Someone Believes In You, I desire to communicate hope, acceptance, steadfastness and encouragement within my writings. Having worked with people from young toddlers to graying seniors intermittently for nearly 30 years, I take great joy when I witness someone attaining fresh levels of confidence, self-esteem and courage.

Being a wife for 25 years and the mother of three older teens offers me many joyous opportunities to experience persistence and determination. Being a current cancer patient & undergoing chemotherapy, I embrace wholeheartedly this precious gift called life. Even owning pets of every sort affords me the opportunity to learn tolerance in many forms.

I come from, and now live in Texas, but through life I have traveled abroad and even lived in Canada and Sweden. I've also lived in Louisiana, North Carolina, and Montana. Many times, I have been the "new girl on the block" and so I am fascinated with people watching. Being a public speaker and aspiring photographer, I am often hidden behind my words and works so I understand the need for personal space and silence.

Described often as a 'holy mess', I am hard headed and controlling, adventurous and spontaneous. I am loyal and committed, loud and bold. I don't like waiting in line although I can do it when I have to. I like old people but not acting old. I love the ocean and the rhythm of the ocean...the colors of the water mixed with the constant change of the beach sand relaxes and soothes me. I think life is a grand expedition and we are all its team members. I need you and you need me. As I get involved in the process of aging, more and more I hang on to the present moments....not focusing often on the uncertainty of what lies ahead and spend even fewer moments looking back in regret. I want you to know that no matter where in life we find ourselves, no matter what comes our way, there is always relentless hope for this life. We have so many wonderful days ahead of us!! Mostly though, I am simply delighted to be writing for you."

Suess Karlsson

If you have been challenged through this book to make a difference with your life, please go to www.5MillionForChange. This division of Together We Can Change The World will provide all the FREE Resources you need to make a difference and give you a community of like-minded people.

5 Million For Change Pledge

I raise my hand for 5 Million For Change

I will take time TODAY to make a difference in the world.

I will take time TODAY to do one thing – for one person.

I will take time TODAY to spread some love & caring in my world.

One thing – TODAY.

EVERYDAY!

Nothing is too small. Nothing is too big.

It is only important to take Action.

I will take time TODAY – to ACT – to create CHANGE!

—————————————

www.5MillionForChange.com

www.5MillionStudentsForChange.com

Other Books By Ginny Dye

The Bregdan Chronicles – a sweeping historical saga that begins in the year leading to the American Civil War...

Storm Clouds Rolling In
1860 – 1861

On To Richmond
1861 – 1862

Spring Will Come
1862 – 1863

Dark Chaos
1863 – 1864

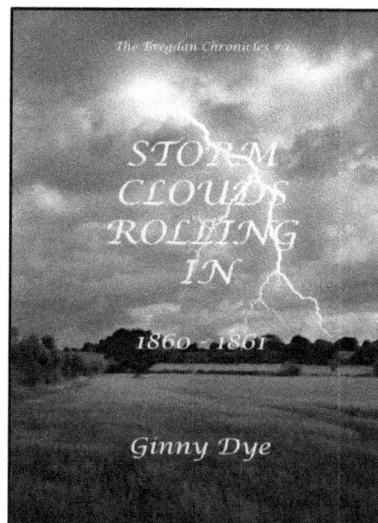

Many more coming as the Bregdan braid of history continues to be woven...

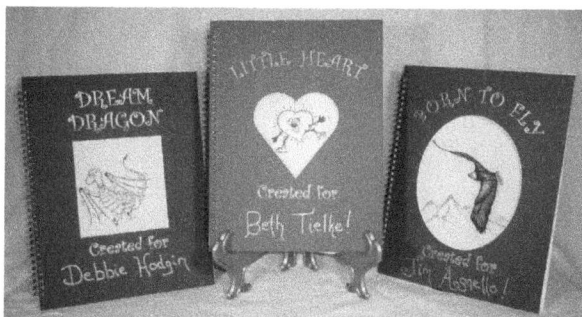

Fly To Your Dreams Series -
www.FlyToYourDreams.com

Dream Dragon
Born To Fly
Little Heart

Other Books by Ginny Dye & Sandi Valentine

101 Ways Series - www.TogetherWeCanChangeTheWorldPublishing.com

101 Ways To Change The World
101 Ways Your Church Can Change The World
101 Ways Your School Can Change The World
101 Ways Youth Can Change The World
101 Ways Women Can Change The World
101 Ways Your Business Can Change The World
101 Ways To Show Appreciation To Your Volunteers
101 Ways To Help Planet Earth
101 Ways Change The World For Animals
101 Ways To Support The Troops

Future Fireflies For The Heart Books

While we have hundreds of stories already written, we are always looking for amazing people who need their stories to be told – all over the world. They don't have to be wealthy. They don't have to be famous. We just want to tell the stories of people who are living life "Full Out". We want to tell the stories of people who have overcome obstacles, or who have simply decided to live a life of purpose and meaning – using their life to make a difference.

If you know someone *we* should know, we'd love to have you tell us!

Together We Can Change The World Publishing
Fireflies For The Heart
1941 Lake Whatcom Blvd. # 207
Bellingham, WA 98229

Or send an email to:
Admin@SomeoneBelievesInYou.com

www.ingramcontent.com/pod-product-compliance
Lightning Source LLC
Chambersburg PA
CBHW062043090426
42740CB00016B/3007